BOUDICCA

*This book is dedicated to
Carol of the Corieltavi,
with love and gratitude.*

BOUDICCA

THE WARRIOR QUEEN

M.J. TROW

SUTTON PUBLISHING

This book was first published in 2003 by
Sutton Publishing Limited · Phoenix Mill
Thrupp · Stroud · Gloucestershire · GL5 2BU

This paperback edition first published in 2005

British Library Cataloguing in Publication Data
A catalogue record for this book is available from the British
Library.

ISBN 0 7509 3400 X

EL
Donation 7.06
38028009225316
936.2

Typeset in 10/12pt New Aster.
Typesetting and origination by
Sutton Publishing Limited.
Printed and bound in Great Britain by
J.H. Haynes & Co. Ltd, Sparkford.

Contents

Acknowledgements

Many thanks to everyone who has helped in the production of this book: to Jaqueline Mitchell and the Sutton team; to Andrew Lownie, friend and agent; to Philip Crummy of the Colchester Archaeological Trust; to David Thorold of Verulamium Museum; to Dick Barton of Colchester Museum; to all those who have allowed us to use their images; and most of all, as always, to Carol Trow, who typed the manuscript, took photographs, dotted all the 'i's and crossed all the 't's.

All quotations from Kipling are reproduced by kind permission of A.P. Watt Ltd. on behalf of the National Trust for Places of Historical Interest or Natural Beauty.

1
𝕸𝖆𝖗𝖙𝖎𝖆 𝖁𝖎𝖈𝖙𝖗𝖎𝖝

> What chariots, what horses
> Against us shall bide,
> While Stars in their courses
> Do fight on our side?
>
> 'An Astrologer's Song' from
> *Rewards and Fairies*, Rudyard Kipling

Boudicca of the red hair stood on her chariot platform, her daughters by her side. She noticed how still they were, and pale. All around them the warriors chanted and whooped in the summer sun; tall, fierce men with lime-streaked hair and blue painted bodies. The women trilled behind them from their positions on the wagons and the children scampered and played. Boys and girls no higher than a Celtic sword acted out their games of war, rolling and laughing under the wagon wheels, sliding on the dry grass of summer.

Still her girls were silent, their eyes at once hard and vacant. They had not been the same since the night the Procurator's men came. She could still smell the sour, watered wine on their breath and the stink of olives. They had laughed at her when she had screamed at them. Even when she knew what they were going to do and had slashed the cheek of one of them with her

1

dagger, they still laughed. One of them had slapped her backwards so that she sprawled on the earth floor. Two more had grabbed her arms, twisting the knife from her grip. A third had ripped her tunic, taunting her in the guttering firelight, fondling her breasts for a moment before throwing her forward to be hauled upright onto her knees. Her arms were wrenched outwards, her long unbraided hair thrown over her face so that her back was bare. She could hear her girls crying, screaming as the caligae *dragged them away. She was crying now, not for herself, but for them, and she did not hear the soft thud as the sticks drove home, biting through her flesh and spraying the ground around her with blood. All she could hear was her daughters' screams coming from the hut. All she could imagine was their little naked bodies side by side, jerked up and backwards by the* caligae's *thrusts. She heard the men laughing as they grunted, egging each other on as the rods rained down on her spine. Each time she twisted to release her wrists, they drove their boots into her ribs and spat all over her long tresses, wet with her sweat and blood.*

She did not know how long it lasted, the scourging of a queen and the raping of princesses. All she knew was that she had to move, to force her tortured body off the bloody ground and find her girls. She could barely stand and every breath was agony. Before her in the darkness the huts stood silent, the royal palace bereft of her people. Only a flaming torch guttered. Only a stray dog whined. The caligae *had gone, their broken rods lying bloody near the strewn dresses of the girls.*

The little ones huddled in the darkest corner, their red hair matted across their faces, streaked with tears. They shivered in their nakedness, infants on the verge of womanhood, hugging each other in their desolation and their fear. She pulled her dress around her so that they shouldn't see the bruising and the blood, and she wrapped them in her arms, all three of them sobbing in the watches of the night. There were no words, for who could find them? No reasons, for who had them? Only a mother, hushing her raped babies and kissing their tears.

She looked at them now, on her chariot in that broad, sunlit field. It had been . . . how long? Only since Beltane, when the caligae *had come with their incomprehensible tongue and their leering. Boudicca had heard those accents many times since and knew that when she had, they had always been screaming for mercy. She could not speak their language, but she understood every word – at Camulodunum, where the veterans had gone down before her warriors' swords; at Londinium where their harlots' breasts had been hacked off; at Verlamion where heads had bounced through the dripping marshes. And over all the screaming, the roar of fire and the roar of her thousands.*

Boudicca looked beyond her spearheads to the hills and the dark mass of trees. This would be it, the final test. Here, drawn up in a glittering mass on the edge of the sacred oaks, was the army of the legate, Gaius Suetonius Paulinus.

The legate shielded his eyes from the fierceness of the noonday sun. In the floodplain of the river below him, the army of the Iceni was huge. What was it . . . four, five times his own? Since Minerva's month this army had been at his back, chasing him northwards. Back home, the farmers would be pruning the vines and sowing the three-month wheat. Through all the weeks that followed, when the weak British sun was in the sign of Aries and his people sacrificed to Sarquis, that army had haunted him. They had attacked the veterans' colony at Colonia Claudia, burning to the ground the great temple of the deified Claudius, slaughtering in their frenzy all that crossed their path. While he and his legions had been tramping through the mountains of the Ordovices, following the gold road to the west, the Horse People had struck south, looting and pillaging as they went. Under the protection of Apollo though he was, Cerialis and IX Hispana had been cut to pieces. At home the sheep were shorn, the wool was washed and sacrifices made to Mercury and to Flora. Cerialis had ridden north, lucky to have a command lucky to be alive.

While the farmers at home mowed the hay and sacrificed to Hercules and Fors Fortuna, she of the red hair had taken Londinium, burning its shops and its houses, impaling and disembowelling the citizens that he, Paulinus, had had to leave behind. Even before he'd left Mona, with its terrifying women and its chanting Druids, he knew that the Horse People and their terrifying queen were on the march. With a tiny cohort of cavalry, what could the legate do but ride north to meet the rest of his army and choose his ground? Under Jupiter in the sign of

3

Cancer, when barley and honey were harvested and feasts held to honour Apollo and Neptune, the Iceni had marched on Verulamium, burning its streets, crucifying its people. And they weren't even Romans.

So here he was, squinting into the sun under the scorching brim of his helmet, sitting his mare in the centre of his legions. The month was under the protection of Ceres, and in the fields beyond the river, he could see the corn unharvested, flattened by the great army that shifted and writhed below him like some terrifying monster. At home, he knew, there would be sacrifices to Diana and, with a sudden realization that wrenched his heart, Hope and Safety. The feast of Volcanalia.

Boudicca knew where the legate was. She knew it by the plain scarlet flag in the centre of his ranks. His troops were spread out in a long solid line against the screen of trees. In the centre were the legions, hard men under their iron helmets, their javelins pointing skywards, their shields scarlet and gold with their wings and lightning flashes. She could hear the barked orders from the centurions standing ahead of their cohort lines. They were wearing full battle gear as if in honour of the day, silver phalerae *dangling on their scarlet tunics. She could even see the torcs on red ribbons around their necks, the trophies of the Celtic dead. She knew their battle standards by heart – the boar of XX Legion copied, like so much else Roman, from the Celts. She knew the* signifers *with their wolf pelts around their shoulders, and the* aquilifers, *with their flashing eagles. In the centre, near the legate's flag, she could see above the heads of the bristling cohorts the image of their emperor, the lyre player who some men said was mad.*

On the legion's flanks the auxiliaries stood, their mail shirts and many-coloured shields a reminder that they were not from Rome. These men were Gauls and Iberians, Pannonians and Batavians, crossing the sea no doubt for women and loot. Beyond them the cavalry on their tough little horses, circular shields catching the sun as their bearers twisted in the saddle, holding their animals steady in readiness for the word.

The barked commands had stopped. The only sound that Boudicca could hear was the rising roar of the Iceni around her and the harsh, clacking tongues of the boar-headed carynxes.

She tapped the shoulder of her charioteer and gripped the rail as they lurched forward, the wheels grumbling over the short yellow grass, and she swung in an arc to the right to face her people.

Paulinus saw her go. He glanced along his line, the grim-faced tribunes of XIV Gemina and XX watching him, waiting for his command. He sensed the cohorts shifting, the bolt-headed pila in their hands wavering as they saw the Iceni mob surge and writhe around their queen. The front rank could hear snatches of her harsh, rasping voice haranguing them, driving them into a frenzy. Paulinus knew his men had faced all this before – on Mona with the sea crashing around their ankles and the blazing torches of the Druids driving them back. They had faced that down; they could do it again. But he also knew that IX Hispana had gone, swallowed up by that monster that vaunted itself in the field now. And he remembered his father's tales of the Teutoburger Forest and the annihilation of three whole legions. This one was going to take careful timing.

He lashed his horse forward, yelling at the top of his voice, 'Ignore their roar. They're just empty threats.' He reached over and clapped a centurion on the shoulder. 'Look, there are more women than warriors!' He heard the rear ranks chuckle. 'When we get in among them, they'll break. They'll run. We've seen it all before, eh, lads?' His silent legions were laughing now, the metal of their tunic plates rattling in the sun. He wheeled his horse to face them. 'Keep in close order. Use your javelins, then march on. Bring them down with your shield bosses, kill them with your swords.' He swung back to the front of his line so that all could see him. 'When you have won,' he bellowed, 'you will have everything!'

Boudicca's chariot hurtled over the rough ground. As her warriors leapt and whooped and roared their battle chants, she yelled at them, 'I am descended from mighty men! But today I am not fighting for my wealth or my kingdom. I am fighting as a wronged woman, with my bruised body,' – she held her shaking girls to her – 'and for my outraged daughters.' She hauled at the reins to spin the chariot round to the right as her people danced around her, clashing their swords on their great wooden shields. 'Old people are killed,' she growled, 'virgins raped. But the gods will give us the revenge we deserve. The ninth legion is destroyed and others cower in their camps, afraid to face us. Afraid even to face our noise and the roar of our thousands.' She swung back along the battle line, unable to hold them much longer. 'Remember what you're fighting for. You will win or you will die. This is what I plan to do!' She laughed with her warriors with their flashing eyes and skyward-pointed swords. 'Let the men live in slavery if they will.'

For a moment, perhaps two, the XIV Gemina flinched, the javelins wavered as the Iceni launched their attack. They came in their thousands, men who stood a head taller than the legions, running forward up the slope ahead of them. The dogs ran too, and the boys, eager for their first blood, their first kill. The high-pitched bray of the Roman trumpets called the commands now, for no one would hear Paulinus again above the noise. The ground was shaking with the thunder of feet and the Iceni horsemen and the charioteers galloped on the wings, outstripping the runners in the centre. At the trumpets' command, the legions slid sideways, extending their line to let the mixed cohorts through to take the centre.

Ahead of them, the centurions' vine sticks were in the air and they hissed down as one, each man in every unit launching his javelin through the blue.

The Iceni met the shock running, the iron-headed pila thudding through their shields and thumping into their unarmoured bodies. The crash of the onslaught was broken, the charge was slowed as the warriors fought to hold their feet and wrench the twisted javelins out of their shields.

As one, the legions' shields swung sideways across the soldiers' chests. As one, the swords slid clear of the scabbards and the trumpets sounded again. The air was full of hissing stones as the Iceni slingers pelted the front line, pebbles bouncing off the tough shields and denting the helmets. Here and there a Roman went down, his eye gone, his head streaming with blood. On the flanks the cavalry moved out against the Horse People, but they had left it late and the Iceni speed jolted them backwards, mailed horsemen crashing into the trunks and branches of trees.

A chariot clattered against the auxiliaries, then another and another, probing for weaknesses, picking off the front ranks, who were too slow or inexperienced. Then the legions formed *their wedges, the cohorts of XIV with XX behind them, marching down the slope into the teeth of the still ongoing charge. Boudicca was with her warriors, shaking her spear at the advancing legions, screaming support for her people. Her daughters clung to the chariot's rim, shouting out in imitation of their mother.*

The crash of arms carried far beyond the deep woods behind Paulinus and far beyond the river at Boudicca's back. A cohort was held here, another knocked sideways there by the impact of the Iceni charge. But the Romans were making ground. Paulinus could tell, watching from the forest's edge, that the Celts had outrun themselves. Pushing forward on aching and exhausted legs, the warriors' long swords bounced and clashed on the moving shield wall. The legate knew what it was like in the centre of all that; the iron shield bosses smashing ribs and crippling lungs, the two-edged swords thudding into the naked bodies, the iron-shod caligae stamping sweating faces into the mud, slippery with the blood of the dead and the dying.

Now the auxiliaries pushed forward too, eight of Paulinus' ten thousand driving their murderous wedges through the tossing, struggling Iceni ranks. The slaughter went on.

Boudicca did not know how long her people had held their ground before they broke. Was it one hour? Two? Nor could she tell who ran first, but the right was breaking, crumbling like bread at Beltane too long in the fire. The legions gathered pace as they sensed the moment, driving the Iceni back and into the arms of the Roman cavalry, pushing in now from the flanks. Boudicca's own horsemen were in disarray, a thousand individual contests going on all over the slope of the ground.

Now the Romans were silent no more. They were smashing their curved shields with their bloodied swords, shouting out in a language that was not their own, the alien war cries stolen from a thousand battlefields. Warriors hurled themselves onto the wedges, hacking at the helmeted heads below, sliding to their deaths on the moving caterpillars of the enemy. And now the legions had reached the wagons. The women and the children snatched up the swords and the spears and the slings of their husbands and fathers. They stood with their wagon circle at their backs and died before the eagles. Still the shield bosses

7

went in, the swords hacking into flimsy bodies, boots grinding children into the dust. The oxen, still yoked, were hacked down, and the legions overturned the wagons as they marched, unstoppable, to the river.

Only then did the trumpets call them back. Only then did the Iceni melt away. Only then did Boudicca of the red hair hold her daughters to her and bury their tear-streaked faces in the folds of her dress. The day belonged to Paulinus. The Iceni were no more, and the guttering torch of freedom had gone out forever.

* * *

Boudicca's last battle with the Romans has passed into legend. Like the life of the queen herself, we have only the briefest of accounts, the most passing of shadows. The account above is probably as close as we are ever likely to get to what happened in that distant past. Such is the infuriating nature of ancient history that we do not know exactly where or when the battle was fought. We cannot be sure of the season or even the year. But our speculation about it, like everything else in this book, is based as closely as possible on the written and archaeological evidence we do have.

To begin with, we must realize that there are no Iceni or Celtic accounts of the battle. The Celts had no written language in the conventional sense, and although their priests, the Druids, might have used a form of Greek in certain circumstances, they did not compile histories or chronicles of events. As we shall see in a later chapter, their traditions and their culture were at once verbal and closely guarded. We therefore have to rely on the only written accounts available and that means the inevitably biased versions of the Romans.

History, they say, is written by the winners. And in this case we have two historians – Tacitus and Cassius Dio. Of these, Publius Cornelius Tacitus is the more reliable, and for two reasons: he had served as a legionary commander himself, somewhere in the provinces, probably between 89 and 93 and his father-in-law was the renowned Julius Agricola, one of Britain's ablest governors and himself a tribune there at the time of Boudicca's rebellion. That said, there are three problems in relying on the record of Tacitus. Several of his books have been lost, and he has the obvious bias of a historian overly influenced by events of his own day. His terse style of writing has lent his name to a sulky lack of communication – taciturnity. We know little about the man's early years. He was probably born in Vasio or Forum Julii (today's Vaison or Fréjus in southern France), part of the Roman province of Gaul some three or four years before the Iceni took on the might of the empire. His father may have been the *procurator* (essentially a tax collector) at Augusta Treverorum (Trier) and paymaster of the Roman armies along the Rhine. He wrote:

> I have no wish to deny that my career owed its beginning to Vespasian [Emperor 69–79] its progress to Titus [79–81] and its further advancement to Domitian.[1]

By 88 Tacitus was a *praetor*, the magisterial rank in Rome preceding consular status which allowed a man to hold a senior command either in the army or governing a province. His absence from Rome from 89 to 93 is doubtless explained by his holding either of these posts. A lawyer of some eminence, Tacitus was also a member of the priestly college in Rome and first went 'into print' in the spring of 98 with his *Life of Julius Agricola*, eulogizing his dead father-in-law. Vitally important as this work is to our understanding of Roman Britain in the period of Agricola's governorship (78 to 85), it must be remembered that Tacitus tends to measure all governors by Agricola's exacting standards and finds several of them wanting. It is here that his bias inevitably creeps in and gives us a distorted view of the years in which Boudicca was a girl and young woman coping with increasing Roman domination. Tacitus' best known works, from which we will be quoting extensively, are the *Historiae* and the *Annales*. The former probably once had a different title and consists of fourteen books written *c.* 105, covering the period 68 to 70. Only four and a half of these survive in full. They describe the chaotic political time of the year of the four emperors (69), when Nero committed suicide and no public Roman felt safe.

The *Annales* (actually titled *Ab Excessu Divi Augusti – From the Death of Augustus*) is his best-known work and the most relevant to us here. Probably unfinished at the time of his death in 120, only the first few books survive – parts of 5, 6, 11, 12 and 16 – out of a total seventeen volumes.

In these years, the historian was living in the relatively benign *imperia* of Trajan and Hadrian, but his bitterness at the memories of Domitian's appalling reign is evident in the *Annales*. It is also refreshing for us, because he often criticizes Roman administration and Roman officials and shows a certain sympathy with the Celts, which would otherwise be totally lacking in the written record.

Tacitus' sources are unknown. Since Agricola was a tribune on Paulinus' staff and very probably present at Boudicca's last battle, we must assume he had seen eyewitness accounts. He had access to the records of the Senate, Rome's 'parliament', and very possibly the *commentarii* (dispatches) of Britannia's governors from Aulus Plautius to Paulinus himself. He had probably read the elder Pliny's epic thirty-seven volume *Historia Naturalis*, the account of the emperor Tiberius' German Wars by Aufidius Bassus and the works of the historian-consul Cluvius Rufus.

The brevity of his style is infuriating and in the context of Boudicca it raises more questions than it answers. He was clearly fascinated by his subject's psychology, but two elements cast doubt on his accuracy in this respect. First, most Romans wrote for an audience, not a readership – the tales had to be exciting, varied and epigrammatic because they were in part oral entertainment at dinner parties. Second, Tacitus was trained as an orator and the speeches he puts into the mouths of his 'actors' have far more to do with the Roman scholarly perception of the world than authentic Celtic attitudes. As always, in the absence of confirmatory historical evidence, we have, in the end, to take some of Tacitus at least on trust.

Lucius Cassius Dio, often referred to today as Dio Cassius, was a Roman historian who wrote in Greek. Born in Bithynia (modern Turkey) in 164, he was the son of Cassius Apronianos, the governor of Dalmatia. He held many offices in Rome after 180, serving as a senator under the Emperor

Commodus and suffect consul under Severus. He was governor of Pergamum and Smyrna and a consul in 220 before taking in the governorship of Dalmatia, as his father had, and of Pannonia (modern Hungary).

His greatest work is the *History of Rome* from the city's legendary founding by Aeneas of Trojan War fame to the reign of Severus (222–245). The eighty volumes took him twenty-two years to write, and again we are left with only a partial record. Books 36 to 54, which cover the period 68 to 10 BC, have survived in full; books 55 to 60, covering the period relevant to us, extend to 46 AD but are merely abridged; the rest exist only in scraps. We are fortunate, however, in that in the cultural renaissance of the twelfth century both the scholars Xiphilinus and Zonarus produced summaries of Dio's work known as *epitomes*. These cover the period of the Boudiccan rising.

Dio is not the master of narrative that Tacitus is, and his judgement does not appear very sound if compared with other texts. He seems to have understood the problem of using tainted sources, although, unlike Tacitus, he lived long after Boudicca's time. Like Tacitus, he believed that brevity was the soul of history and he leaves out a great deal that we would love to know. Part of the problem, as historian Michael Grant says,[2] is that 'during the third century AD it was not very safe to write about facts', and Dio may have veered away from them as a result.

The 'raw material' then for the account of the battle above comes from these two men. What do they say? In *Annales XIV* Tacitus wrote:

> Suetonius [Paulinus] collected XIV legion and detachments of XX together with the nearest available auxiliaries – amounting to nearly ten thousand armed men – and decided to attack without further delay.

He does not tell us what time of year this was, merely that the Boudiccan revolt had begun under the consulships of Lucius Caesennius Paetus and Publius Petronius Turpilianus in Rome. This makes the year 61, but other evidence today suggests the previous year, extending the rebellion by perhaps six months. Even so, it is logical to assume that the battle was fought in the summer of 61, perhaps in August, near the Roman feast of Volcanalia. In an era of physical, hand-to-hand warfare fought over heavily wooded terrain with virtually no roads, summer was the usual campaigning season. Celtic warriors who survived went home to gather the harvest and lick their wounds over winter, telling tall tales around the home fires with their beer and their choice cuts of pork. Then the whole process began again in the spring when the swords were sharpened.

> [Paulinus] chose a position in a defile with a wood behind him. There could be no enemy, he knew, except at his front, where there was open country without cover for ambushes.

The legate knew perfectly well that the Celts were at their most deadly in thick woodland, and ambush was their speciality. Quintus Cerialis had lost his IX Hispana Legion that way only weeks before, and Paulinus was not going to make the same mistake.

We do not know where the battlefield was. Given the details of the earlier campaign when Boudicca's army had destroyed Camulodunum (today's Colchester), Londinium (London) and Verulamium (St Albans), Roman expert Malcolm Todd surmises a site in Hertfordshire, not far north of the last place of attack. Folklore places it much nearer to London, perhaps close to the present King's Cross station. Most experts today, however, favour Mancetter, along Watling Street, the Roman road in Warwickshire. Any battle walker today has to contend with 'progress'. The Roman army's cobbled road is now the busy A5 running past Daventry to the south and swinging north-west towards Tamworth. The whole area is a mass of industrial development, a legacy of the nineteenth century, with a railway line and the Coventry canal cutting across the site. The area is no stranger to battles, however; five miles to the north-east lies the field of White Moor, better known as Bosworth, where Richard III was killed in another August, that of 1485. It is an ironic reminder of history's cycle that his boar standard fluttered so close to that of Paulinus' XX Legion at Mancetter and perhaps another carried by the Iceni opposite them.

The village is easy to miss; the battlefield even more so. Today it is a dormitory of Atherstone, a medieval settlement exactly 100 miles from London, Lincoln and Liverpool. Between 1955 and 1980 a series of excavations was carried out here establishing the likelihood of two auxiliary forts, one built over the other on the slope of the ground between the River Anker and the present railway line. Three complete amphorae (wine vessels) were found by chance in 1955 and the subsequent excavations by Keith Scott and his team revealed at least three periods of timber buildings. Another, with a latrine pit which could indicate a centurion's quarters, was discovered along Quarry Lane with what was clearly the second, larger fortification square bound by a double-ditch system. The pit had been deliberately filled in, but still retained its wooden cover and twelve two-handled flagons. There are obvious signs of deliberate demolition, as though the larger fort, perhaps legionary, was replaced with the smaller, for an auxiliary unit. Graham Webster believes that this was the home of XIV Gemina Legion before their subsequent move to Wroxeter, to the north-west.

The problem with using archaeology, as opposed to the written record, however biased, is that precise dating is unlikely. Despite a coin hoard being found near the road itself, between the church and the manor house, we cannot put an exact date on these fortifications. Perhaps the auxiliary fort was built first, as part of the forward positions of the governor Aulus Plautius in the mid-'40s and the larger legionary base ten years later. If both sets of buildings fall within the period 50 to 65, it still begs the question of whether it was there – and defended – by the time of Boudicca's battle. Neither Tacitus nor Dio mentions any such fortification, so we conclude that either it did not figure in the action or that the battle was fought elsewhere.

When we visited the site on a bright day in late February, a well-meaning local sent us in what we believe was the wrong direction. Along the slight ridge of Quarry Lane are a number of bungalows which we were told effectively marked Paulinus' position. We didn't expect to find a thick wood still on the site, but neither was there any sign of Tacitus' defile, and the ground which would have marked Boudicca's line of advance was such a gentle gradient that it would have posed no difficulties whatsoever. Tacitus implies that Paulinus chose the ground, as any experienced commander would, to provide the best advantage. The ridge of Quarry Lane would not have given him this. Following the road further, past the centurion's latrine, we crossed the railway line; here the ground took on a far more familiar shape. The road itself winds up through a sudden escarpment that is still thickly wooded with oak and ash. On our second visit the ground was carpeted with bluebells. The road veers away on the bank of what was clearly Tacitus' defile, and Paulinus' troops must have marched over the brow of the hill – now utterly disfigured by the extent of the quarrying at the top.

Walking this way we had an extraordinary view of miles of countryside across which the Iceni would have marched and a clear view of what would have been Boudicca's position on the flat flood plain of the meandering Anker; the Iceni view of the Romans, conversely, could have been almost entirely screened by trees. Whereas Tacitus gives the clear impression that this ground was carefully chosen by Paulinus, Dio says that he was short of food and that he 'feared their numbers and their desperation' but was nevertheless forced to engage the Iceni (whom Dio merely calls 'barbarians') 'contrary to his judgement'.[3]

Archaeologists Anne Ross and Don Robins put a further gloss on the site of the battle. Mancetter's Celtic name is Manduessedum, the place of the chariots, perhaps a reminder that the Iceni were still using this rather obsolete form of warfare in 61. Manduessedum, they contend, is clearly visible as a high ridge beyond High Cross, the all-important junction of the two military roads of the Fosse Way and Watling Street. There is of course over twenty miles between the two – a good day's march even for a fit legion that had not just exhausted itself with fighting on Mona (Anglesey), as XIV and XX had, and with a rapid forced march across Wales. Ross and Robins are vague about the precise site, but ask whether Paulinus deliberately drew the Iceni to Manduessedum because it had special religious significance for them. This all depends on our view of tribal conflicts. Manduessedum is in the territory of the Corieltavi, ancient enemies of the Iceni, so would Boudicca even know of their shrines? The whole vexed question of Celtic religion and the possible overarching power of the Druids is discussed in a later chapter.

Tacitus wrote that '[Paulinus] drew up his regular troops in close order with the light-armed auxiliaries at their flanks and the cavalry massed on the wings.'[4] Dio saw it differently:

Paulinus could not extend his line the whole length of [Boudicca's] for, even if the men had been drawn up only one deep, they would not have reached far enough, so inferior were they in numbers; nor, on the other hand, did he dare join battle in a single compact force, for fear of being surrounded and cut to pieces. He therefore separated his army into three divisions, in order to fight at several points at one and the same time, and he made each of the divisions so strong that it could not easily be broken through.

The backbone of the Roman army was the legion (meaning 'levy'). The original units were, according to legend, raised by Servius Tullius, a king of Rome in the fifth century BC. Membership was based on the ownership of property, and the legion operated along the lines of the Greek phalanx, using the *triplex acies* formation which Dio implies Paulinus used at Manduessedum. Fighting in subdivisions called *maniples*, and armed with swords, spears and oval shields, the legions were reorganized by Gaius Marius into a truly professional force some three centuries later. Various changes were already under way by his day, the most obvious of which were the creation of the cohort and the dropping of the property qualification. Instead, legionaries had to be Roman citizens, an honour much prized even by potential enemies like Cogidubnus, king of the Atrebates in southern Britain.

The men who fought for Paulinus on the slopes above the Anker that day in the summer of 61 were ideally five foot ten inches tall (six *pes* in Roman measurement) with good eyesight and a strong, well-proportioned body. Most of them were recruited and inspected by army boards at the age of eighteen and, by Boudicca's time, came from all over the empire. There were probably Gauls and Iberians, ancestors of today's Frenchmen and Spaniards; huge Batavians, bearded Germans from the Rhine whose speciality was fording swollen rivers; Pannonians and Thracians from further east. They had all sworn allegiance to their emperor, thumping their chests with their clenched fists and saluting the gilded eagle, which was their legion's most coveted standard. They would have learned to dig ditches and earth ramparts and build wooden stockades for the permanent and marching camps. They would be experts at marching up to twenty-five miles a day with the *impedimenta* of a campaign – a pole from which dangled their kit (weighing up to 40 pounds and consisting of cloak and other spare clothing); a leather wallet containing razor, tools and any personal effects; a netted bag with rations of grain; a bronze *patera* (or mess tin) for eating, and a metal water canteen.

The fourth-century Roman writer Vegetius[5] described the typical legions of his day, which had changed little in three hundred years:

. . . a young soldier who is chosen for the work of Mars should have alert eyes and should hold his head upright. The recruit should be broad-chested with powerful shoulders and brawny arms. His fingers should be long rather than short. He should not be pot-bellied or have a fat bottom. His calves and feet should not be flabby; instead they should be made entirely of tough sinew. When you find all these qualities . . . you can afford to take him even if he is a little on the short side . . . Fishermen, birdcatchers, sweet-makers, weavers and all those who do the kind of job that women normally do should be kept away from the army. On the other hand, smiths, carpenters, butchers and hunters of deer and wild boar are the most suitable . . .[6]

Some of the most faithful depictions of a Roman army of the period come from the extraordinary bas-relief of Trajan's column in Rome. The monument records in breathtaking detail figures on campaign against the Dacians (today's Romanians) in 101 and 105. Re-enactment groups like the Legio XIIII Gemina Martia Victrix, organized in 1982, work very hard to reproduce the battle and marching gear of Paulinus' cohorts, and have proved by experience that some of the acrobatics shown on Trajan's column are merely artistic licence, unless of course the human body has undergone more changes than we realize in 2,000 years!

The legion, under the command of a legate, comprised at full strength 5,500 officers and men. It is difficult to equate the legion and its ranking system with modern armies, and comparisons quickly cause problems. In terms of numbers, the legion is roughly twice the number of most western European regiments of the last 200 years, but in terms of *élan* and *esprit de corps*, a legion and a regiment are virtually synonymous. The only full legion with Paulinus was XIV Augusta Gemina, so called because it had been raised as one of a pair in the reign of the Emperor Augustus. The other was XX, which, until Boudicca's time, had no nickname, unlike most other legions. Both these units had probably been stationed in Britain since 43 and the Claudian conquest. If the legate was the rough equivalent of a colonel commanding the regiment (and in reality he was far more of a general, allowed wide latitude in tactical and even strategic decisions), the six tribunes below him were rather superior to modern majors. These men were of equestrian rank in the civilian world, with at least five years' military experience, and one of them, *tribunus laticlavius*, was the second in command of the legion and bound for a senatorial career. War and politics went hand in hand in the Roman Empire. Below the tribunes the legion was divided into ten cohorts, each, except the first, of 480 men and with its own distinctive battle standard. The first cohort comprised 800 men or five double centuries, all the other cohorts being subdivided into six centuries.

Perhaps the best-known image we have from various *stele* (military gravestones) is of the centurion with his transverse plumed helmet, the *phalerae* or battle honours on his tunic, the iron greaves that protected his shins and his notorious gnarled vine stick used to beat slow or unruly soldiers into discipline. By Paulinus' time the century was actually composed of eighty men, not the accepted hundred, and it is difficult to be precise about the type of man who led them. He is something between a junior commissioned officer and a long-serving sergeant major in modern times: recent armies have no one quite like him. Foremost among this group was the *primus pilus* (first javelin), who commanded the first century of the first cohort.

The legions drawn up in the centre of Paulinus' line below the woods at Manduessedum wore the *lorica segmentata*, the overlapping, hinged plates of iron, laced and buckled back and front, which have been shown in *stele* and other art forms all over the empire. The term is actually a modern one meaning sectional breastplate, as there are no clear contemporary terms for this piece of armour. Their heads were protected by the 'Imperial Gallic' helmets, examples of which are not uncommon throughout Europe. They had a brow ridge to deflect downward blows, ear pieces to protect the lobes, huge cheek plates with deflecting flanges and a wide brim at the neck. From the legionaries' waists hung the leather and iron groin guard to deflect blows to the genitals, and on their feet were the elaborately laced boots called *caligae*, made of leather with inch-thick soles studded with iron hobs.

The weaponry of Paulinus' legionaries never varied. Originally equipped with two spears, one for throwing, the other for thrusting, soldiers now carried a single, 7-foot *pilum* (javelin) with a wooden shaft and a small iron triangular head balanced by a block a third of the way down. From a belt on his right hip the legionary carried a *gladius*, a short, double-edged sword with a razor point designed for thrusting. He could twist the scabbard housing and draw this with his right hand while steadying his shield with the other. On his left, the shorter *pugio*, or dagger, could be used for close-quarter killing should the sword fail. The legionar's weak spots were his arms and legs and his partially exposed face, and to protect all these he carried the most brilliantly designed part of a Roman fighting man's equipment, the *scutum*, or shield. By Paulinus' time this was made of several thin layers of wood (in effect an early form of ply) curved to fit snugly around the body. It was large and rectangular with rounded corners, usually brightly painted with totemic or religious symbols (the most usual of which, at least for re-enacters, is the wing and lightning flash design) and with a central iron boss which was a weapon in itself. In siege situations, these interlocked shields, called *testudos* (tortoises) could protect a unit of men smashing its way through the gates of a Celtic hill fort with little damage other than bruised knuckles.

Fanning out on each side of XIV Gemina and XX at Manduessedum were the *auxilia*. The image we have of these fighting men is that they were less well equipped than the legionaries and somehow inferior to them. This is not actually so. Most of the empire's frontiers were manned by these men. They mounted guard on lonely outposts and, as in the case of Boudicca, helped to put down rebellions. Neither were the *auxilia* 'light infantry' in the accepted sense. Re-enactment groups have made armour and equipment from archaeological specifications and found that an auxiliary's mail shirt is actually heavier than the legionary's *lorica segmentata*; moreover, it is far more cumbersome, all the weight in mail armour hanging on the wearer's shoulders. The *auxilia* served in units of 500 or 1,000, often in mixed cavalry and infantry formations. It has been suggested that the *auxilia* were kept in smaller units so that the legions always outnumbered them; in the event of an internal insurrection, the 'foreign' troops would be defeated. Such men were given the promise of the coveted Roman citizenship after twenty-five years' service, assuming they survived that long. Specializations these men brought with them from various parts of the empire included archery, sling marksmanship and, in the curious case of the Batavians, the ability to cross rivers with ease. As the legions themselves contained men who were trained as artillerymen, carpenters, engineers, architects, clerks, bookkeepers and doctors, it is little wonder that the Roman army was so successful in the ancient world. Its troops were multi-taskers, trained to perfection and imbued with an iron discipline wholly lacking in most of their opponents.

Beyond the *auxilia* in Paulinus' battle formation at Manduessedum sat the cavalry, the horsed soldiers, in units, called *alae*. Commanded by the *praefectus alae*, there were normally 120 horsemen with each legion, not including the auxiliary units whose names reflect their origin.[7] At the time of Marius' reforms in the first century BC, there appears to be no legionary cavalry at all, but probably by the time of Claudius' invasion of 43, they were back. The Jewish warrior-turned-Roman-historian Flavius Josephus[8] describes them nine years after Boudicca's defeat as being divided into *turmae* (troops) of thirty men, but as there were so few of them, their role can only have been that of escorts and messengers. On the march, they would have ridden ahead of the legion and on the flanks, watching for signs of the enemy. They would have sighted the Iceni on their flood plain beyond the Anker first. The bulk of cavalry work was carried out by the auxiliaries, and their role was to harass the enemy on his flanks and turn a defeat into a rout. In common with all 'barbarians' whom they faced, Roman cavalry did not know the use of stirrups at this time and relied instead on a Celtic-style four-pronged saddle to achieve balance. Apologists for Roman cavalry say that this made them perfectly capable of delivering a charge at the gallop. We beg to differ – it was the ability to *stand* in the stirrups that gave the horseman the edge over foot soldiers. The best that can be said is that they were as competent horsemen as most of the enemy they met; they were not better.

Written about four centuries before Boudicca, the magnificent description of a warhorse from the Book of Job still thrills:

Hast thou given the horse strength? Hast thou clothed his neck with thunder? . . . The glory of his nostrils is terrible. He paweth in the valley and rejoiceth in his strength; he goeth on to meet the armed men. He mocketh at fear and is not affrighted; neither turneth he back from the sword. The quiver rattleth against him; the glittering spear and the shield . . . and he smelleth the battle afar off, the thunder of the captains and the shouting.[9]

Tacitus tells us that most European cavalry rode horses of Numidian origin, from Spain, but Gallic and German breeds were also used. They were descended from wild breeds, with upright manes and short legs. Archaeological remains suggest a norm of thirteen to fourteen hands – ponies by the standards of cavalry horseflesh in the nineteenth century.

The poet Virgil[10] wrote of the warhorse about ninety years before Manduessedum, 'his neck, is carried erect; his head is small; his belly short; his back broad . . . A bright bay or a good grey is the best colour; the worst is white or dun . . .' Such animals were well fed, receiving an astonishing 20 pounds of barley a day, nearly twice that provided by the British cavalry in the First World War, and that was for animals of fifteen to sixteen hands.

Tacitus wrote of Manduessedum:

On the British side, cavalry and infantry bands seethed over a wide area in unprecedented numbers. Their confidence was such that they brought their wives with them to see the victory, installing them in carts situated at the edge of the battlefield.[11]

Here, as throughout this book, we are hampered by the lack of evidence about Celtic armies written by the Celts themselves. We only have the word of the Romans, and the Romans were at pains to stress the discipline and superiority of their men, even when they lost! We have no idea of any command structure, names, or even the existence, of Boudicca's generals or captains, or whether the Iceni had anything approximating to fighting units such as the Roman cohorts. But there was a tribal hierarchy, and this was presumably transmitted in some way to the battlefield.

As we shall see in Chapter Three, the Iceni, in common with all Celts, had an extended family or clan system in which blood was infinitely thicker than the water that they held to be sacred. The Graeco-Roman historian Polybius[12] wrote:

[The Celts] treated comradeship as of the greatest importance, those among them being the most feared and most powerful who were thought to have the largest number of attendants and associates.[13]

These attendants, present in their thousands at Manduessedum, operated with the tribal leaders in a client relationship not unlike the feudal system of the eleventh-century Normans, in which the lower orders pledged allegiance and gave military support in exchange for protection and employment. On the battlefield, there must have been many clientage groups, but they never acted as cohesively or with such training as the Roman cohort.

What we do know is that the Celts throughout Europe lived for war. They were fantastically brave and terrifyingly fierce: the bas-reliefs of Celtic warriors on Trajan's column show superb specimens of naked manhood trading blows with the heavily armoured legionaries along the Danube. Whether Boudicca's men fought naked we do not know, but it was probably part of the ritual of warfare that they did. It may be that they had religious reasons for doing so, trusting that the blue designs pained over their bodies in *insalis tinctalia*, known usually as woad, somehow served to keep them from harm. It was also a symbol of bravado. According to various Roman commentators, Celts were vainglorious, boastful and arrogant. Strabo wrote:

> To their simplicity and vehemence they add folly, arrogance and love of ornament. Around their necks they wear gold collars, on their arms and wrists they have bracelets and those of good position among them clothe themselves in dyed garments, worked with gold. Their fickle, impressionable nature makes them intolerable in victory and faint-hearted in defeat . . .[14]

When telling tall tales around their campfires and smoky huts of a winter's evening, what better than to declare honestly that such and such an enemy was brought low in single combat by a hero armed only with a sword and shield?

The Greek philosopher Poseidonius[15] wrote:

> They sit in a circle with the most influential man in the centre, whether he be the greatest in warlike skill, nobility of family or wealth. Beside him sits the host and on either

side of them the others in orders of distinction. Their shield bearers stand behind them while their spearmen are seated on the opposite side and feast in common like their lords . . . The Celts sometimes engage in single combat at dinner. Assembling in arms they engage in a mock battle drill and mutual thrust and parry. Sometimes wounds are inflicted and the irritation caused by this may even lead to the killing of the opponent unless they are held back by their friends . . . When the hindquarters [of a boar] were served up, the bravest hero took the thigh piece; if another man claimed it they stood up and fought in single combat to the death.[16]

They limewashed their hair, these Celtic warriors, which made them taller and more fierce than ever and, swarming over the flood plain, they danced and shouted and taunted the Romans, clashing their long iron swords against their hexagonal wooden shields.

Writing of the Gauls of the previous century, the Greek historian Diodorus Siculus[17] would probably have recognized Boudicca's warriors at Manduessedum:

The Gauls are tall of body, with rippling muscles and white of skin. Their hair is fair, not only by nature but also because of their custom of accentuating it by artificial means. They wash their hair in lime water, then pull it back so that it differs little from a horse's mane. Some of them shave their beards, others let them grow. The nobles shave their cheeks but let their moustaches grow until it covers their mouths.[18]

The bulk of Boudicca's army was probably made up of men the Romans called *soldurii*, foot troops with no body armour and armed with sword or spear. Diodorus Siculus noted that:

Their arms include man-sized shields decorated according to taste. [This was probably a totemic tradition]. Some of these have projecting figures in bronze, skilfully made not

Outline of a bronze sword hilt first century BC showing a human figure, common in Britain and Europe. Found in Ballyshannon, Co. Donegal.

only for decoration but also for protection. They wear bronze helmets with large figures, which give the wearer the appearance of enormous size. In some cases horns are attached, in others the foreparts of birds or beasts . . . some of them have iron breastplates or mail while others fight naked. They carry long swords held by a chain of bronze or iron hanging on their right side . . . They brandish spears which have iron heads a cubit or more in length and a little less than two palms in breadth. Some are forged straight, others are twisted so that the blow does not merely cut the flesh but on withdrawing will lacerate the wound.[19]

The accent for those men was on personal deeds of valour, crashing into the enemy line at full running speed and breaking up formations where possible. The nobility rode at the head of what the Romans called *trimarcisia* (from the Celtic 'three horses') originally a system among the Celts in which the warrior was accompanied by two servants who each rode a spare horse, to remount their lord should he become unhorsed. The cavalry of the Iceni was probably large, as we might expect from a people whose name is associated with horses, and the breed they rode was as tough and short-legged as that of the Romans, the forerunner of modern breeds like the Dartmoor and New Forest ponies.

Most tantalizing of all at Manduessedum is the use of the chariot. Tacitus refers only to one – that of the queen herself, but Dio implies they were used in numbers. We know from Caesar[20] that the British used chariots in huge numbers at the time of his invasion in 54 BC. He was fascinated by them because of the speed and agility with which the Celts brought them into play and also because they were obsolete elsewhere in Europe by his day, the Gauls having abandoned them a century earlier.

In his famous commentaries on the Gallic Wars, Caesar wrote:

In chariot fighting the Britons begin by driving all over the field hurling javelins. Generally, the terror inspired by the horses and the noise of the wheels are sufficient to throw their opponent's ranks into disorder. Then, after making their way between the squadrons of their own cavalry, they jump down from the chariots and engage on foot. In the meantime, the charioteers retire a short distance from the battle and place their vehicles in such a position that their masters, if hard-pressed by numbers, have an easy means of retreat to their own lines. Thus, they combine the nobility of cavalry with the staying power of infantry.

The Romans called such charioteers *essedarii*, but in Rome by this time the vehicle was only used for racing, for example in the famous Circus Maximus in the City. Chariot burials have been found much further north in Yorkshire among the Parisii, recent Belgic arrivals on the east coast, but an important grave from Iceni territory implies that Boudicca's people used them extensively too. And Manduessedum, after all, means the place of the chariots.

The chariot platform was a wooden square about 3 feet 4 inches, mounted on axles whose wheels were about 3 feet in diameter. The wheels were spoked and iron-rimmed, the chariot's sides made from double hoops of bent wood, perhaps reinforced with wickerwork or leather strapping. The floor was probably leather too, providing a rudimentary suspension, and front and back were open for ease of access. Caesar tell us[21] that while the charioteer drove his chariot into an enemy flank the warrior with him dashed along the pole between the horses and hurled his javelins or hacked with his sword before wheeling away to another part of the field. In Irish mythology, it was the custom always to wheel the chariot to the right, to copy the clockwise movement of the sun and to invoke the power of the Celtic Otherworld.

Both Tacitus and Dio put speeches into the mouths of their combatant leaders and it is likely that Paulinus and Boudicca said *something* along those lines. It is interesting, however, that much of the legate's advice is practical, while Boudicca's smacks of rhetoric and passion in righting wrongs. In what follows we have taken Tacitus' version because he at least had access to someone (Agricola) who was probably there.

'Disregard the clamour and empty threats of the natives,' Paulinus told his men. 'In their ranks, there are more women than fighting men.'

It was the noise and terror of the first Celtic charge that might rattle Paulinus' men. The Iceni would have spent upwards of an hour taunting and berating the silent, immobile Romans on their slope, working themselves up into a frenzy not unlike the chanting of the Zulu at Rorke's Drift or the Maori *haka* before an international rugby match.[22] Diodorus Siculus wrote that 'Their trumpets are of a peculiar kind, they blow into them and produce a harsh sound that suits the tumult of war.'[23]

Shown on the famous Gundestrup cauldron, the war horn, or *carynx*, was a long, straight instrument ending in an animal head. An excellent specimen in bronze from Deskford, Scotland, is in the form of a stylized boar with a movable lower jaw and a wooden tongue that clattered when vibrated.

The Roman historian Livy[24] wrote of the Gauls much earlier, 'They are given to wild outbursts, and they fill the air with hideous songs and varied cries.' Of other Celts, the Galatae in Asia Minor, he wrote, 'Their songs as they go into battle, their yells and leaping and the dreadful noise of arms as they beat their shields . . . all this is done with one purpose: to terrify their enemies.'[25]

Paulinus' reference to women is instructive. There were indeed whole families with Boudicca, perhaps an example of her arrogance, but very definitely a miscalculation. On the other hand, as the Greek historian Ammianus Marcellinus[26] had already written, a Celtic woman with her blood up was, if anything, more dangerous than her man:

> A whole troop of foreigners would not be able to withstand a single Celt if he called his wife to his assistance; the wife is even more formidable. She is usually very strong and with blue eyes; in rage her neck veins swell, she gnashes her teeth and brandishes her snow-white robust arms. She begins to stroke blows mingled with kicks, as if they were so many missiles sent from the string of a catapult. The voices of these women are formidable and threatening, even when they are not angry, but being friendly . . .[27]

Boudicca's words at Manduessedum deserve more consideration and will be analysed later. They cannot be genuine but they are important for all that. Agricola would have been too far away to hear them and as far as we know he did not speak the Iceni tongue; so for Boudicca, in effect, read Tacitus. 'We British are used to women commanders in war,' she begins – an astonishing statement. The only other Celtic woman whose name we know from the Roman record is Cartimandua, whom Tacitus describes as 'flourishing in all the splendour of wealth and power'.[28] She was a contemporary of Boudicca and queen of the Brigantes in what today is Yorkshire and Lancashire. As we shall see, this pre-Roman woman had faced an internal rebellion some years before and would again in the years that followed. Whether Tacitus is referring to her or to other figures known to him but not recorded cannot now be resolved. Tacitus' version of Boudicca's speech has been closely paraphrased above, and he stresses her total faith in the Celtic battle system: 'They will never face even the din and roar of all our thousands, much less the shock of our onslaught.' She was wrong.

Dio's version of Paulinus' speech puts the fear of the gods into his soldiers' minds:

It would be better for us to fall fighting bravely than to be captured and impaled, to look upon our own entrails cut from our bodies, to be spitted on red-hot skewers, to perish by being melted in boiling water – in a word, to suffer as though we had been thrown to lawless and impious wild beasts . . . for in any case our bodies shall for ever possess the land.

Tacitus' account of the battle is, typically, eleven lines long. Dio's is more detailed, but bears little resemblance to what must have happened. Tacitus implies that the Romans stood still, partly defended by the narrow defile, as the Iceni ran up the slope. Dio says both sides moved forward. Diodorus Siculus wrote of the Celts:

When the armies are drawn up they are wont to advance in front of the line of battle and challenge the bravest of their opponents to single combat. When someone accepts the challenge, they recite the heroic deeds of their ancestors and proclaim their own valour, at the same time abusing and belittling their opponent in an attempt to rob him of his fighting spirit.[29]

Although the Roman historian Livy gives an account of a Roman accepting such a Celtic challenge (and killing his man) Paulinus showed no such inclination at Manduessedum. His was the only effective legionary force left north of Exeter and he was not about to risk it with hare-brained heroics.

Dio, no military historian and clearly with no understanding of Celtic tactics, pictures the Iceni advancing at a walk, a suicidal method against the legions. Both men refer to the accuracy of Roman *pila* throwing, which would have slowed the wild Iceni charge, warriors throwing away their skewered shields to give them unlimited access to the enemy. At Mons Graupius twenty years later, the Pictish troops facing Agricola's legions had learned a tough lesson. Tacitus wrote:

> The fighting began with an exchange of missiles. The Britons showed both steadiness and skill in parrying our spears with their huge swords or catching them on their little shields, while they themselves rained volleys on us.[30]

Clearly at Manduessedum, the lesson had not yet been learned.

Dio's picture is of evenly matched sides in terms of contests – 'light-armed troops exchanged missiles with light-armed, heavy-armed were opposed to heavy armed, cavalry clashed with cavalry'. Romano-British battles were just not like that. According to Dio, the charioteers were seen off by the Roman archers, but not before they had crashed into Paulinus' ranks, 'knocking them helter-skelter'.

> Horsemen would overthrow foot soldiers and foot soldier strikes down horsemen; a group of Romans, forming in close order, would advance to meet the chariots, and others would be scattered by them; a band of Britons would come to close quarters with the archers and rout them, while others were content to dodge their shafts at a distance . . . They contended for a long time, both parties being assisted by the same zeal and daring.

In this, Dio is right. Had Paulinus lost this battle, it is entirely possible that the Emperor Nero would have pulled his battered troops out of his troublesome province 'beyond the ocean' as not being worth the candle. Had Boudicca won, she would have driven the hated Romans out, avenged the insult to her and her family and perhaps halted progress by an untold number of centuries.

A battle like Manduessedum cannot last for long. When Aulus Plautius fought his two-day battle on the Medway eighteen years earlier, people commented. Tacitus' brevity implies a very swift affair, which is unlikely given what had happened so far and what was at stake. Dio says the battle ended 'late in the day' and it is reasonable to accept three or four hours as a maximum for a struggle of this type. The exact instant when the Iceni cracked and fled is not recorded. Such a moment happens in all battles, but it is indefinable, a rising sense of loss and panic that translates into hysteria coupled with exhaustion. The rolling tide of the advancing legions had a momentum of its own and, once the Iceni fell back, this quickly turned into a rout.

Hemmed in by their semicircle of wagons and their women and children, the Iceni were slaughtered in great heaps. The Belgic tribe called the Nervii had chosen a similar dogged resistance against Caesar in the previous century:

> But the enemy, even in their desperate plight, showed such bravery that when their front ranks had fallen those immediately behind stood on their prostrate bodies to fight; and when these too fell and their corpses were piled high, the survivors still kept hurling javelins as though from the top of a mound and flung back the spears they caught on their shields.[31]

Tacitus similarly recorded. 'The Romans did not spare even the women. Baggage animals, too, transfixed with weapons, added to the heaps of the dead.' And Dio noted how '. . . they slew many in battle beside the wagons and the forest, and captured many alive.'

The fate of captives after a Roman battle will be discussed later, but essentially it involved slavery or death, even though a few escaped and prepared to fight again. Five centuries later the Bardic poet Aneurin wrote of the fate of other Celtic warriors, this time fighting the invading Saxons at Catraeth (today's Catterick, in Yorkshire): 'Though they were killed, they slew, and until the end of the world they will be remembered.' Among the survivors were Boudicca and her children. 'So much', wrote Dio, 'for affairs in Britain.' A delighted Gaius Paulinus gave new honours to the legions who had fought her. The XX were made Valeria Victrix and XIV Gemina, Martia Victrix – the winner of the war.

What led to Manduessedum? What brought Boudicca, her raped daughters and her vengeful people to that hillside above the Anker in that summer of 61? It all began with Roman destiny, a belief in racial superiority so strong that it demanded these dazzling conquerors concern themselves in precisely these 'affairs in Britain' of which Cassius Dio wrote; that insatiable thirst that he accords to Paulinus – 'for in any case our bodies shall for ever possess this land'.

2
A Landing of Eagles

> And see you, after rain, the trace
> Of mound and dike and wall?
> O that was a Legion's camping-place,
> When Caesar sailed from Gaul!
>> 'Puck's Song' from *Puck of Pook's Hill*,
>> Rudyard Kipling, 1906

Caesar remembered in *De Bello Gallico*, 'It was now near the end of summer, and winter sets in early in those parts . . .' Nevertheless, Caesar made active preparations for an expedition to Britain, because he knew that in almost all the Gallic campaigns the Gauls had received reinforcements from the Britons.

Any understanding of Boudicca's rebellion must begin with the bare fact that Rome invaded her territory and that that invasion began either as a reconnaissance in strength or as a publicity stunt, depending on one's view of imperialism generally or Julius Caesar specifically, in 55 BC.

Views on empire change with the weather. The British in the twenty-first century are still reeling from the loss of theirs and are trying to find themselves again in a world dominated by others. Some Roman writers were as sure of their right to conquest, to create the *Pax Romana*, as the British were nineteen centuries later. We even borrowed their language to express it – *Pax Britannica*. Today, obsessed as we are with the concepts of self-determination and political correctness, *any* sort of imperialism is denigrated as racist, harmful and destructive, and an awful lot of babies have disappeared with the bathwater.

The image of the Roman expansion to the west which held sway in the apogee of later European empires – the British, the Austro-Hungarian, the Russian, even the Ottoman – was that the Romans were reluctant imperialists. The flag, or more accurately, the eagle, followed the call of trade and if rebellious tribes rose up, like the Iceni in 60 AD, it was the Romans' sacred duty to put them down. Straight roads, public baths, central heating, aqueducts, a written language and strong laws, not to mention an incomparable army, were the benefits of such imperialism; everyone was better off.

Today, we are perhaps more wary or more cynical and it is possible to see in the Roman wars in Gaul and Britain, as elsewhere, the greed and ambition of military adventurers, with Caesar at the forefront. His views on the Celts of Britain are important in the story of Boudicca for two reasons. First, the 'divine Julius' exerted a huge influence on Romans long after his death. His attitudes to the Celts remained essentially those of all Romans up to and including Boudicca's time. Second, the pace of life in the ancient world was measurably slower than today. Four generations separate Caesar's invasion from that of Claudius, when Boudicca was already in her late teens, but given the slow pace of society's development, this would have made little difference. Caesar was only yesterday.

There may well have been British Celts with the Atrebates, Caesar's excuse for his invasion of Britain. But there were also legends of fabulous wealth in the Pretanic Islands across what the Romans called Oceanus Britannicus, and it is likely that Boudicca's people, the Iceni, were among the richest of its tribes. The islands promised untold riches and limitless opportunity. Who knew what lay beyond that shifting sea and those constant mists?

Caesar's attempt to find out in 55 BC had achieved nothing. The whole venture was badly planned, was certainly beyond his remit as governor of Gaul and twice had come very close to disaster. There was no permanent landfall, no booty worthy of the name, almost no hostages and an unspecified number of casualties. The most remarkable event, and it was this that probably accounts for the adulation demonstrated in Rome at the time, is that Caesar had crossed the Oceanus Britannicus and lived to tell the tale. Caesar and his eagles would be back the following year, this time with the largest armada ever to land on Britain's shores. His campaign of 54 saw the legions cross the Thames and establish what would become a permanent foothold in the country.

Historians and archaeologists can form only the vaguest of maps of Celtic Britain. Caesar had the leisure to write three years later that

The population is exceedingly large, the ground thickly studded with homesteads closely resembling those of the Gauls, and the cattle very numerous.[1]

But we have no idea where these homesteads were located or whether any of them was large enough to equate with what the Romans would consider a town.

What had Caesar and the 'civilized' heart of Rome learned about the people at the edge of the world? 'The interior,' he wrote three years after he left Kent, 'is inhabited by people who claim, on the strength of an oral tradition, to be aboriginal; the coast, by Belgic immigrants who came to plunder and make war – nearly all of them retaining the names of the tribes from which they originated – and later settled down to till the soil.' He is describing the traditional immigration pattern of newcomers to Britain – handfuls of marauders who came to kill and pillage and who were, astonishingly, accepted by the communities nearby. Of the many invaders of Britain, only two, the Romans and the Normans, came in the form of an all-conquering army and en masse.

For money [and cash economics were never far from Caesar's mind] they use either bronze or gold coins or iron ingots of fixed weights. Tin is found inland [only, in fact, in

Cornwall] and small quantities of iron near the coasts [the Sussex Weald]; the copper they use is imported. There is timber of every kind, as in Gaul, except for beech and fir. Hares, fowl and geese they think it is unlawful to eat, but rear them for their pleasure and amusement. The climate is more temperate than in Gaul, the cold being less severe.[2]

Some of this information Caesar would have obtained first-hand, seeing it himself. The rest would have been gleaned from the Trinovantes and the minor tribes who flocked to the protection of his eagles; but much of it was mistaken. Whether this was genuine ignorance or an attempt at 'misinformation' is impossible to say. Certainly, his geographical details are very wide of the mark:

The island is triangular with one side facing Gaul. One corner of this side, on the coast of Kent [where he landed twice so would know well] is the landing place for nearly all the ships from Gaul, and points east; the lower corner points south. The length of this side is about 475 miles. Another side faces west towards Iberia [Spain]. In this direction is Hispania or Insula Sacra [Ireland], which is supposed to be half the size of Britain and lies at the same distance from it as Gaul. Midway across is the Isle of Man [Caesar wrongly calls this Mona, which was actually Anglesey, off North Wales] and it is believed that there are also a number of smaller islands, in which according to some writers there is a month of perpetual darkness at the winter solstice. Our inquiries on this subject were always fruitless, but we found by accurate measurement with a water clock[3] that the nights are shorter than on the continent. This side of Britain [i.e. the west coast] according to the natives' estimate, is 665 miles long. The third side faces north; no land lies opposite it, but its eastern corner points roughly in the direction of Germania [Germany]. Its length is estimated at 760 miles. Thus the whole island is 1900 miles in circumference.[4]

Caesar accepted contemporary geographers' views that the coast of Gaul was virtually vertical on a north-south axis, so the south coast of Britain ran parallel to it and this slewed the whole country's axis; hence the 'west' coast facing Spain.

Of the people who would become polyglot British in the centuries ahead, Caesar found the Cantiaci 'by far the most civilized' and very similar in their way of life to the Gauls, itself strong evidence for the pan-Celtic European tradition, but the tribes of the interior

> . . . do not grow corn but live on milk and meat and wear skins. All the Britons dye their bodies with woad, which produces a blue colour and shave the whole of their bodies except the head and the upper lip.

There is a sense of 'beyond the pale' about this description. The natives sound barbaric and primitive and this is precisely the image that Caesar wanted to give of Celtic peoples, which made slaughtering them all the more acceptable. During his *imperium*, the squint-eyed geographer Strabo added to Caesar's commentaries:

> Most of the island is flat and covered in forests, though there are many hilly areas. Grain, cattle, gold, silver and iron are found on the island. They are exported together with hides, slaves and excellent hunting dogs . . . The Britons are taller than the Gauls, their hair is not so yellow and their bodies more gangling. To give some idea of their size, I saw some of them in Rome, just young boys, but they towered half a foot above the tallest people there. What is more, they were bandy and their bodies all crooked.[5]

Deformed bodies such as these have been found in Iron Age graves at various sites in Britain, implying perhaps some sort of primitive euthanasia. Alternatively, the bone malformations in graves could be the cause of a natural death, and it is likely that the slave boys Strabo saw had the rickets associated with the poor diet of many ancient peoples. Unlike Caesar, Strabo did not visit Britain and his ignorance and reliance on hearsay are evident:

Their way of life is a bit like that of the Gauls, but much cruder and more barbaric. For example, although they have plenty of milk, some of them do not know how to make cheese, nor do they know anything about keeping gardens or farms.

Their cities are their forests. They cut down the trees and fence in a large round space. In this enclosure they build their huts and corral their cattle, but they do not stay in any one place for very long. They have more rain than snow and on days when there is no rain the fog hangs about for so long that the sun shines for only three or four hours around midday. Apart from some other small islands around Britain there is a large one called Ierne [Ireland]. About this island I can say nothing definitely except that the inhabitants are fiercer than the Britons and that they are maneaters.[6]

The ninety-seven year gap between the two Roman invasions can only be mapped in the vaguest terms, but archaeology tells us what the written record does not. Between the invasions of Caesar and Claudius there was ongoing trade with Rome which led to luxury items reaching the south of Britain in ever larger quantities. The client kings of Rome were happy to carry on this trade and even to pay the annual tribute as long as the *caligae* and the eagle were not planted on their soil.

As politics in Rome settled down[7] and the Roman world came to accept that imperialism and the cult of the emperor were already a way of life, 'she of the seven hills' turned again to that distant province that was not truly a province – yet – and, as Horace had written, to 'the Britons, who are savage towards foreigners'.[8]

Aulus Plautius, a greatly respected senator, commanded an expedition against Britain. For a certain Berikos, who had been driven out of the island during an uprising, had persuaded Claudius to send a force there.[9]

As with Caesar's account of his incursions nearly a century earlier, Dio's is the only narrative of events we have for the

Claudian invasion of 43 AD and it limits us. Like the whole story of Boudicca, we only have one version, the enemy's, on which to rely, and Dio raises as many questions as he provides answers.

By the time Aulus Plautius brought his legions from Portus Itius in the summer of 43, Boudicca was probably already a wife, a queen and possibly even a mother. Working backwards from the physical description of her given by Dio and the fact that her daughters were raped in 60/61, we can assume that she was born between 25 and 30. News of the rapid events of 43 would have been highly relevant to the Iceni, poised as they were on the edge of the Roman world, whose frontier was creeping inexorably north.

As we shall see, the Iceni were cut off from the Romanization that was increasing through trade in the south, but Claudius' arrival would have forced Boudicca's tribe to sit up and take notice. How much of the detail of the invasion she would have known, and how long news would have taken to reach her, we cannot tell, but like all the tribes in the path of Roman civilization, the Iceni faced a stark choice – to fight or capitulate.

Tiberius Claudius Drusus Nero Germanicus rejoiced in the names of four other emperors besides himself and must have been one of the most unusual rulers of Rome. A most dramatic representation of him was found in the River Alde in Suffolk and may well have been a casualty of Boudicca's rebellion in 60. Only the head of the life-size bronze statue has survived, raising all kinds of possibilities about rivers, votive offerings and the cult of the head which we will examine later. It shows a man of about thirty, clean-shaven and with the characteristic forward-combed hair of the time. The mouth is sensitive, the chin small and pointed. His large eyes, which may originally have held coloured glass balls, are hollow, giving the face an unusual, masklike quality. His ears are very large, like the handles of amphorae. He does not have the commanding face of a general – and he was not a natural leader; that he was emperor at all was due to a quirk of fate.

Suffering from a condition which gave him an air of imbecility, his appearance was a mass of contradictions. He had a stoop and a severe limp. His nervous tic and stammer were the causes of frequent hilarity, before he became emperor at least. He was a heavy drinker as an adult, incoherent and incapable sometimes for days on end. Some of his behaviour was irrational, although how much was merely play-acting for self-preservation is difficult to gauge. He was tall and imposing, however, commanding respect in his more self-assured moments.

Vicious infighting among Rome's leading family is the real reason for Claudius' invasion of the vaguely outlined province at the edge of the world. As we have seen, Roman influence continued to be established in Britain through trade, but not through politics. After the civil war, the Emperor Augustus' eyes occasionally turned to the Oceanus Britannicus, but this was not translated into action. Tiberius, likewise, while presumably he continued to collect the annual tribute from various British tribes, was content to let sleeping Celts lie.

By the time of his death, however, attitudes among the British Celts had changed, and the death of Cunobelin, Rex Britannorum, probably in 39, marked a crucial turning point. Either before or after the death of this British king, whose extensive capital was at Camulodunon, a rift had developed between his three sons. Judging by subsequent events, it is likely that the Catuvellauni and Trinovantian lands north of the Thames were now ruled by Togodumnos, and the land to the south, as far as the Atrebates' territory, by a man whom Rome would come to fear, his younger brother Caratacus. Clearly, these brothers belonged to a rising anti-Roman group in Britain, perhaps whipped up by their priests, the Druids, who had more to lose than anyone should the eagles return.

A projected invasion in 40, mounted by the increasingly unstable Caligula, failed to materialize, but three years later the portents were more favourable.

The probable hostility of the new war leaders in Britain drove a refugee into the arms of Rome. This time the writer is Cassius Dio, the emperor was Claudius and the exile was Berikos, almost certainly Verica, the king of the Atrebates in the south. Claudius seized the opportunity with great enthusiasm. Clearly not the idiot he had been painted as by fashionable circles in Rome, he nevertheless had no other reputation. He was succeeding an apparent lunatic (Caligula) and was all too aware that strong republican feeling was growing in the Senate. The army had put the stammering scholar on the imperial throne; it could now win laurels for him. Above all, Claudius admired Caesar, and even Caesar had not been able to conquer Britain. What a triumph that would be . . . and it would be a *personal* triumph. Though not in the first wave ashore, the emperor himself would command in the field.

Under the highly respected Aulus Plautius, ex-governor of Illyrium along the Danube, with brilliant legionary commanders like Vespasian and Caius Geta, an army of four legions sailed from Portus Itius in the summer of 43. The bull-necked Titus Flavius Vespianus, the future Emperor Vespasian, came from a humble army family. His background did not make him a natural to command a legion, but he had the backing of the consul and crony of Claudius, Lucius Vitellius, as well as the emperor's extraordinary 'secretary of state', Narcissus. Accordingly, Vespasian's promotion was rapid; he was *quaestor* (financial magistrate) in 35, *aedile* (law and order magistrate) in 38 and *praetor* in 40. The last two qualified him for a seat in the senate. Caius Hosidius Geta's family came from Histonium in southern Italy. His brother Gnaeus was probably the same Geta who was busy conquering Mauritania at roughly the same time as the British invasion, but the similarity of names makes it possible to conclude that they are the same man.

Roman expert Guy de la Bedoyere is doubtful as to which legions crossed with Plautius, but other authorities have no problem on later evidence of citing II Augusta, IX Hispana, XIV Gemina and XX. The II, raised by Augustus during his reign, marched to the Gallic coast from its headquarters in Argentoratum, today's Strasbourg. Led by Vespasian, it would strike out from the main body of the invasion to penetrate the hillforts of the south-west. The IX had clearly served in Spain at some point and had tramped across Europe from its base in Siscia (modern Sisak) in Pannonia (Hungary). The legion is particularly associated with Aulus Plautius and may again have been selected by him because of their experience in river crossings. The XIV, called Gemina by Augustus because it had been raised by the amalgamation of two other legions, came from Moguntiacum (Mainz) on the Rhine. From further along the great river frontier came XX stationed at Novesium (Neuss). It had been raised, either by Augustus or Tiberius, to crush the revolt in Pannonia in 6 AD. These were the legions, together with their *auxilia*, that faced the fury of Boudicca's rebellion seventeen years later.

But Plautius' troops at first refused to sail. Mutiny in the Roman army was not new, and it could prove disastrous. Its fortunes were at their lowest in AD 9 when three legions – XVII, XVIII and XIX under Publius Quinctilius Varus – were wiped out in the Teutoburger Forest, putting paid to Augustus' German policy for the Rhine frontier. Tacitus had written grimly in the *Annales*:

> On the open ground were whitening bones, scattered where men had fled, heaped up where they had stood and fought back. Fragments of spears and horses' limbs lay there – also human heads, fastened to tree trunks. In groves nearby were the outlandish altars at which the Germans had massacred the Roman colonels and senior commanders.[9]

On the death of Augustus five years later, the Rhine and Pannonian troops mutinied and Tiberius was forced to execute the leaders to restore order.[10]

Plautius seems to have been getting nowhere in begging his men to cross the Oceanus Britannica. He sent dispatches back to Claudius in Rome and the emperor sent his freed slave Narcissus to use his diplomatic skills on the nervy, disgruntled legions. The fact that he probably arrived with large chests of cash was a huge incentive.

The expeditionary force sailed in three divisions, which Dio explains by claiming that a single force could be prevented from landing; the reality is that Plautius wanted a reserve in case he was met at the beach as Caesar's first arrival had been. But a flash of lightning, or perhaps a meteor over the Channel, was seen as a good omen and gave the worried soldiers heart, and they landed unopposed, probably near Richborough in the north of the Cantiaci territory, today's Kent.

Of the enemy, there was no sign – Plautius had to find them. To the army's left flank, to the south of the Isle of Thanet, a large bay existed, now reclaimed as the levels of Romney Marsh. Inland from here was the dense forest of oaks later called Andredsweald, so thick that it was not likely the Celts would attack there. It was also possible that this area, with its groves of trees, was sacred to the Celts and not suitable battle country. Whatever the reason, that first Togodumnos, then Caratacus, were defeated separately, suggests delaying tactics. The Celts had dispersed to gather in the harvest, so it must have been late August or early September by now, and recalling these men from the fields must have been difficult and time-consuming. The Romans were advancing with at least two divisions, possibly all three, parallel to the Thames and towards Caratacus' territory of the Catuvellauni. They had to be slowed down until the entire British army could be assembled. This is why the victories that Dio records are no more than skirmishes. The main battle would be fought at a river crossing, with its likely sacred connections, and logically that river had to be the Medway.

If Plautius' army had been following the ancient trackway that would later take medieval pilgrims to Canterbury, he would have reached the Medway between Snodland and Halling. To his left flank, the river executes a series of sharp meanders to the south, and being heavily wooded on both banks provided difficult country for his legions and impossible country for his cavalry. To his right and to the north, the river widened to a possible 500 feet. The enemy faced him on the far side, waiting for him to cross. He sent in the Batavians.

These troops were auxiliaries from the Rhine, variously referred to as Celtoi by Dio Cassius, and were probably attached to XIV Gemina. In the field they fought as cavalry and may have been lent out to the legions for certain specialist qualities. Among them was their ability to swim swollen rivers in full armour, and in this context they crossed the Medway downstream of Plautius' massed ranks, who were probably feigning a full-scale crossing further south.

The left flank of the army may have been II Augusta under

Vespasian, ordered to be the first legion across the river. They would have been waiting in formation somewhere near the modern village of Wouldham. Where the river widened, on the right flank, XIV were busy drilling with as much noise and bustle as possible, holding the enemy's attention there. XX were held in reserve to the south of II on the slope of Blue Bell Hill. Plautius orchestrated the whole from the lower hill of the Great Lines, with a clear view of the river and the British force on the slope of Broom Hill between Rochester and Strood.

The Batavians' orders may have been to outflank the British and cut off their retreat north to the Thames, but their likely small numbers precluded this and instead they attacked the enemy chariots and their horses, which were tethered some way away from the main body of Togodumnos' army. The ruse seems to have worked, and the entire Celtic army may have been drawn in the direction of their screaming, whinnying horses, bleeding, hamstrung and useless for swift cavalry attacks. In all this confusion, the Batavians probably swam back and Plautius' legions, led by II Augusta under the brothers Vespasian and Sabinus, crossed the river and clashed with the Britons on the west bank.

A second legion, probably XX, under Hosidius Geta, reinforced the Flavian brothers, crossing the river where they had, and at dawn the next day launched their columns into Togodumnus' whirling, yelling ranks. So impressive was Geta's personal bravery in driving the Britons back that he was the first to receive from Claudius the *ornamenta triumphalia*, the battle honours awarded only to a few and the rough equivalent of our Victoria Cross.

Togodumnus, his blue-streaked warriors mauled and exhausted, fell back to the Thames, but whereas the battlefield on the Medway is relatively easy to pinpoint, the site of the next one is difficult. Dio says the next battle was fought on the Thames, 'near where it flows into Oceanus and where a lake is formed at high tide'.[11] The most likely area seems to be near Tilbury. The area around Higham Marshes to the east of modern Gravesend was a patchwork of reedy islands visible only at low tide. There were similar marshes on the northern bank of the Thames at East Tilbury.

Somehow, Plautius crossed the Thames and threw the Britons back again. He probably lost too many men in the pursuit across the dangerous Essex mudflats, but the defenders had lost Togodumnos and with him the will to fight any more pitched battles. The loss of this king may have been more important than some commentators have made clear. It may explain why resistance north of the Thames seems to be so limited and why Camulodunon fell so easily. Did the Catuvellauni, with the notable exception of Caratacus and no doubt a sizeable following, throw in their lot with the Romans and cause a rift with the Trinovantes which would simply play into Plautius' hands?

The Roman commander halted and licked his wounds. This in itself requires explanation. Were the Romans seriously mangled after two battles, probably both fought in one week? Did they still face serious opposition from the Catuvellauni-Trinovantian confederacy? Or was this merely the expected 'half-time', when Plautius judged it safe to send for the Emperor?

It was necessary for Claudius to be seen at the front of the army, even in a carefully stage-managed 'thick of the action', so that his triumph would seem genuine. And with him he brought the imperial kitchen sink.

Surrounding Claudius as he sailed from Portus Itius, probably in mid-September, were the *comites*, the companions, although many of them were there because it was simply not safe to leave them behind. The Praetorian Guard were there under their commander Rufrius Pollio, possibly a prime mover in the declaration of Claudius as emperor three years before. Seneca, playwright and stoic philosopher, tells us that Pollio was executed four years after the Claudian invasion. Unfortunately, he does not tell us why. There were leading senators like Valerius Asiaticus, the first Gaul to be made consul. Wealthy and powerful, Asiaticus was probably a leading conspirator against Claudius' predecessor Caligula, and removal of emperors may have become his stock in trade. His friend and co-conspirator against Caligula was Marcus Vinicius, senior magistrate in Rome in both 30 and 43. Didius Gallus, who would later invade the Crimea before governing

Britain, was also with Claudius on his crossing, as was Marcus Licinius Crassus Frugi, who had fought in Mauritania and had been decorated with the *ornamenta triumphalia*. The last of the named *comites* in Claudius' glittering entourage was Lucius Sulpicius Galba, for whom the emperor delayed his departure because he was ill. To Claudius he was vital – a war hero and disciplinarian. It must have been the end of September before the emperor set out, leaving the trusted consul Lucius Vitellius to govern Rome.

Claudius' royal progress would have been slow. His entourage was huge, the *comites* no doubt bringing servants and all the comforts of home with them. Many of these men had been serving officers, but roughing it was no part of their duty now. Claudius sailed to Ostia at the mouth of the Tiber and on to Massilia in southern Gaul. Hitting two severe storms from the Mistral on the way, the imperial ménage crossed Gaul, partly by river, partly by land, to Portus Itius, where Claudius probably collected a number of elephants which accompanied the crossing.

We do not have the reactions of the disbelieving Celts to these beasts, but they could not have seen them before and the sight of them must have been awesome. Was there nothing the Romans could not accomplish? The animals were probably the now extinct North African forest elephant, too small to carry fighting towers and probably ridden by a single rider, like horses. There was no intention to use them in warfare. Hannibal the Carthaginian had terrified the Romans with these beasts in the Punic Wars, but they were too skittish to be reliable in battle situations. It would be another 1,200 years before inhabitants of these islands saw an elephant again, as part of the royal menagerie of Henry III in the Tower of London.

We do not know where Claudius landed or where he reached the army. Hailed several times as *imperator* (emperor), which Dio says was unusual, he crossed what may have been the River Chelmer on a bridge probably by now built by Plautius' engineers and drove the scattering Catuvellauni back, perhaps at the place later called Caesaromagus, today's Chelmsford. The classical writers were not fooled by this showmanship. Dio wrote, 'Claudius joined his legions . . . and led them across the river to engage the Britons who had assembled there. Having defeated them, he took Camulodunum.' Suetonius is probably nearer still: 'He fought no battle nor did he suffer any casualties.' There is an air of theatricality about all this. Some authorities have suggested that Claudius was needed by Plautius to direct the next phase of operations north of the Thames, but this seems unlikely. The emperor was no general – two-thirds of his *comites* and all his legionary officers had more military experience than he had. The whole invasion was a political gesture designed to impress, and Claudius lost no time in sending his sons-in-law Gnaeus Pompeius Magus and the sixteen-year-old Junius Silanus back to Rome with news of his triumph. Suitably impressed, the Senate would grant Claudius the title of Britannicus, 'British'; he had succeeded in the eyes of the world where even the great Caesar had failed.

The height of Claudius' campaign, indeed the crowning glory of his sixteen-day stay in his new province was the taking of Camulodunon, now given the Latin 'um' ending. We know little about the Trinovantian capital that would one day become Colchester. Named after Camulos, the Celtic god of war, it became the headquarters of Cunobelin and possibly the largest settlement in Britain.[12] We know it produced coins as early as 20 BC, and the area was defined by a series of ditches between the rivers Colne and Roman. At Sheepen, three miles away, were thriving 'industrial', trading and religious centres. The place was sufficiently impressive for Claudius to believe this to be the British capital and to make it his own. Boudicca would burn it to the ground seventeen years later. Neither Dio nor Suetonius mentions any Celtic resistance here in 43, so it is likely that the place was surrendered without a fight, the Catuvellauni leadership in temporary disarray.

More oddly, neither of the classical writers mentions the eleven-strong deputation sent to Claudius at Camulodunum. For that evidence we have to go to Rome itself, where a triumphal arch was built on the Via Lata and dedicated in 52. The monument itself no longer stands, but a depiction of it is shown on silver coins from Claudius' reign, a mounted emperor between trophies of arms. And enough of an inscription survives to give us the essence of what happened at Camulodunum in the autumn of 43. Eleven kings of the Britons came to the emperor in submission – *'in deditionem'* means capitulation or surrender – but it is not clear whether this was with or without a fight. *'Sine ulla iactura'* (without any loss) implies that this was a peaceful surrender, but some experts have questioned whether it meant without loss of face. Either way, events at Camulodunum were rather a damp squib after the initial stands at the Medway and the Thames.

From the emperor's point of view, 'his' invasion of Britain had been an enormous success. For the mere risk of a sea crossing he had gained a province and more importantly established himself as Claudius Britannicus, *Praetor Recept* (sheltering emperor), Claudius the God. The Senate was genuinely impressed and got carried away with the euphoria of the moment. The arrival of Magus and Silanus in Rome kick-started preparations for a triumph that was probably held in 44. A special sitting of the Senate saw eulogies of Claudius read out and triumphal arches planned, one in Rome and one on the Gallic coast from which the emperor had sailed with his elephants and his entourage. He and his son were hailed Britannicus, and the architects, master-masons and die-cutters of coins were soon at work to commemorate the brilliant achievement of the emperor, once again, as with Caesar, as much a triumph over the wild, tempestuous Oceanus as over the warlike Celts.

Claudius himself took six months to get home and probably visited his legions along the Rhine to receive yet more military adulation. The triumph itself, based on the earlier festivals of Augustus, Tiberius and Germanicus, was the first held in Rome for twenty-seven years, and no doubt the archivist in Claudius planned all the ritual with a great deal of historical care. On his procession to the Capitol, the steps of which Claudius had to climb on his creaking, 54-year-old knees, the emperor rode in a gilded *quadriga* beside Messalina, his wife, who was also granted honours. Curiously, in a state where women had no official place, she was allowed a seat in the Senate. She was also allowed to ride in Rome in a *carpentum*, a mule-drawn cart reserved for the Vestal Virgins[13] and for consuls, even though she was neither. Behind them came the *comites* and generals who had received *ornamenta triumphalia* in the campaign, although it is likely that Plautius and Vespasian at least were still in Britain at the time.

Before he left Britain, the emperor's orders to Plautius were to conquer *reliqua pars*, the rest. Whether he meant merely the south or the whole island, or even whether he knew the exact extent of the island, we do not know. It is probably a measure of Claudius' lack of grasp of military matters that he thought his four legions could do this without difficulty. That said, what had been achieved so far was impressive and the capitulation of the eleven kings undoubtedly painted a picture rosier than reality. Even brilliant soldiers have made the mistake of leaving 'mopping-up operations' to subordinates in the mistaken belief that all is well behind them.[14] It was not. Soon after Claudius' arrival in the territory of the Cantiaci, Plautius sent Vespasian and II Augusta into the south-west.

The future emperor's chronicler, Suetonius, tells us that the general 'conquered two very powerful tribes, more than twenty *oppida*[15] and the island of Vectis which lies near the coast of Britain.' For these victories Vespasian was awarded the *ornamenta triumphalia*.[16] The man was every inch a soldier. On one occasion when his grumbling legionaries complained about the chafing of their sandals, he made them march barefoot. They loved him nonetheless.

He fought thirty battles, but the scale of these was likely to be small. With a single legion and its accompanying auxiliaries, he is unlikely to have commanded more than 12,000 men, and, increasingly far from his support base at Camulodunum, he had to be careful with them. We do not know precisely the tribes against whom Vespasian and II fought. The bulk of the Atrebates had long been friendly to Rome and their king was probably one of the eleven who paid homage to Claudius at Camulodunum. Beyond them, in today's Dorset, were the Durotriges; to their north, in Somerset and Avon, the Belgae; and in the far west of Cornwall, the Dumnonii.

The exact sequence of Vespasian's conquest is unknown, but it is likely that he marched II Augusta south from the Thames into the friendly kingdom of the Regini under Cogidubnus. There is some confusion over the man and his tribe, but the available evidence points to a kingdom centring on modern Chichester, the Roman Noviomagnus Regensium, with an important trading port at Bosham Harbour. An inscription found under the colonnade in the wall of the eighteenth-century Assembly Rooms records Cogidubnus' name. A complex system of ditches, not unlike that at Camulodunum, implies Roman building, but whether this dates to 43/44 is impossible to say. Cogidubnus adopted the Roman names Tiberius Claudius, in honour of the emperor whose man he undoubtedly was. It is likely that he became a full Roman citizen because of his support of the Claudian invasion, although in fact he may have been a Gaul. Remains of a very large palace at Bosham may have been his, as might the elaborate villa at Fishbourne. The palace is one of the truly astonishing relics of Roman Britain. The nearby Celtic shrine on Hayling Island, dating from the first century BC was possibly converted to a Romano-Celtic temple dedicated to Mars, the Roman god of war. Ritual finds here include chariot fittings, horse trappings, currency bars and 170 coins, together with pork and mutton joints and jars of food and drink. Later generations might see Cogidubnus as a quisling,[17] treacherously welcoming a stronger enemy in order to survive and to benefit; and, judging by Fishbourne, he certainly did that.

Further west, the picture is clearer. Both the Belgae and the Durotriges put up stiff resistance, but they faced exactly the same problems that Togodumnus and Caratacus had faced whenever they confronted the Romans. The enemy were apparently unbeatable either in open country or in siege situations. The *oppida* to which Suetonius refers were probably hill forts, fifty of which have been found in Durotriges territory alone. The problem with these for the defenders is their immense size – the stronghold at Maiden Castle in Wiltshire is a prime example. For any tribe to defend all sections of the ramparts would require thousands of men, which no single tribe could muster. This problem would not be solved adequately until the invention of gunpowder, when bastions had cannon angled to rake along linking ramparts. The Romans were experts at smashing their way through timber gates and palisades, and it is likely that resistance in these hill forts was short-lived and may only have been token gestures of defiance.

Aulus Plautius with IX, XIV and XX legions was moving north-west into the territory of the Coritani, today's Lincolnshire, leaving command in the London area to an unnamed officer who may have been Cnaeus Sentius. His name appears as a commander with Claudius in the *Survey of Roman History* written by the fourth-century writer Eutropius.[18]

Plautius' and Vespasian's advances were probably coordinated and in three phases. The first was effectively achieved by the time Claudius went home. The second was to establish a temporary frontier roughly along the ancient Icknield Way that ran from Dorset to the Wash. The third and final objective was to establish a second frontier beyond the Jurassic Way to form a defendable line from the Severn to the Trent.

Vespasian established an important base at Lake Farm on the Stour near Wimborne, where he could establish links with the Classis Britannicus (the Roman fleet) from nearby Christchurch Bay. By this time it was probably the spring of 45 – perhaps the year that saw the birth of the elder of Boudicca's daughters – and Vespasian may have wintered here on the edge of Durotrigan territory until the worst of the weather was past.

The hill fort at Badbury Rings probably fell without a fight, but at Spettisbury over eighty skeletons were found with weaponry which included fragments of a legionary shield when navvies built the Central Dorset Railway in 1857.

Maiden Castle and Hod Hill were also taken, although dating of the finds in both places is difficult. These and other strongholds were attacked three times, by Vespasian in 43, Ostorius Scapula in 48 and Suetonius Paulinus after Boudicca's revolt. Maiden Castle, described by Thomas Hardy as 'like loosely clasped fingers, between which a zigzag path may be followed – a cunning construction that puzzles the uninformed eye',[19] was excavated by the first of the 'television archaeologists', Mortimer Wheeler, in the 1930s. Near one of the gates, he found twenty-eight graves, clearly the hurried burials of twenty-three men and eleven women. Obviously, the fort was not purely a military stronghold, but a settlement.

The absence of children's bodies may mean that the Romans spared the children, perhaps to sell as slaves, or that the children were evacuated before the fighting started. Dramatically, an iron *ballista* bolt was imbedded in the vertebrae of one of the skeletons. Wheeler proved that the ramparts were destroyed by the Romans to make the place useless in the future. A camp was built nearby, at what may have been the Durotrigan tribal capital, which would develop into Durnovaria, today's Dorchester.

At Hod Hill, near Blandford Forum, the attack by II Augusta caught the defenders by surprise. Ian Richmond excavated the area in the 1950s and discovered that the ramparts at the north-east corner came to an abrupt end in a Celtic spoil heap. The presence of fifteen *ballista* bolts in a concentrated area may imply that this was the centre of resistance, either in the form of a chieftain's headquarters or a determined stand by a body of troops. Unlike Maiden Castle, no bodies have been found here, and unlike Maiden Castle, Vespasian retained the site as a military base. Large quantities of Roman gear have been found on the slopes below this camp, much of it bought by the British Museum in 1862. Both coins and Samian-ware pottery in the finds date the Roman presence to Claudius' reign and suggest that the camp may have been abandoned by 50. The idea of building a Roman camp in the corner of a larger Celtic one is unique in Britain, and Richmond's discovery of legionaries, cavalry and staff remains imply that this was, however briefly, an important centre. It was large enough to house a cohort of infantry and perhaps a half *ala* of cavalry.

It seems from the excavated sites of the 40s that what Vespasian was doing was taking on the major strongholds in a broad sweep from the Hamble river as far west as Taunton in Devon. In terms of territory, he accomplished far more than Plautius, though both men received sizeable honours. His ultimate objective remains in doubt. The wily Caratacus was still at large and was possibly harassing Vespasian's right flank as he struggled west.

We do not know exactly when Aulus Plautius left Britain, but Rome was still on a high after the Claudian triumph and the emperor took the unprecedented step of walking out of the city to meet his general, who rode ahead of Claudius in the procession to the Capitol. He was given his own ovation, a mini-triumph last granted sixty-six years earlier, and in future only given to members of the emperor's family. The strait-laced but competent general retired to his estates after this accolade and we can only imagine how horrified he would have been at the indiscretions of his wife, Pomponia Graecina. Tacitus tells us[20] that she 'was charged with foreign superstition and referred to her husband for trial'.

We do not know what this 'superstition' was. A scratched graffito of a similar name in the catacombs in Rome may indicate that she was an early Christian, but this cult would hardly have reached the elevated circles of a general's wife by 57. Perhaps it was an Egyptian cult we know to be popular in Rome at this time; it has even been suggested that the superstition was Druidism, a result of her husband's links with Britain. Plautius' commission acquitted his wife, but she seems to have become deranged with grief after the murder of her relative, Livia Julia, by the machinations of Messalina, and 'her long life was continuously unhappy'.[21]

Vespasian's achievements led to his being awarded the *ornamenta triumphalia* and election to two *pontifex* posts in Rome. In 51 he was given a consulship, a remarkable achievement for a relatively low-born Roman. Some of this success is no doubt due to the influence of his friend, the Machiavellian imperial freedman Narcissus, but much of it must be his dogged taking of the hill forts of western Britain and his conquest of the Durotriges and the Belgae. Famously nodding off during one of Nero's musical performances (almost a death sentence under that emperor) Vespasian would rise to the purple himself on the death of Vitellius. Among his lasting monuments to the grandeur that was Rome was the Colosseum, denounced in our politically correct days as a centre of all that was wrong with Roman society.

What of Claudius Britannicus, the unlikely emperor who joined the 'two worlds' of Britain and Rome? The army may have learned to love him, but the Senate never did. His triumphs of 44–5 quickly faded and a rash of executions of his political enemies followed. Most justified among them was that of his third wife, Velina Messalina, in 48. Married to Claudius at fourteen, her name is associated with the murderous *realpolitik* of ancient Rome. A nymphomaniac and sadist, she publicly married a favourite, the consul-designate Silius, while Claudius was away from the city. It was the last straw.

If there was one thing the emperor was appallingly bad at, it was choosing wives. His next bride was his own neice Agrippina, the mother of Nero. She persuaded Claudius to adopt her son Nero as heir, in preference to his own son by Messalina, Britannicus. Unlike Messalina, Agrippina was a hands-on murderess, if we are to believe contemporary Roman gossip and subsequent classical writers, poisoning a number of Claudius' enemies and eventually, with a plate of poisoned mushrooms, the emperor himself, to serve Nero's succession. With typical filial gratitude, Nero had her executed in 59, perhaps because she knew where too many bodies were buried.

Of the eleven kings who swore allegiance to Claudius at Camulodunum, it is likely that one of them was Prasugatus, king of the Iceni in East Anglia, the tribe whose lands bordered the Trinovantian territory now conquered by Rome. His wife was called Boudicca whose red hair, harsh voice and indomitable courage, the Romans would come to know all too well.

3

'Under a Different Sky . . .'

> And we bring you news by word of mouth –
> Good news for cattle and corn –
> Now is the Sun come up from the South
> With Oak, and Ash, and Thorn!
> 'A Tree Song', Rudyard Kipling

Boudicca springs fully formed in the accounts of both Tacitus and Dio, a woman already grown and regal. In the *Epitome* of Book LXII, the latter historian wrote:

But the person who was chiefly instructed in rousing the natives and persuading them to fight the Romans, the person who was thought worthy to be their leader and who directed the conduct of the entire war, was Boudicca, a Briton woman of the royal family and possessed of greater intelligence than often belongs to women.

Tacitus is even less helpful, and the first we know of the queen from him is that '[Prasutagus'] widow Boudicca, was flogged and their daughters raped.'[1]

Although little can be said for certain about Boudicca's life before 60, we can at least offer some speculation. If, as we know, her daughters were raped in 60/61, the younger of them is likely to have been twelve or thirteen. We may presume that their mother was perhaps sixteen when the elder, who may have been fifteen in 60/61, was born. On this guesswork, we have posited a birth date for Boudicca of between 25 and 30 BC.

What is impossible to state definitively is where she was born or from which tribe she came. Dio's throwaway line that she was 'of the royal family' perhaps implies that she was royal in her own right and not merely the consort of the king. This would explain the apparent readiness with which not only the Iceni but the Trinovantes and other tribes followed her in 60, although we know little of the Celts' relationship with their leaders. The clientage system described in Chapter One must have operated among the Iceni as it did throughout Celtic society, but does not help us to understand the nature of Celtic kingship. Among other ancient peoples, such as the Egyptians, the role of pharaoh had deeply religious significance; the man was literally a god. After the expulsion of Tarquinius,[2] the Romans regarded 'king' as something of a dirty word, yet later, albeit unstable, emperors like Caligula had themselves formally declared divine. By the Middle Ages, kings walked a difficult line between 'first among equals' and 'the Lord's annointed', creating endless tension between ruler and ruled. We simply do not know how the Iceni reacted to their royal family or who belonged to such a family.

Whether Boudicca was of Prasutagus' own family of the Iceni or whether she was an alien 'import' is another unanswerable question. Antonia Fraser speculates that there may have been a cousin kinship between Boudicca and Cartimandua, which would make her Brigantian. There is no evidence that intertribal marriages of this type took place, and, bearing in mind the warring nature of the internecine Celts, this seems unlikely. Hector Boece, the Scottish chronicler who wrote of Boudicca in the sixteenth century, states that Prasutagus took her as a slave or prize of battle, which is entirely possible. Would the Iceni, however, have rallied to such a chattel? Thousands of Russians followed the German Catherine 'the Great', widow of Tsar Peter II, but that was 2,000 miles away and 1,800 years later; we are not comparing like with like.

Whoever Boudicca's parents were, they were likely to have been of royal or at least aristocratic blood, and if Gaelic legends and folklore are based on fact, then her mother would have made the sexual running in whatever ritual courtship was carried out. Celtic legends, best preserved in Ireland, the *'insula sacra'*, because they were uncontaminated by Roman influence, are an important strand in our understanding of Boudicca and her people. In the absence of an Iceni alphabet, folk tales, albeit garbled and distorted by time, are the only sources we have. In various Irish stories, some of this courtship is rather unceremonious – Deirdre grabs Naoise by the ears and tells him she is a cow who wants him as her bull; the queen of Ulster and the ladies of her court appeared bare-breasted before the great mythical hero Cúchulainn and lifted their skirts, such exposure supposedly a sign of veneration for him. Caesar tells us that the Celts practised polygamy, and in various parts of Ireland, Wales and Scotland marriages were seen as temporary affairs and changes of partner common until well into the Middle Ages.

The Celtic pattern of equality in sexual matters appalled the Romans,[3] and, while it may be overstressing the point, many of the Celtic deities were female – as in Boudicca's calling on Andraste, a goddess, at the start of her campaign in 60. The central deity of the Romans, Jupiter, was singularly male. Christianity followed this tradition. Women (other than the Virgin Mary) had little status in the life and times of Jesus Christ, and it is still considered blasphemous or preposterous by many to refer to God as 'she'. Vague though it is, Boudicca was probably conceived and grew to womanhood in a society classed by some sociologists as a 'mother-identifying, guilt-free group'.[4]

The oldest known reference to the British Celts comes from Pythus of Massilia (the Greek colony of Marseilles in southern Gaul) about 325 BC, who visited Belerion (Cornwall) in search of tin. Archaeological evidence has provided much older links between the West Country and Brittany, most spectacularly Barry Cunliffe's find of a Sicilian hand axe made of bronze off Hengistbury Head, Dorset. Bronze and silver coins in the area all point to fairly extensive trade between Britain and Cisalpine Gaul and Italy. More complicated and immeasurable is the westward migration of people.⁵ Debate still rages about the origin of the Celts, but by about 500 BC an Iron Age culture of the Hallstatt and La Tène types was already in place and with it, probably, a spoken Celtic language or languages.

Hallstatt, on the shore of the Hallstättersee in Austria, was an Iron Age-salt production centre of some importance. Excavated in the nineteenth century by Johann Ramsauer, the extraordinarily rich graves found on the site led, by 1872, to the generic application of the name Hallstatt to all Iron Age archaeology of that type. The oldest finds there date from the Bronze Age.

La Tène (the name means 'the shallows') is the name given to the type of Celtic artwork associated with the finds by Hans Kopp on the banks of Lake Neuchâtel in Switzerland in 1857. The astonishing range of finds and the reason for their being in the lake's waters will be discussed elsewhere, but the typical style of art, on mirrors, jewellery and weapons, has an unmistakeable appearance, described by Frank Delaney as

> a tendril of a plant teased into itself, then spun outwards until it becomes a pattern, a whorl, a whole inner world, leaping, coiling, dancing.⁶

Many examples of artwork of this type have been found in the territory ruled by Boudicca. Mirrors were coveted by her women, weapons were prized by her men.

The Iceni: warlike, rebellious, primitive. Some of them may have been ranged along the banks of the Thames when Aulus Plautius got there in 43, screaming and cursing, with Togodumnos and Caratacus, ritualistically tattooed in woad, brandishing their long swords and their broad-headed spears in the air. This was the picture facing a Roman soldier and this is a Roman interpretation, the view of Agricola as told to Tacitus. But did Agricola know who he faced, and what would Tacitus have written if his father-in-law had looked closer?

The Iceni: farmers, artisans, spiritualists. Fearlessly defending a culture steeped in powerful ritual beliefs, producing beautiful craft, embodied by the flowing designs on their shields and the twisted gold torcs around their necks.

Although the pre-Roman Iceni remain highly enigmatic, consigned to mystery because of their lack of a written language, archaeology has allowed us to catch a glimpse of a culture in a particularly unique part of the Iron Age world. Much must be left to suggestion, logic, speculation and even imagination, but the clues are there and they can paint a tangible picture of Boudicca's people.

The archaeological landscape of what would become East Anglia, the territory of the Iceni, is notably void of the monuments we see elsewhere in the Iron Age world. The flat landscape means there are no imposing promontories that were often used for the building of hill forts such as Danebury and South Cadbury, the death traps of other Celtic tribes who had tried to stand against Aulus Plautius and Vespasian. The preservation in the soil is generally poor, so even aerial photography and fieldwalking do not always yield results. For this reason, excavation is not as widespread as it could be. Because of expense, many sites have been extended in areas where evidence has already been found, rather than breaking new ground. Allowing for problems of archaeological research which are common to the whole of the modern industrial world, Iceni territory has nevertheless revealed a fascinating collection of artefacts which form the building blocks of any study of Boudicca's people.

Using the excellent work of earlier generations of archaeologists, we can attempt to give a clearer picture of a culture which has left no overriding physical mark on the landscape. To appreciate the extent to which the Iceni were developing in terms of their interaction with the landscape and extension of their cultural identity, it is important to look for evidence not only before the Claudian invasion, but before the first Roman came into contact with the tribes of modern Norfolk; into the late prehistory of Britain.

It is unlikely that Iron Age Britain was a landscape of bustling townships with wide-reaching trade and strong social bonds. Early Roman commentators noted that the Celts' 'towns' were their forests. It is this that made the creation of Claudius' colony at Camulodunum all the more alien to the Trinovantes in whose territory it was established. Looking at

Iron Age Britain in terms of the sparse and sporadic settlement evidence, it would seem that we are dealing with small individual groups who existed in an ever-changing territorial landscape. This does not mean that these people were nomadic in the sense of following their herds and flocks to different pasture; that has always been the lifestyle of mountain or desert people. Nor does it necessarily square with Caesar's *De Bello Gallico*, in which he compared the coastal tribes of Britain, largely the Cantiaci south of the Thames, with those relatively civilized kingships he had encountered in Gaul. In the interior, he believed, the savage nature of the tribes was notable. Caesar probably never encountered the Iceni, and his conclusions are odd in that the trans-channel contact between Gaul and Britain would have been small. Where 'civilized' influence had spread, namely via the Belgic peoples, it was not confined to Kent but had penetrated far inland and certainly as far north as modern Yorkshire, in the shape of the Parisii.[7] The people of the interior probably had royal and even industrial centres, which are indicative of population growth, and indeed urbanization was very high on the agenda between the time of Caesar's invasion and that of Claudius almost one hundred years later. Forestry, agriculture and settlement design all developed in this period, from house shape and structure to what crops to farm and how to farm them in the face of more mouths to feed. The idea of a fast-changing tribal landscape from the Iron Age well into the Roman period is suggested by the appearance of different coinage representing different individuals, but from the same area and period. This denotes a shift in the centres of power, and the many subtle differences in craftsmanship can be used as an indicator of territorial boundaries.

The Iceni seem broadly to have been based in what is now Norfolk, the north of Suffolk and north-east Cambridgeshire, a part of their frontier at least of being marked by the rivers Lark and Gissing. We have become used over the centuries since the Norman invasion to thinking in terms of the counties they created, based loosely on earlier Saxon shires. In that thousand years, regions have acquired reputations and 'flavours' of their own which have no bearing on Celtic society. The tribes of East Anglia as a whole share many characteristics which make them unique among other regions of ancient Britain, but the Iceni show an individuality all of their own. This is apparent not least in their cultural development, which seems to have been far more independent than that of neighbouring peoples who were heavily swayed by more than one external influence. This could explain why the Boudiccan revolt was so successful in its formative stages, because the Iceni were the embodiment of independence and freedom, and inspired support from others.

The landscape brings us the first unique element of Iceni culture and that of others in East Anglia. The topography, the land itself, is flat here, leaving little room for the hill fort enclosures identified all over the rest of the British isles. There is evidence of enclosures, and therefore we can speculate that they were built for defence, but it is harder to define without a well-represented model such as the hill forts of Cadbury and Maiden Castle, to where defence is attested not only by associated material and topographical evidence but with the historical, written record too. The importance of settlements with large defended enclosures suggest refuge, but they do not tell us who lived there, nor precisely why they needed to be defended. They could be royal or aristocratic sites, perhaps producing high-quality items in precious metals, or they could be settlements of dense occupation, which often went hand in hand with trade and production. The hill fort models rarely yield evidence of continuous occupation, which suggests they were probably points of last-ditch refuge, if they were used for defence at all. Other interpretations include ritual practice and burials. For example, Maiden Castle presents both ritual evidence – Mortimer Wheeler found burials within the enclosure – and defence in its reuse by Vespasian's II Augusta. In the Iceni region, Thetford has evidence of construction from the Late Iron Age to the period of Roman colonization. However, it has little occupation in the centre, so perhaps Thetford was used only in times of tribal crisis. Some historians have suggested that Boudicca launched her campaign of 60 from there. Elsewhere, the territory of the Iceni paints a different picture of the nature of defence. South Creake, Narborough and Warham are all enclosed sites with a bank and ditch, and the extent of these, between 1.5 to 6 hectares, would suggest fortifications of some sort.

Without the presence of high ground, natural defence seems to have been a significant consideration. Warham has a river to the west and is surrounded by marshland. The earthworks are exceptionally high to the east to compensate for surrounding high plateaux, but the natural defensive features and possible means of escape and supply provided by the river are great natural advantages. South Creake is near a crossing of the river but presents no other natural defence and may have been difficult to protect as a result.

We know that water had great significance to the Celts in general and very probably to the Iceni specifically. Rivers present travel routes and obvious logistical considerations in terms of supply for armies as well as the water itself for drinking and a source of fish for food. There is a heavy use of rivers by the Celts: evidence of predominance of ritual votive offerings in the campaign between Boudicca's army and that of Rome may well outstretch coincidence. Could it be that to the Iceni, as to all Celts, water was seen as an unstoppable force and a protector? It was revered by the Iceni and the Romans alike, as we can prove with evidence from the tokens in the Roman spas, Bath in particular, with its dedication to Sulis Minerva. Large numbers of coins and brooches have been recovered from waterways. No less than one-third of all vessels belonging to the Iron Age have been found in river silt. Did the Iceni put more stock in water as a magical element than Rome did, or did it represent a completely different set of beliefs? Did Rome learn to put more religious faith in water because of the Iceni? As we shall see in a later chapter, the legionaries were as superstitious as their enemies and readily adopted other people's deities to avoid giving offence and risking defeat. The later cults of Mithraism and Christianity are proof of this. It is certainly true that sites which have been interpreted as having been ritual sites before the arrival of the legions remained significant to the continental conquerors, for exampl, Fison Way at Thetford.

The morphology of the sites themselves also poses questions about ritual. Towards the end of the pre-Roman Iron Age, circular enclosures were replaced by square or rectilinear ones. In parts of Gaul such as Champagne and the Moselle[8] so-called *'viereckschanzanzen'* sites have been connected with burials, inhumations or cremations. Ceremonial sites in Norfolk such as Wighton, between Fakenham and the coast, are likely to have had a similar importance.

In other cases the date of construction can aid interpretation. Thornham,[9] further west near Hunstanton, appears to have been added to around the mid-first century AD. These defences could have been in response to Rome, which in turn possibly points to the importance of the site as a centre of opposition, or at least a proposed one. The problem arises, as so often, in the absence of accurate dating possibilities, that Thornham may have been a centre in the Iceni revolt of 47–48 or a desperate refuge in the bloody aftermath of Boudicca's campaign. Other 'open' sites also existed, for example, Great Bealings in the Trinovantes territory near Ipswich, and Barham further to the west. These could represent smaller farmsteads or sites that were ritually protected; interpretation of sites like these is as multifaceted as enclosed sites. They could even represent areas that regularly changed hands due to territorial movements and so were not seen as being worth defending by any one group.

The sites begin to increase both in number and size as the Iron Age progresses. This shows not only population growth but also a possible centralization of the disparate groups which had existed before. This unification could be significant in that the rebellious forces could well have been cross-cultural army made from different tribes, rather than one. For example, it seems more likely that Trinovantian aid was proffered to Boudicca because of the Roman support given to their age-old enemies, the Catuvellauni, than because of the loss of land to Rome and the heavy-handed moneylending tactics of Paulinus and Catus Decianus which helped spark Boudicca's revolt.

Elsewhere, large sites appear to have been developed either under the auspices of or actually by Rome. Saham Toney, almost certainly a ritual centre, was defended by a Claudian fort, but was that to protect the centre or to watch its occupants? There is a concentration of deposition near

Woodcock Hall[10] on the banks of what would have been a substantial river two millennia ago. This concentration can be dated broadly between 40 and 50 AD. Could these inhabitants, too, have been people praying for a successful outcome of the rebellion in 47? The outcome was that Rome crushed the rebels and disarmed many tribal groups in accordance with common imperial policy. It depended on who was placing votive offerings into that river as to whether the fort commanding high ground over the centre was for defence or observation.

Such centres were obviously heavily influenced by Rome. The Trinovantian capital of Camulodunon, modern Colchester, was renamed, as we have seen, first Camulodunum, then Colonia Claudia, and became home to the temple of Claudius, which was much reviled by the indigenous population. So, too, the Catuvellauni saw their beloved Verlamion become Verulamium, the home of a bathhouse and a theatre in a later development after its centre was razed to the ground by Boudicca. The fact that Boudicca focused on these two suggests that they were very significant centres of Roman influence and that their destruction would be an important symbolic victory.

When turning to the question of the capital of the Iceni, we are faced with an insuperable problem: we don't know where it was. Prasutagus' city is mentioned by both Tacitus and Dio, but not its location. There are many possibilities for this. First, the Iceni had proved such a thorn in Rome's side that, when Tacitus and Dio wrote, the tribe did not warrant enough respect to have mentioned anything as civilized as a capital city. Secondly, that there were no overriding elements of Roman influence on the scale of Camulodunum and Verulamium before the revolt makes it hard to postulate a possible location. Claudius regarded Camulodunum as the capital of Britain, and there were Roman-style retail outlets and workshops on the banks of the Ver. It could also be that territorial fluidity or the presence of more than one Iceni aristocracy could mean that there was no single centre. When Caesar wrote of the Cenimagni in *De Bello Gallico*, was he referring to a single all-powerful group or did 'the great Iceni' imply that there was a lesser sept, or tribal subdivision, in the area? After all, Prasutagus was a client king, put on the throne or at least supported by Rome. Coins minted in the area and period-stamped with SUBIPASTO-ESICO may refer to him, but equally may have equine roots pertaining to a horse cult which will become clearer when we come to look at Iceni material culture.

There are possibilities, however, for the capital of Prasutagus. The most common one is Caistor St Edmund, for which there is tangible place-name evidence: 'Caistor' is a corruption of the Latin *castra*, meaning 'camp'; St Edmund of course belongs to a much later period, but the Romans referred to it as Venta Icenorum or 'marketplace of the Iceni'. The idea of a large trade centre for industry and commerce was beginning to emerge in the last century BC and the first AD. There is evidence of coin minting and of production of commodities, those of high-status quality and everyday objects, as well as a concentration of settlement around them. These *oppida* were heavily influenced by Rome after Claudius' invasion, as well as by increased trade with areas of Gaul and the Belgic peoples who were present among other tribes in the area. Market towns may well have come together to form a capital, as trade and wealth were becoming central to a culture which previously looked only to subsistence as a priority. In one sense the weather and the harvest still governed all, but life was becoming much more multifaceted. This all ties in with the sophisticated craftsmanship of the Celtic peoples, especially in East Anglia, which will be our focus later.

Caistor St Edmund is at the confluence of the Tas and the Yare. It had a long-established ritual significance, the nearby Arminghall henge being home to Norfolk's largest concentration of Bronze Age barrows. Despite the area's deep stratigraphy, which means that evidence is difficult to identify individually as occupational patterns are so complex, a plethora of Iron Age finds associated with the Roman and pre-Roman layers, including coins and fine imported Samian ware, suggests that this was a significant site. We shall see that after the Boudiccan revolt there was a strong Roman presence – Caistor St Edmund was a significant Iceni centre. After Boudicca's death, the area around Caistor St Edmund fell out of favour with Rome as administrative and developing centres. This could show that

Rome had given up trying to Romanize and therefore support the area, using Caistor St Edmund as a single centre to monitor the peoples living there, rather like a semi-permanent black or Jewish ghetto in the twentieth century.

Another suggested site for Prasutagus' capital is Snettisham. This site is associated with many rich hoards, one in particular containing a torc (which we would love to imagine being worn by Boudicca herself). The sheer wealth of these hoards suggests an important production site if nothing else. However, as for its being the capital, sites associated with high-status artefacts do not automatically signify capitals. The site may have had royal connections – as was the case with Verlamion – or royal patronage, as did cities associated with mints, but the lack of other evidence of high-status buildings for defence would tend to preclude this.

But it is not only the settlement as a whole that we should look at to appreciate elements of the Iceni culture, but the microcosm, the individual house, the artisan's shop and the small enclosed site.

Barnham, south of the probable religious site at Thetford, stands on a hill with no discernible evidence of defence. The small hectare site gains strong religious overtones from what was perhaps a ritual deposition of a complete human jawbone in the corner of an outer ditch, along with horse bones. There is also evidence of domestic buildings here from the rings of post holes. The subsoil within is stained and sandy, suggesting domestic use, waste deposition and fire, possibly for small industrial production. The initial date for this is early Iron Age and derives from a pit containing possible ritual deposition of pots and animal bones. Similar domestic buildings have been found at sites such as Hacheston, north of Ipswich, which may have been in Trinovantian lands. Elsewhere, the buildings are on a grander scale. Pakenham, near Bury St Edmunds, is home to a building whose outer trench has holes suggesting the appearance of a continuous wall. It is associated with a Boudiccan-era fort; perhaps this was home to an aristocrat of the Iceni or the head-quarters of an the officer.

Elms Farm, though far to the south at Maldon in Essex and generally thought to be Trinovantian territory, lies along what was possibly the boundary between the tribes. It is on the confluence of the Chelmer and Blackwater, which has been identified as a likely major trading route due to its natural proximity to Chelmsford (the Roman Caesaromagus), where much fine Samian ware has been found. However, no such evidence has been found at Elms Farm in what was almost certainly a temple. Initially circular in shape, and dating from the pre-Roman period, it subsequently became rectilinear, as did the possible ancillary buildings associated with it. Was this a ritual site used by pilgrims, the ancillary buildings representing places for them to stay, or was it an inhabited site, the buildings housing the Druids, who were the priests of the Celts? Was it the religious centre for nearby Caesaromagus?

West Stow is a more anomalous site. Today, its Iron Age buildings have been rebuilt, along with later dwellings, and it makes a fascinating open-air museum. Its irregular pattern, with a rectilinear trench around an oval arrangement of post holes, encloses a rectangular pit. Is this a grave, a ritual site, a functional defence or a mixture of all three?

Burial practices varied, but the most common method seems to have been cremation. Archaeologist and historian Guy de la Bedoyere estimates that as many as 90 per cent of the Britons' bones were destroyed by fire, leaving us a particularly sparse record. The Belgic peoples, whose art and ritual practices penetrated both Trinovantian and Catuvellaunian territory, did not have much impact on the Iceni. However, there are examples of burials, in places with no real territorial identity, which have elements of Belgic influence. At Elveden, south of Thetford, a find in 1888 was recorded as a cremation burial with three globular urns of double striated decoration and the remains of a large gold-handled tankard. As with many Victorian finds, this one has since been lost, only the recording of it remaining. However the burial's situation, away from any grave concentration, suggests that the differing materials could be representative of foreign or aristocratic burial. What is more likely, after all, than that an important tribal leader should be buried alone in pride of place? The appearance of a Roman-style brooch in the form of a dragon in the grave could indicate the veneration of an individual family with Roman contacts. Alternatively, it could reflect changing socio-political trends, with bodies being cremated on the borders of all three territories as a mark of special significance. The possibility of an outcast burial is unlikely, due to the richness of the associated material. As it lies between territories and if it was a tribal individual the idea of an overall elite is very attractive. Sadly, the site was excavated in the nineteenth century and only reappraised in 1939, so some of the possible advantages of modern archaeological techniques are missing.

There is also evidence of inhumation. Barnham yielded an articulated human leg. This could be evidence of a crouching burial similar to those found all over prehistoric Europe. In 1814 at Mildenhall the burial of a human of 'large dimensions' with two horses, an iron sword, axe and golden torcs was discovered. This not only suggests the appearance of a warrior elite but confirms the idea of horse worship.

The Uffington Horse[11] is not the only example of horse veneration in Britain. At Saham Toney in Iceni territory, horse furniture from chariots provides a tangible link with Manduessedum. There is material evidence in abundance. Firstly, there is the plethora of horse furniture, particularly terrets (the rings from chariots through which reins were slipped), which appear to us in the archaeological record. And these items are not just in base metals but highly ornate gold and enamel decoration. They draw artistic parallels with the torcs worn by the Iceni nobility, such as those from Snettisham. It has been argued that these were functional; however, gold is very soft and an iron sword would make quick work of them. Could they be interpreted as some kind of parallel to horse furniture, the eyelets being linked to a bit or bridle?

Archaeological evidence has linked Boudicca's people with the horse to such an extent that we can perhaps surmise that horse and chariot races were a part of Iceni social life. The Gaelic word for a horse is 'Each'; is it a flight of fancy, we wonder, to imagine that the word Iceni is derived from it? Some patterns of coin found in the area carry the spelling ECENI. In the 1920s, the archaeologist and journalist Arthur Weigall, who had worked in the Valley of the Kings in Egypt, wrote with confidence that the Icknield Way, Ickbur, Icklingham and other place names in the east of the county originated in the tribal name. Today we doubt this. The coins of Prasutagus and his predecessors show the horse as a common motif.

The burial of dogs with horses points towards the hunt as an aristocratic way of life, and we have already seen horses' terrifying potential as weapons of war. The power and the sexuality of the horse are reflected in Beltane, the spring festival of fertility and mating – and the horse goddess Epona was alike the 'patron saint' of cavalrymen and the mother goddess of all things. Many of the Iceni horses from Manduessedum were probably rounded up and driven fifteen miles south to the Roman camp of the Lunt, near modern Coventry, where a cavalry barracks was built around the time of Boudicca's last battle. Cartimandua, Boudicca's contemporary and queen of the Brigantes means, in Celtic, 'sleek pony'.

The coinage of the Iceni has in the past been used to plot broad tribal territories. This is a very difficult task, as subsequent research shows that gold was in use between 65 and 40 BC and silver by 35 BC; by Boudicca's time, with colonization fully under way, indigenous coinage was largely abandoned in favour of Roman coinage. However, it can give us an insight into what form the currency took, and suggest significant sites where rituals could have been carried out, such as Snettisham, where a considerable amount of gold coinage has been found. It can also give us the merest glimpse of personalities whose names are stamped on the coins. From pre-Roman coinage we have CAN DVRO, ANTED, AESVED and SAENV. Whether these are the names of kings or mint sites is impossible to say. And, if kings, we have no idea of their relationship with Prasutagus and Boudicca. It is interesting to note that hoards, which are as common as stray finds, are either purely silver or gold. This not only implies a preference for different metals at different times but also the different significance of the coins. By virtue of their being in hoards, they could have been hidden from Rome or saved perhaps as ransom or bribe money. In fact, some gold hoards have been associated with Caesar's expedition in 54 BC and are known as

Depiction highlighting the
design of a horse-style coin.

'flight hoards', essentially taken and hidden from Rome by
British kings and leaders. Equally, in some cases their
deposition could have been a ritual undertaking.

The vast majority of gold hoards deposited for ritual
purposes are found along the coast. Although we have already
established that water is ritually significant, there is little
evidence that the sea features as a ritual element. There are
many reasons for this. If archaeological evidence did exist,
tidal changes are likely to have removed it; erosion has swept
settlements away. In the period we are dealing with,
seasonality was no longer an issue. The Iceni were a settled
people, no longer nomadic, and with sedentism came the need
for settlements that yielded the maximum in terms of food
production. Fish was more likely procured from inland waters
than by building camps on the coast, although there could
have been coastal exploitation. The poor preservation of
organic material in the area means that evidence of boats is
sadly absent. We know that it was reported to Caesar that the
tribes of the south coast had nothing approximating to an
ocean-going fleet. The Norfolk Broads represent a large body
of inland water at various times of the year where votive
hoards could have been deposited. Some of these hoards,
however, could represent offerings to the sea.

Silver hoards belong predominantly to the first century AD. Half are purely Iceni and half mixed with Roman *denarii*. Ten hoards have been loosely connected with Boudicca, either hidden from her or by her. They will be discussed more fully elsewhere.

Whatever the interpretation, one thing seems clear. It is unlikely that coins formed what we would recognize today as a currency – there is no evidence of 'small change', meaning lesser coins in bronze. This suggests the coins were used for the reasons already posited.

Another question immediately arises in the context of coin hoards and elaborate works of art such as torcs: where did the gold and silver come from? It seems clear that the tribes of East Anglia were skilled and revered craftsmen in precious metals. This is apparent from the intricate Battersea shield which stylistically shows many Celtic elements, though its symmetry of design suggests it could have been influenced externally, perhaps by a Roman commissioning his own design from a local craftsman. The Celts' artwork in general is notoriously asymmetrical, as in the La Tène finds from Switzerland. The hoards at Snettisham are indicative not only of skill but volume. Coin production in East Anglia seems to have included only the actual striking, as the precious metals were not mined there and even the lead ingots used for moulds were shipped in. A shipwreck found off Sept Iles, Brittany, had 271 lead ingots as part of its cargo, five of which are stamped with ICENES. Old Sleepford in Lincolnshire, north of the Iceni territory in the Brigantian lands, has evidence of mould fragments and could be connected with Iceni minting sites. Were these the moulds used to produce the metal ingots, and were they sent to the Iceni for striking?

This makes the royal or hierarchical importance of the area seem considerable, as well as suggesting how far Iceni influence may have spread. The gold could have been Irish and could also explain a possible connection with Anglesey, which will come into play with the synchronicity of the Iceni and Druidic rebellions on opposite sides of the country, a theme explored later. Does the skill and wealth of Boudicca's people explain why Caesar, noting what his Celtic clients told him, called them the Cenimagni?

It is also through material culture that we can partially identify territories. The rivers Alde, Deben, Stour and Lark[12] may mark the boundaries of the Iceni territory. It was in the first-named river that the severed head of Claudius was found, almost certainly 'liberated' from Colonia Claudia and placed in the water as a votive offering. By looking at the material evidence, regional differences can be deduced. It is difficult to do the same with coins alone because of their short periods of circulation (as far as we are aware). In general there are more Iceni coins in North Suffolk and more Trinovantian in the rest of the county. However, Iceni territory can be identified as having more horse ornaments, whereas Trinovantian territory reveals more Belgic and Roman influence, for example, with more amphorae. The differences in their brooch production and pottery design have also raised some interesting questions.

We have focused on the archaeological evidence of the Iceni because there is little else. The physical appearance of Iceni settlements followed the pattern of Celtic villages everywhere. Most Iron Age houses were circular, built of upright oak posts with a conical roof covered in thatch. The walls between the uprights were of wattle and daub, a mesh of split sticks plastered with a mixture of clay, chalk, straw and animal hair. The floor was merely beaten earth, and within the dark, smoky, damp home, beehive-shaped clay ovens cooked the food. Reconstructions of such houses at Butser Hill in Hampshire and Stow on the Iceni-Trinovantian border have shown them to be surprisingly durable, at Butser the house withstood the freak 100 mph winds of the hurricane of 1987. So successful was Celtic building that the principle of timber frame and wattle and daub infill lasted for sixteen centuries.

By the time of the Claudian invasion, when Boudicca would have been in her late teens, rectangular buildings were also being erected, although most of these seem to have had religious significance. Royal residences were probably simply larger, more impressive versions of the conical house; the tiles and mortar we associate with the Romans played no part in Iceni life.

Boudicca's people were farmers who planted crops and

raised animals. Cattle were particularly prized among the Celts, and large herds probably indicated the status of their owner. Strabo wrote of the Celts, 'Their pigs are allowed to run wild and are noted for their height, pugnacity and swiftness. It is dangerous for a stranger to approach them.'

The boar was the most common totemic animal in Celtic ritual, and from various finds in the area we know the Iceni carried talismans in boar form. At Manduessedum, as we have seen, it is likely that both sides faced each other across the field with essentially the same battle standard.

Fascinatingly, bearing in mind the heavy, twisted gold necklaces worn by Boudicca and other British and Gallic leaders, the Gaelic word for boar is *'torc'*. Although a male animal, the boar represents a goddess whose skin can heal. He represents raw power and his tusks are the inbuilt weapons of the warrior. We know from Celtic burials that joints of pork were placed in warrior graves and the helmets often had boar crests. The sixth-century bardic poet Taliesin was able to describe one of the many magical animals into which he turned himself: 'I have been a wild boar.'[12]

We shall see in a later chapter that the Celtic year was divided into four and marked by key feasts, the notion of sacrifice and a belief in a vast pantheon of gods and a dark other world. The image that outsiders had of Celtic peoples – and this is certainly true of the Iceni – is that they drank heavily, feasted wildly and boasted outrageously. We have seen from Diodorus Siculus and Ammianus Marcellinus that feasting often became violent and that tall tales told around the campfires led to duels to the death. It is likely that the Iceni 'Celtic temperament' followed this pattern.

The 'Boar horse' and 'Patten Horse' forms of coin appeared around 35 BC, the 'Face Horse' slightly later and possibly copying the Roman republican *denarii* by featuring a crude face on one side of the coin. Horses were clearly, like cattle, status symbols, and horse and chariot burials in Iceni territory, like those in the Parisii lands in Yorkshire, clearly indicate the animal's revered position.

Because Roman sources tell us nothing of Boudicca before her rebellion and because archaeology has so far failed to reveal anything personal about her, we have no option but to speculate. We know that Celtic women were accepted as equals with men, in terms of physical strength, leadership skills and sexual voraciousness. Exactly how we do not know, but Celtic attitudes foreshadowed those of the modern world. It was the Romans, and particularly the Christians, who demanded that women should be childbearers and little else. The astonishing grave of the anonymous 'princess' from Vix, near Mont Lasois in Gaul, is proof of the accord given to high-ranking women. The princess was small (under five feet) and deformed, but her 3-metre-square burial chamber contained a dismantled four-wheeled chariot, a superb 24-carat gold torc, a Greek *Krater,* or wine jar, and relics of luxury fabrics – and all this five centuries before Boudicca was born. Another female chariot burial, from the Hömicele Barrow in Germany, contains drinking vessels, pots, jewellery and textiles of silk imported from China. At Reinheim near the River Blies, an oak-lined chamber held over two hundred items of gold, amber, coral, glass and bronze, and is again associated with a female burial. These astonishing finds make it all the more galling that nothing of the kind has been found in Iceni territory.

If we turn from archaeology, and the silence of the Roman chroniclers, to Celtic law as it had developed in the early Christian period, there is a precedent in Welsh tradition for Boudicca's stand in 60. There is doubt about when such a position first appeared, but Aneurin Owen argues that *arglwyddes*, literally 'female lord', meant a 'chieftain in her own right',[13] and it is feasible that both Boudicca and Cartimandua are early examples of this. The first Celtic ruler recognized by classical writers was Onomaris, meaning 'rowan tree', who was a warrior queen of the Scordisci in what today is Serbia. A later ruler in the same area, although she is far less well chronicled than Boudicca, was Teuta, who fought the Greeks in Illyria two and a half centuries before the Iceni rebelled. Polybius had the typical sexist view of her: 'She suffered from a typically feminine weakness, that of taking the short view of everything.'[14] Her name is more important to us than what she achieved. The name 'Teuta' is linked with the Celtic *teutates*, meaning 'people', and the Irish-Gaelic *tuath*, 'the tribe'. So Teuta is literally the people's queen. Similarly, Boudicca means 'victorious' (which helped kindle renewed interest in her in the nineteenth century); in Welsh, the word is *buddugol* and in Irish *buach*. It may be that both Teuta and Boudicca are actually nicknames and not their given names at all, rather as the semi-legendary Arthur means 'the bear' and may simply refer to his battle standard.

There is no problem then in accepting the leadership of the Iceni by Boudicca in 60; the problem lies in our total lack of knowledge of her beforehand. Novelists from Anya Seton to Manda Scott have, as a result, had a blank sheet on which to let their imaginations work. Considering no doubt Diodorus Siculus' famous description of gargantuan Celtic women spitting and scratching in all-out brawls, Manda Scott has the young Boudicca killing her first man at the age of twelve. In that great time warp of history, no doubt Tacitus and Dio are nodding approvingly in their graves. Assuming that Boudicca was born in 27 or 28, she would have been very much of marriageable age by the time the eleven kings paid homage to Claudius in 43. We do not know if Prasutagus was one of them or whether it was his predecessor, who may have been Anteios. We do not know whether Boudicca was his consort first or whether her regally independent status meant that she automatically became Prasutagus' wife later. Whether Boudicca married once or twice, and whether she was the only wife of either king in what was probably a polygamous society, we also do not know. We have little direct knowledge of Celtic marriage vows or ceremonies. With the Celtic love of feasts and music, we can be sure there would be plenty of both.

Julius Caesar, writing of Gaul a century before Boudicca, claimed that in Celtic marriages both parties put an agreed sum of valuables aside in equal proportions and the survivor received both shares as a built-in pension. Since he also claimed that men had the power of life and death over their wives and could use torture on them, which was a typically Roman practice, much of what he says must be doubted. The role of Celtic women is admirably described by Peter Beresford Ellis, but his examples inevitably come from much later, the earliest nearly five centuries after Boudicca, by which time the world had changed significantly.

Boudicca was certainly no shrinking violet, combing her long auburn hair in front of one of the elaborate bronze mirrors belonging to her time and admiring the pretty torc around her neck. In the effete-late seventeenth century she would be depicted in this way. Nor can we be sure she was the guttural, spitting tomboy whose barbarity is for ever associated with the torture and slaughter of thousands of her fellowcountrymen in Camulodunum, Londinium and Verulamium.

It is this very enigma which fascinates.

4
The Wicker Men

The smoke upon your Altar dies,
  The flowers decay.
The Goddess of your sacrifice
  Has flown away.
What profit then to sing or slay
  The sacrifice from day to day?

'L'Envoi', Rudyard Kipling

When the Roman governor of Britannia, Gaius Suetonius Paulinus, heard of Boudicca's revolt, he was in Anglesey, the Roman Mona. Tacitus takes up the tale:

The enemy lined the shore in a dense armed mass. Among them were black-robed women with dishevelled hair like Furies, brandishing torches. Close by stood Druids, raising their heads to heaven and screaming dreadful curses . . . For it was their religion to drench the altars in the blood of prisoners and consult their gods by means of human entrails.[1]

As we shall see, it was probably more than coincidence that the only sizeable Roman army in Britain was nearly 300 miles away when the Iceni rising began, but to understand why

Paulinus was so far away from friendly territory, and indeed to understand Boudicca herself, we need to understand those strange, shrieking women and the cursing men who accompanied them.

According to Roman sources, when Boudicca launched her campaign against Rome in the spring or summer of 60, she called upon the goddess Andraste, one of over 400 Celtic deities whose names we know. We should not see the Boudiccan rebellion purely in terms of revenge, nor of economics, nor of politics, but as a mix of all three, and, from what we know of Celtic religion, all her actions would have been overlaid with mysticism and faith.

Boudicca's religion is a mystery to us. Two thousand years and a lack of written record have left cold trails, dead ends. But some things are certain and others likely. Of the Celtic Gauls, Caesar wrote:

> The god they reverence most is Mercury. They have very many images of him as the inventor of all arts, the god who directs men upon their journeys and their most powerful help in trading and getting money. Next to him they reverence Apollo, Mars, Jupiter and Minerva . . . Apollo averts illness . . . Minerva teaches the principles of industries and handicrafts . . . Jupiter is king of the gods . . . Mars the lord of war.[2]

With this Romanization of Celtic gods, Caesar had caused confusion. It is an example of what Tacitus calls *interpretatio Romana*. We have seen that both Gaul and Britain were exposed to Roman trade, coinage and customs long before the legions came, but this is unlikely to have extended to a wholesale acceptance of alien gods.

> The Gauls claim all to be descended from Dis Pater, declaring that this is the tradition preserved by the Druids.[3]

Dis Pater was the Roman god of the dead and the underworld. That he should also have been seen as the common ancestor of man, as Adam in the Judaic tradition, is not anomalous. In

Irish mythology he was Donn, the dark one, creator of storms and protector of cattle.

Some experts have tried to equate Caesar's gods with those of the Celts he was unable or unwilling to name. In our view this is misleading. All pagan societies had gods and goddesses associated with aspects of life and nature – their similarity to one another is the result of the shared experience of existence. The sun and the moon are physical realities, and ancient peoples saw them as deities, an infinitely more logical explanation than the invisible monotheistic creation of the Hebrews and subsequent Christians, whose inexplicable machinations were awesomely described as 'moving in a mysterious way'. As historian and archaeologist Guy de la Bedoyere has written, 'It is almost impossible to measure the quality and nature of symbolism, ritual and belief. One man's religious symbol is another man's decorative motif and yet another man's nightmare.'

So what do we know of Celtic religion, of the gods whom the Iceni worshipped? We know that it was a shamanistic tradition, an animism that lay somewhere between the worship of elemental nature and veneration of the divinities believed to inhabit natural things. No doubt it was based on an older tradition of Neolithic and Paleolithic origins of which we know virtually nothing. In archaeological terms, the various henges with which Britain is richly endowed are just a tantalizingly vague smudge on an otherwise blank canvas. The sun, the moon, the wind, the rain, the seasons and the eternal circle of life and death were central to Celtic belief. It is highly likely that each tribe had its local gods, to which symbols like the horse and the boar testify. The Romans, not averse to the alien religions they encountered in conquest, found no difficulty in assimilating these local deities – as at Bath, where the natural spring was dedicated to Minerva Sulis. Further north in the territory of the Brigantes, the less impressive spa at Buxton was called Aquae Arnementiae, and here in particular lies a clue to the core of Celtic faith.

The name 'Arnementiae' refers almost certainly to *nemeton*, the Celtic word for a sacred grove. Here we strike a chord with the classical writers, many of whom comment on Druidic ceremonies in such holy clearings in woodland, especially where the oak and the mistletoe coexisted. In a country far more heavily wooded than today, such groves were common, although probably some sites were more sacred than others. Gaius Suetonius Paulinus knew this when he moved against Mona: by hacking down the sacred trees, the legionaries were destroying a way of life. Boudicca had done the same thing at Camulodunum as Paulinus struck, smashing the temple of the deified Claudius in an orgy of destruction.

But Aquae Arnementiae has a double importance. Like Bath it was a source of water, and water, too, was sacred to the Celts. We have already noted the finds at La Tène in Switzerland; a strip of about a hundred yards along the riverbed of the Thiele produced 382 brooches, 8 cauldrons, 41 axes, 29 shields, 166 swords and 269 spearheads. No evidence could be found that this was an arsenal, and today we believe that the objects at La Tène were votive offerings – objects placed in the water deliberately to appease a terrifying god.

The debate rages as to the quality of these goods. Some archaeologists claim that the goods offered to placate the gods were worthless or obsolete trash, rather as we still throw small change into 'lucky' fountains. This flies in the face of both human emotions and archaeological fact. If men believed in the need to appease the gods at all, they would offer their best equipment, not their worst, for fear of giving the gods offence and increasing their wrath.

Examples of votive offerings in water can be found nearer to home. The extraordinary Battersea shield dredged from the Thames is the bronze face of what was probably a wooden artefact. Dating from the third century BC and now in the British Museum, it has been called, rightly, 'the noblest creation of late Celtic art'. Appositely, in the case of Mona, excavations have revealed votive offerings there. In 1942, when a new runway was being built by the RAF at Valley, 142 metal objects were found. The blasting and quarrying involved almost certainly disturbed the site, and it is possible that Llyn Cerrig Bach ('the lake of the little stones') was indeed a Druid headquarters, as Tacitus implies. The fact that none of the finds postdates Paulinus' destruction of the island in 60 shows what a thorough job his legions did, but the 200-year 'lifespan' of the site also indicates that this was an important place for the Celts long before the eagles landed.

At Llyn Cerrig Bach eleven swords have been found, a dagger, two shields, horse harness and parts of twenty-two two-wheeled war chariots. The bronze decoration in the form of twisted spirals may well be from ceremonial ash wands or staffs carried by the Druids slaughtered by Paulinus' troops. We have already discussed the use of Celtic chariots by the Iceni and have seen them in inhumations throughout Europe, but it is likely that the wheel motif had a secondary purpose in these grave goods – its spokes symbolized the rays of the sun, and may have represented one of the Celtic gods whose name we know – the 'thunderer', Taranis.

Of the 400 Celtic deities whose names we know, 300 of them only occur once in the historical record, and in archaeological terms not at all. Once again, we are at the mercy of a society without a written tradition, which leaves us groping in the dark. Among the classical writers, Lucan, mentions three gods in particular, but whether these represent a kind of trinity, and indeed hierarchy, or whether this is merely the accident of historical commentary, is difficult to say. There is a theory that the number three had special significance for the Celts: certainly, finds of a three-faced god and artwork of the La Tène type in which there are three whorls or loops, are commonplace.

Taranis, according to Lucan, was Jupiter Optimus Maximus, the all-powerful, the father of the gods, 'lifted' from the Greek Zeus. In Welsh *taran* means 'thunder' (the equivalent Irish word is *tarann*), and it is typical of pagan societies to attribute divinity to something they did not understand and of which they were afraid. A pottery mould found at Corbridge in Northumberland has been identified as Taranis. He carries a decorative shield and vicious-looking club, with the sun-wheel motif beside him. Similar art forms dedicated to him have been found all over Europe.

In *De Bello Civili*, Lucan equated the god Teutates with Mercury, the god whom Caesar says was most worshipped in Britain. Linguistically, he is linked with the people (*tuath*, in

Irish, means 'a province' or 'tribe'; *tudri*, in Welsh, 'the ruler of a province') and so perhaps comes closest to the concept of a god for all seasons. As a result, it has been suggested that the pre-Roman Celts were moving towards some sort of monotheism; with a panoply of 400 gods, however, this is not entirely convincing. Among a number of archaeological finds in Britain, the TOT rings are unusual. Again, there is the theory that these were worn in honour of Teutates in the alternative spelling of Totatis. Interestingly, most of them have been found in Iceni territory around East Anglia and Lincolnshire. As Guy de la Bedoyere points out, however, the initials TOT could have other meanings now lost, and he cites *terras obscura teneret* (darkness holds the land) or the Aeneid phrase *tonat omne tumultu* (heaven thunders with the noise) as possibilities. Intriguingly, both phrases have a resonance with the year 60 and the rebellion of Boudicca – in the path of her destruction, the darkness of smoke covered the land and heaven shook with the thunder of her chariots. Other experts claim that TOT signifies a religious site, as at Totnes in Devon.

Esus is the third of Lucan's Celtic gods. Lucan is as scathing of him as he is of Taranis and Teutatis – 'uncouth Esus of the barbarous altars' – and we must remember that he was writing for a sophisticated Roman readership who expected their enemies and their enemies' gods to be beyond the pale, taking comfort in the superiority of their own. Esus is associated with woodland, and two carved reliefs from the first century show him as a woodcutter. While this would certainly tie in with the notion of the sacred groves, his name only occurs in a single inscription, and it is impossible to know the extent to which he had a cult.

Beyond these three specified by Lucan, three others must be mentioned in relation to the Iceni – Lug, Epona and Cernunnos. Lug was probably Mercury in Caesar's estimation of the British tribes he encountered. In Irish mythology he is Lugh; in Welsh Lleu. The 180-foot giant carved into the chalk above Cerne Abbas in Dorset may well be this god. Like Taranis, he carries a club, but the most obvious thing about him is his erect penis. At over 12 feet long, this was too much for the Victorians, who partially covered him with a bush!

There is a great deal of evidence for the importance of this god – Carlisle on the Pictish borders was named after him, as was Leignitz in Germany; Londinium may have been originally a sacred site linked with him. In Celtic mythology, the Irish called him 'of the long arm', the Welsh 'of the skilful hand', and if his other name really was Vin, he became Finn McCool, hero of the Fianna who guarded the high kings of Ireland. It may even be that the most famous of the legionary forts along Hadrian's Wall, Vindolanda, was consecrated in his honour. The Romans, every bit as superstitious as their Celtic enemies, took no chances. As Guy de la Bedoyere says, 'A soldier at Housteads fort on Hadrian's Wall would have struggled not to trip over the shrines, altars and dedications cluttering the slope below the stronghold.'[4]

As a god associated with fertility, he also gave his name to one of the four principal feasts of Celtic religion, Lughnasadh on 1 August. When the Emperor Augustus made Lugos (today's Lyon) capital of Romanized Gaul, he appropriated the god's feast as his own, rather as later Christians stole 25 December, the midwinter solstice, as Christ's birthday. The Christians also adopted Lug's festival, renaming it Lammas. The date is significant for a people as bound to the earth as the Celts were. The Iceni, as we have seen, were farmers before all else as a matter of survival. The harvest and the good weather to make it grow were vital. Lug's feast was the chance to make devotions to him so that food would be plentiful before the darkness of winter.

On 1 May came Beltane, propitious for the spring growing. This was the feast of another deity, Belenus, whom Caesar equated with Apollo, the god of prophecy. It is possible that Billingsgate in London was named after him. *Tane* in old Irish means 'shining' or 'brightness', and the god seems to have been associated with fire. Samhain was another great festival of the Celts, on 1 November. All-Hallows Eve to the Christians, this feast became associated with the night on which the witches rode, and witchcraft is believed by many to be the survival of pagan religion long into the Christian era. Samhain marked the end of the summer and looms largest of the four feasts, associated as it was with the other world and the dead. Imbolc, celebrated on 1

February, is unimportant by comparison, although it was the day associated with birth, especially of livestock.

Epona is a goddess who may be linked more directly with Boudicca. She was a horse deity, always portrayed as riding or petting horses. In Irish she is Edain Echraighe; in Welsh Rhiannon, but there is a mixed tradition as to whether she was merely a rider or a zoomorphic goddess in the form of a horse. The beautiful chalk carving of the white horse at Uffington in Oxfordshire may be in homage to her. Unsurprisingly, the Roman cavalry adopted her as their totem. In a stone statuette from Alésia in eastern Gaul, she is shown riding side-saddle, a fashion not known in England until the fourteenth century.

The Gundestrup cauldron is one of the most remarkable and tantalizing of Celtic finds. Discovered in a peat bog in Denmark in 1891, it belongs to the first or second century BC and its copper sides are richly decorated with motifs that are probably religious. The cauldron itself was a cult object associated with the Druids and was probably used in any or all of the festivals referred to above. The heads around the bowl's exterior surface may have a significance in themselves, and one of the principal figures, shown sitting cross-legged and surrounded by a plethora of wild animals, is the horn-headed Cernunnos, with a torc in one hand, a serpent in the other. Like Epona, a zoomorphic creation, he is linked with the animal world and the hunt. In folklore, he is Herne the Hunter, whose ghost (allegedly!) last appeared in Windsor Great Park in 1962. In a wider context, the horned god is the herd leader, associated with procreation and fertility. It may be from Cernunnos and his horns that the Christians invented the embodiment of evil, the devil.

How much of Celtic religion can we link directly with Boudicca and the Iceni? It is tempting to see the queen as linked with Epona, the horse goddess, and it may be that the timing of her rebellion, like the timing of all Celtic events, was influenced closely by the seasons and the festivals of Samhain, Imbolc, Beltane and Lughansadh. We know that the Druids counted time by night (reflected in our word 'fortnight') not in days, and this may have a bearing on Boudicca's attacks, too.

Some clues come to us over the centuries from folklore, an important element all too often ignored by historians obsessed with the 'paper trail' of written evidence.

At Aylmerton near the north Norfolk coast are the Shrieking Pits, Neolithic flint mines allegedly haunted by a female figure in white who has been seen wringing her hands and peering into the depressions in the ground. We cannot know if the Iceni had similar legends associated with older religions that 'predated their own society'. In the hills overlooking the fens of Cambridgeshire to the west is the Iron Age fort of Wandlebury, probably one of Boudicca's strongholds. Somewhere beneath its windswept summit lie, according to legend, the bodies of Gog and Magog, the last of a race of giants who were probably Celtic gods. In the 1950s archaeological and psychic researcher T.C. Lethbridge visited the Gogmagog Hills and discovered three figures, one of whom he equated with Epona the horse goddess and another with a beaked horse and chariot. The latter figure he dated to the second century BC, but Epona to only about eighty years before Boudicca's birth. The legendary golden chariot buried at Mutlow Hill nearby is almost certainly a link with the Iceni.

Andy Mould already had a reputation for finding bodies when he unearthed 'Pete Marsh', a potently tangible link with Boudicca and her rebellion. It was Friday 1 August 1984, the feast of Lughnasdh, and the place was Lindow Moss, below the great sweep of Saddleworth Moor, itself a graveyard.[5] A year earlier the peatcutter had found part of a woman's skull, a discovery that had prompted a local man to confess to murdering his wife twenty years previously. In the event, the skull was not hers and her body has never been found, but it is a grim example of race memory, perhaps, that sacrifices are still being made in watery places.

Since the 1950s spectacular finds have emerged from similar peat bogs in Jutland and Denmark, at Tollund and Grauballe, for instance, where the chemical combination of peat and water have led to extraordinary levels of preservation. The body found at Lindow was carefully excavated, and samples were sent to three separate laboratories at Harwell, Oxford and the British

Museum. Carbon-dating, though inconclusive at first, eventually narrowed the likely age to the first century AD; 'Pete Marsh' was a contemporary of Boudicca. The forensics were fascinating. Despite inevitable distortion caused by 2,000 years of the weight of waterlogged peat, the neck was clearly broken, as was the jaw. The skull was fractured and the ribs on the body's right side were shattered. Nothing below the waist was found at first because the excavator had sliced right through the body. Sections of leg and buttock were found subsequently.

The state of the bones and teeth indicated that 'Lindow Man', as archaeologists called the find, was a healthy adult male in his late twenties or early thirties, suffering from mild osteoarthritis, which is often found in inhumations – a common problem for Bronze or Iron Age man. What was riveting was that Lindow Man had been murdered – and with a degree of overkill. There were two deep lacerations in the peat-brown leathery skin of the scalp and corresponding splits in the skull below. These blows had been delivered from above and behind while the victim was still alive, possibly in a kneeling position. The base of the skull had a similar fracture, caused perhaps by an axehead rather than its edge. The teeth were crunched together by the impact of these three blows, and around Lindow man's neck was a garrotte of animal gut, tied with three knots for the inclusion of a stick to be twisted as a ligature. Death would have been very quick, the airways closing before the spine snapped, but to make triply sure of death, an incision had been made in the jugular vein in the neck, just above the ligature. The weapon used was pointed and very sharp, and the victim was still alive as the blade went in. He was then immersed in the bog of Lindow Moss.

Further analysis provided knowledge of the victim's last meal. Archaeobotanists were able to tell from the starch grains still present that Lindow Man had eaten a small amount of bread not long before he had died. Using ESR (electron spin resonance) it was possible to tell that the bread had been cooked to a heat of 200°C and that it was unleavened, parts of it cooked to a 400°C heat; in other words, it was burned. The most bizarre find, however, also came from Lindow Man's stomach – grains of mistletoe pollen.

Archaeologist Dr Anne Ross and chemist Dr Don Robins have followed every step of Lindow Man's journey from that casual find by Andy Mould twenty years ago. Although it is likely that some 230 parts of human bodies have been found in British peat bogs since Victorian times, none has been analysed as thoroughly or so famously as 'Pete Marsh'. In *The Life and Death of a Druid Prince*, Ross and Robins turn an anonymous leathery corpse into a flesh and blood individual whose links with Boudicca are very real. They are able to tell us that he was five feet six inches tall, with a large head and deep-set eyes, and that his beard was cut shortly before death. He would have weighed about eleven stone and his blood group was O.

Using current knowledge of Celtic religion, Ross and Robins notes the 'triple death' – three cuts to the head, three knots in the gut garrotte, three elements to the attack (blunt instrument, strangulation, throat slitting) – and speculate that this was a ritual sacrifice to three of the greatest gods in the Celtic pantheon. The fire of Taranis the Thunderer is explained, not by burning a wicker man in a giant effigy, but by Lindow Man's swallowing the *burned* bread before death. The garrotting (found in several Danish bog burials, too) has links with Esus, whose victims were hanged from trees. His immersion in the marsh clearly recalls Teutates. Indeed, one of the carvings on the Gundestrup cauldron clearly shows a god plunging one such victim into a barrel.[6]

To Ross and Robins the triple death means that the victim's sacrifice was especially meaningful. But their speculation does not end there. Because his fingernails were immaculate, they cannot believe that he was a tiller of the soil. There were only two occupational groups who did no manual labour in Celtic society, warriors and priests. It is difficult to believe that a warrior could have survived thirty years of life, at least fifteen of them as a fighting adult, without getting a scratch. Yet, other than the wounds that killed him and the slice of the cutter that disinterred him, Lindow Man was unmarked. This means that he was a priest, and the presence of mistletoe grains merely confirms the Druidic link, since, as we shall see, the Druids believed the mistletoe to be holy.

Ross and Robins believe that Lindow man died in 60, the

'black year' of the Druid Prince. And the hinge is the events of that year, the timing of those events and the geography of Romano-Celtic Britain. Assuming that Paulinus made his move against the Druids of Mona in March (the earliest likely campaigning month because of the weather and assuming it took him a minimum of two to three weeks to defeat the force there and secure the island), he now, according to Tacitus, heard of Boudicca's rebellion and hurried south-east to find her. The messenger had brought news of the destruction of Camulodunum, and no one could know where she might strike next. Setting aside for the moment the question of whether the Mona campaign was a diversion to enable her to act, Paulinus set off across a 250-mile tract of country with only a small cavalry retinue. Speed was of the essence and the infantry would take too long to deploy.

A commander as experienced as Paulinus would not have abandoned the island he had just lost men in taking. If Anglesey was as sacred to the Druids as everybody believed and if it had been, as we shall see elsewhere, the 'granary' of Caratacus' campaigns with the Silures, the Romans would have left troops there, just in case of trouble, either adapting the hill fort on Holyhead mountain or building a camp of their own. Ross and Robins believe that Lindow Man arrived from Ireland with a 'retinue of Druids',[7] realized it was too late, because the Druids were dead and the groves felled, and made votive offerings at Llyn Cerrig Bach before moving on to the mainland. Here, the authors of the *Druid Prince* believe, he may have deposited the golden torc, which was an emblem of his rank, and escaped by boat at night to reach north Wales.

It would still be spring, perhaps April by now – but here the whole *Druid Prince* theory collapses. Boudicca had time to destroy a vexillation of the IX Legion, Londinium and Verulamium, turn north to catch Paulinus and be defeated by him, all in time for Lindow Man to be sacrificed at Beltane (on 1 May). This sequence of events is unlikely, but Ross and Robins are unclear as to whether they believe the sacrifice was made at Beltane in 60 or 61. If it was 61, what was the victim doing for twelve months before he ended up in Lindow Moss, bludgeoned and strangled?

Ross and Robins contend that Lindow was chosen because it was a wild, isolated place far enough from prying Romans to be safe. The actual killing, they contend, took place at nearby Alderley Edge, perhaps near the present villages of Mabberley or Wilmslow. The bog itself, argue Ross and Robins, had a special significance because of its geographical location – it lies at the 'triple boundary' of the territories of three tribes: the Corieltavi of what is today the West Midlands, the Brigantes in modern Lancashire and the Cornovii who straddled the area where the Saxon king Offa would build his dyke eight centuries later.

More interesting than the sacrificial death of Lindow man, which may or may not have any link with the Iceni rising, is the theory that Ross and Robins promulgate on the ferocity of Paulinus' attack on the Druids. We know that the Romans were – not iconoclasts they were quite happy to absorb native gods and even dedicate shrines to them – so why destroy the Druids so totally? The 'official' propaganda, from Caesar, Lucan, Pliny and other writers, is that their human sacrifices were so abhorrent to the Romans that it was nothing less than a Roman duty to stamp out the whole cult. However, the Romans were among the most barbarous peoples of the ancient world, so this version does not wash. Who were the Druids and what is their link with Boudicca? Over centuries, these ancient priests have been 'discovered', 'rediscovered' and 'invented' so many times that tracing their real roots is almost impossible. Certainly they bear no developmental links with the fancy dress of today's Gorsedd or the myriad modern Druidic organizations around the world.

According to various observers, they kept their arcane secrets to themselves by prodigious feats of memory and the spoken word, and only 'borrowed' written language, largely Greek, for mundane 'business' matters. Of course, the men who observed the Druids were the Romans, their spiritual and political enemies, and any accounts by them must necessarily be taken with various sized pinches of salt. The fact remains that in the written historical record almost all we have comes from Roman sources, or Greek sources based on them.

Dion Chrystosom (354–407) wrote in his *Orations*

On the other hand, the Keltoi have men called Druids, who concern themselves with divination and all branches of wisdom. And without their advice even kings dared not resolve upon nor execute any plan. So that in truth it was they who ruled, while the kings, who sat on golden thrones and fared sumptuously in their palaces, became mere ministers of the Druids' will.[8]

It was this power of the Druids that gives us a clue to Paulinus moving against them on Anglesey in 60.

Ammianus Marcellinus wrote in the fourth century of Druid organization:

It was the custom of the Bards to celebrate the brave deeds of their famous men in epic verse accompanied by the sweet strains of the lyre, while the Euhages [Orators] strove to explain the high mysteries of nature. Between them came the Druids, men of greater talent, members of the intimate fellowship of the Pythagorean faith; they were uplifted by searchings into secret and sublime things and with grand contempt for mortal lot they professed the immortality of the soul.[9]

A century earlier, Diogenes Laertius put stylus to parchment:

[the] Druids make their pronouncements by means of riddles and dark sayings, teaching that the gods must be worshipped and no evil done and manly behaviour maintained.[10]

A number of classical writers were genuinely appalled by the excesses of Druidic practice, a little ironic perhaps in a nation that inspired blood and circuses as crowd pleasers. Marcus Lucianus, the poet and philosopher who won a poetry competition in the Neronian games in the year of Boudicca's rebellion, published his *Pharsalia* two years later:

And you, Druids, now that the clash of battle is stilled, once more have you returned to your barbarous ceremonies and to the savage usage of your holy rites. To you alone it is given to know the truth about the gods and deities of the sky . . . The innermost groves of far-off forests are your abodes . . .

Lucan's contemporary, the geographer Pomponius Mela, wrote in his three-volume *De Situ Orbis* ('The Place of the World') about ten years after the Iceni revolt:

There still remain traces of atrocious customs no longer practised and although they now refrain from outright slaughter [he is writing chiefly of Gaul] yet they still draw blood from the victims led to the altar. They have, however, their own kind of eloquence and teachers of wisdom called Druids. These profess to know the size and shape of the world, the movements of the heavens and of the stars and the will of the gods. They teach many things . . . in a course of instruction lasting as long as twenty years, meeting in secret either in a cave or in secluded dales. One of their dogmas has come to common knowledge, namely, that souls are eternal and that there is another life in the infernal regions, and this has been permitted manifestly because it makes the multitude readier for war. And it is for this reason, too, that they burn or bury with their dead things appropriate to them in life . . . Indeed, there were some of them who flung themselves wilfully on the funeral piles of their relatives in order to share the new life with them.[11]

Another geographer, Strabo, understood the whole Celtic temperament better than he knew when he wrote his *Geographica*, probably before Boudicca was born

So confident are the people in the justice of the Druids that they refer all private and public disputes to them; and these men on many occasions have made peace between armies actually drawn up for battle. All murder cases are referred to them. When there are a large number of these . . . they imagine that the harvest will be plentiful.

They would strike the victim in the back with a sword and divine from his convulsive throes. They never sacrifice without the Druids. It is said they have other manners of sacrificing their human victims; that they pierce some with arrows, crucify others in their temples and that they prepare a stack of hay and wood which they set on fire after having placed cattle, all kinds of animals and men in it.[12]

Diodorus Siculus, approaching the Druids of Gaul from an historical viewpoint twenty years before the birth of Christ, agrees with most of Strabo, but is more graphic in his description of Druidic divination:

> . . . they practice a strange and incredible custom, for they kill a man by a knife-stab in the region above the midriff and after his fall they foretell the future by the convulsions of his limbs and the pouring of his blood, a form of divination in which they have full confidence, as it is of old tradition . . . It is not only in times of peace, but in war also, that these seers have authority and the incantations of the bards have effect on friends and foes alike. Often when the combatants are ranged face to face and swords are drawn and spears bristling, these men come between the armies and stay the battle, just as wild beasts are sometimes spellbound. Thus even among the most savage barbarians anger yields to wisdom and Mars is shamed before the Muses.[13]

Even more details of the Druids and their practices come from Gaius Plinius Secundus, Pliny the Elder. A contemporary of Boudicca, he commanded a cavalry unit and was something of an authority on mounted warfare. At the time of the Iceni rebellion he was in Spain, and in 77 produced his epic forty-seven volume *Historica Naturalis*, a monumental ramble through history and science, fact and fiction, the mundane and the miraculous, with no attempt at qualification or separation. In volume 16 he wrote:

> The Druids – for so their magicians are called – hold nothing more sacred than the mistletoe and the tree that bears it, always supposing that tree to be the oak. But they never perform any of their rites except in the presence of a

branch of it, so that it seems probable that the priests themselves may derive their name from the Greek word for that tree . . . The mistletoe, however, is found but rarely upon the oak and, when found, is gathered with due religious ceremony, if possible on the sixth day of the moon (for it is by the moon that they measure their months and years and also their ages of thirty years). They choose this day because the moon, although not yet in the middle of her course, has already considerable influence. They call the mistletoe by a name meaning, in their language, the all-healing . . . They believe that the mistletoe, taken in drink, imparts fecundity to barren animals and that it is an antidote for all poisons.[14]

No doubt Pliny was willing to accept the reality of the huge Roman pantheon of gods but poured scorn on the faith of others – 'Such are the religious feelings that are entertained towards terrifying things by many peoples.'

Whereas much of Pliny's information in the *Historia* was obtained second-hand by prodigious study, he had travelled in Spain and what today is Germany, so he may have seen the Druids in person. Most of his references are to Gaul, but we know the importance of pan-Celticism, and it is likely that British Druids carried out similar rites:

Similar to savin is the plant called selago.[15] It is gathered without using iron and by passing the right hand through the left sleeve of the tunic, as though committing a theft. [Clearly, Pliny had seen plenty of pickpockets working the crowds in Rome!] The clothing must be white and the feet washed and bare and an offering of wine and bread must be made before the gathering. The Druids of Gaul say that the plant should be carried as a charm against every kind of evil and that the smoke of it is good for diseases of the eyes.

Of particular fascination for Pliny was the Druid's egg, supposedly an entwining of snakes 'glued' together by secretions from their bodies, which had sacred and powerful properties, said to be particularly favoured by the Celtic hierarchy. Pliny himself was less impressed, and on two counts. He had seen one: 'It was round and about as large as a smallish apple. The shell was cartilaginous and pocked like the arms of a polypus.' Secondly, it patently did not work:

> . . . because a man of the Vocontii [a Gallic tribe] . . . kept one of these eggs in his bosom during a trial and was put to death by the Emperor Claudius, as far as I can see, for that reason alone.

The Druid's egg was probably the egg case of the whelk (*buccinum undatum*), which fits the philosopher's description fairly well.

In *Historia* 30, Pliny makes the point that the Emperor Tiberius issued a decree banning Druids 'and the whole tribe of diviners and physicians', but his writ had not reached Britain. The Roman wrote:

> At the present day Britannia is still fascinated by magic and performs its rites with so much ceremony that it almost seems as though it was she who had imparted the cult to the Persians. [The smugness kicks in again] Therefore we cannot too highly appreciate our debt to the Romans for having put an end to this monstrous cult, whereby to murder a man was an act of the greatest devoutness and to eat his flesh most beneficial.[16]

Pliny's intellectual curiosity would kill him in 79 when he got too close to the erupting nightmare of Vesuvius and choked in its fumes.

This mistaken belief that Druidism had its origins in Britain came from a theory from the Roman who knew them well, Gaius Julius Caesar. He had inside information in the form of the Gallic Aeduan Diviciacus, a man, according to Caesar, 'of exceptional loyalty, fair-mindedness and moderation'. It is highly likely that Diviciacus was himself a Druid. In Book 6, Caesar writes:

> The Druids officiate at the worship of the gods, regulate public and private sacrifices and give rulings on all religious

questions. Large numbers of young men flock to them for instruction and they are held in great honour by the people. They act as judges in practically all disputes, whether between tribes or individuals. Whenever a murder takes place or a dispute arises about an inheritance or boundary, it is they who adjudicate the matter and appoint the compensation to be paid and received by the parties concerned. Any individual or tribe failing to accept their award is banned from taking part in sacrifice – the heaviest punishment that can be inflicted in Gaul. Those laid under such a ban are regarded as impious criminals . . . All the Druids are under one head, whom they hold in the highest respect. On his death, if any one of the rest is of outstanding merit, he succeeds to the vacant place; if several have equal claim, the Druids usually decide the election by voting, though sometimes they actually fight it out . . . The Druidic doctrine is believed to have been found existing in Britain and thence imported into Gaul; even today [57 BC] those who want to make a profound study of it generally go to Britain for the purpose.

Here, from a man who knew them as well as any Roman could, is a description of a wise and omnipotent class, every bit as powerful as the later Catholic Church throughout Europe. Being a Druid, Caesar tells us, has its attractions – they do not fight or pay taxes. This explains why well-to-do families sent their sons to the Druidic colleges which later adherents imagined were dotted all over Britain. Such teaching involved prodigious feats of memory and the training could take twenty years:

The Druids believe that their religion forbids them to commit their teachings to writing . . . because they [do] not want their doctrine to become public property . . .

This elitism – like that of scholars of later centuries who wrote in Greek or Latin to protect their wisdom (and so their salaries) from the hoi polloi – is, infuriatingly, responsible for our lack of knowledge of the Druids and Celtic society in general. Caesar said that

[The Druids] hold long discussions about the heavenly bodies and their movements, the size of the universe and of the earth, the physical constitution of the world and the power and properties of the gods . . .

He also noted that

As a nation, the Gauls are extremely superstitious [this from a man cavalier enough to ignore warnings of the Ides of March in 44 BC] and so persons suffering from serious diseases, as well as those who are exposed to the perils of battle, offer, or vow to offer, human sacrifices, for the performance of which they employ Druids . . . some tribes have colossal images made of wickerwork, the limbs of which they fill with living men; then they are set on fire and the victims burnt to death. They think that the gods prefer the execution of men taken in the act of theft or brigandage or guilty of some offence; but when they run short of criminals, they do not hesitate to make up with innocent men.[17]

Strabo implies that by his day, some thirty years after Caesar's death, the wicker man burnings were already obsolete, but his evidence does not refer to Britain, which was 'still fascinated by magic', as Pliny said. There can be little doubt that human sacrifice involving fire was carried out in the teeth of Boudicca's rebellion. Lindow Man may have been one example; the luckless defenders of Camulodunum, Londinium and Verulamium yet more. Only the wicker men have not survived to become the testimony of the spade.

Archaeologist Sir Cyril Fox threw an intriguing theory into the ring sixty years ago. If we take the legionary road of Watling Street as a starting point, it is possible to plot a pre-Roman way marked by Celtic shrines and holy places. The route stretches west to Mona and perhaps beyond that, across the Irish Sea to Dublin. Interestingly, the name Dublin means the same as Lindow, 'the black pool', and the Wicklow Hills beyond are the source of gold production according to Irish bardic mythology. Because the Romans did not land there en masse, the Druidism and bardism of Ireland had an altogether longer life. They were not destroyed by the legions and therefore may represent a survival of the priesthood and indeed faith of Boudicca's people. Fox contended that what the Romans established as a military road lay not on a Celtic sacred way but on an economic route every bit as real and important as the later Silk Road to China; and it was based on gold, one of the reasons for the Roman invasion of Britain in the first place. Was the Druids' hold over the people, then, economic as well as religious and political? Did they, in effect, run the gold route and dominate this most valuable trade rather as later Venetian and Genoese merchants dominated spices and silks in the Middle Ages? Is this why Caesar believed Mercury, the god of journeys and wealth, was the principal deity of Britain? Is this the real reason that Paulinus smashed the Druid groves and wiped out the British priesthood? And was the gold of the Iceni King Prasutagus brought along this road from the sacred island?

The Celtic cult of the head[18] is a subject that a number of classical writers mention. The head was the centre, or the soul of all things, and for this reason warriors lopped off their enemies' heads in battle, taking the grisly objects as trophies, dangling them from their horse harness, embalming them in cedar oil and displaying them outside their houses. The Amerindians of the Great Plains, with their penchant for scalping had a similar belief and if, as the rumour persists, this was first done by French trappers, it merely confirms a long-standing Gallic tradition! Heads of traitors were for centuries nailed to spikes on London Bridge and Temple Bar, intended perhaps to act more as deterrent than trophy. There are intriguing survivals in the medieval concept of the Mandelion, the Head of Christ, supposedly carried by the Templars on crusade. This cult was widespread in the Celtic world, and archaeology has uncovered examples of severed heads from the Rhône Valley to County Cavan in Ireland.

Most commentators believe that Boudicca sacked Verulamium because it was a Roman *municipium*, badly defended and more or less on her route north in pursuit of Paulinus. No doubt there is an element of truth in all this, but in Folly Lane, St Albans, a grave has been found which might change our perception of her campaign. The grave is less than a mile from the town that Boudicca's army destroyed. Dated to about 50, ten years before the Iceni attack, it contains an aristocrat lying on a couch inside a mortuary house built in a pit. The body itself, in keeping with most Celtic burials, had been burnt and placed in a pit next to the funerary chamber, which showed marks of ritual destruction. The whole site was large, extending to five acres, and its west entrance was guarded by three human skeletons. Forty years after Boudicca, a Romano-Celtic temple was built here, typical as we have seen of the assimilation process the conquerors followed. Inside the temple, and dated to about 100, was the head of a teenage boy impaled on a pole. His hair and skin had been removed but the face was intact. If, as excavator Rosalind Niblett believes, this was a site dedicated to head worship, was Boudicca's attack on the area motivated by religion and magic as much as by the thrill of destruction and the lure of booty? And does not the evidence point, in the sacrifice of 'Lindow Man' and Boudicca's calling on Andraste, to the possibility at least that the queen was a priestess in the eyes of her people?

5

The Last of the Celts

> We are the worm in the wood!
> We are the rot in the root!
> We are the germ in the blood!
> We are the thorn in the foot!
> 'A Pict Song' from *Puck of Pook's Hill*,
> Rudyard Kipling

We have no clear physical description of the man the Romans called Caratacus and the Welsh Caradwc. The coins minted by him, too few and scattered to enable us to pinpoint his kingdom with any certainty, show a heavy-boned face and moustache, though the head is wrapped in a lion's skin and may be a Celtic copy of Hercules, a common enough representation among Caratacus' enemies. The fact that the coins' reverse shows a displayed eagle with a serpent in its talons is fascinating; is this a military trophy, the *aquila* of a legion the warrior king had defeated, or a grudging mark of respect for the might of the military nation against which he found himself pitted?

In Welsh folklore, the name Caradwc appears as the son of Bran and grandson of the sea god Llyr. When Bran sailed to Ireland to avenge the mistreatment of his sister by a high king, Caradwc was left behind as chief steward. He was defeated by Caswallon, son of Belin, the god of death. Somewhere in this distorted La Tène mirror of Celtic mythology, are we looking at the story of Caratacus and his defeat by Rome?

Boudicca would have been in her early twenties when Aulus Plautius left Britain in 47 to return to Rome for his well-earned ovation and the undying gratitude of his emperor. In accordance with custom, the new governor could not land on the province's soil until the outgoing one had left. And the new governor was Publius Ostorius Scapula. Little is known about this man, but the fact that he was chosen at all indicates that he was considered both competent and loyal to Claudius. Quintus Ostorius Scapula, either his father or grandfather, had been *praefectus* of Egypt, appointed by Augustus two years before the birth of Christ. Scapula may have been related to the consul Lucius Vitellius, who ruled Rome in Claudius' absence in 43, and was a suffect consul, probably in 45. There is speculation that he may have accompanied Claudius in his expedition, which would explain his being given the post of governor. From his actions, it seems that he was hasty and quick-tempered, without the patience or tenacity needed for a protracted guerrilla war.

What Scapula faced on his arrival clearly indicates how well-informed the disaffected Britons were. Far from the quiescent, subdued peoples of which Plautius may have spoken, Britannia was now seething. It seems likely that the Celts knew that not only was there to be a new, less-experienced governor, but that there was also a sizeable turnover of troops. We know that men served in the legions and the auxiliaries for twenty-one years, and the respite of 47 gave an opportunity for some of these veterans to retire, either to go home or, more usually, to live on as unpaid reserves in this country. No doubt, just as Plautius had brought men from the Danube whom he knew and trusted, some of these would have gone into honourable retirement with him. Likewise, Scapula, whatever his military experience had been, may well have brought his own people over, adding to the nucleus of four legions – II Augusta, IX Hispana, XIV Gemina and XX – which were already based here. Tacitus refers to these troops as *exercitu ignoto*, an untried army, which gave the nod to fugitive Celts on the frontier margins to take advantage of the situation.

It was probably autumn or the early winter before trouble began, and the uncharacteristic timing of the attack has all the hallmarks of Caratacus. We do not know where the king was after the battle on the Medway. He presumably fought at the Thames, where his brother died, but it is unlikely that he hung around to witness Claudius' farcical entry into Camulodunum, and he would have regarded the genuflection of the eleven kings as contemptible. Like the will-o'-the-wisp he was, he was probably in the Severn Valley in the winter of 47, striking terror into the hearts of those fickle rulers who had become the 'clients' of Rome. Tacitus is as brief as ever: 'the enemy had invaded allied territory with particular violence'.[1] Either Caratacus was punishing the quisling stance of the Cornovii and Dobunni or he was relaunching the kind of aggressive assimilation that he and Togodumnos were probably already undertaking before 43.

We know little of the Cornovii, settled along the upper reaches of the Severn and into what today is Cheshire. There were hill forts in the area but it is not known whether they were occupied in the 40s. Well and truly beyond the pale in Roman eyes, the Cornovian pottery was of poor quality and no coins have been found. The Dobunni, of course, were subject peoples of the Catuvellauni, and whether or not the settlements burned by Caratacus were those of the defectors to Plautius on the Medway, the whole tribe can have expected little else but fire and the sword from their overlord. Here in the lower Severn Valley, Caratacus was deliberately provoking the Romans; they had established a series of forts or at least marching camps in the area, and at Kingsholm, north of Gloucester (Roman Glevum), was a camp of some importance, almost certainly a base of XX Legion around this time. As the new man with new troops, Scapula knew he had to strike fast. Waiting for spring, the conventional campaign season, could have been disastrous. Tacitus makes it sound all too easy: 'He killed those Britons that had resisted, pursued those that were scattered.'[2] Other details are totally lacking.

Caratacus' levies drew back into the mountains of Wales to begin a merciless guerrilla war that would last for nine years.

There must have been rumblings of discontent in the Roman territory. Perhaps the Druids, arbiters of all things as we have seen, fanned the flames of rebellion; perhaps Caratacus was able to sow dissent by some other means. But Scapula's next decision only makes sense against the background of tension. The occupied areas, that of the Cantiaci in the south-east, the Catuvellauni north of the Thames and probably a portion at least of Tiberius Claudius Cogidubnus' Regini and Atrebates, had been disarmed by Plautius, as was the Roman custom and a sensible precaution. Now the new governor extended this edict to other client kingdoms and this brought him head-to-head with the Iceni.

Tacitus, as we know, describes them as 'a tough people who had never been crushed in war', but it is likely that their king, Prasutagus, was not the leader of the rebels. We know nothing of the nature of the client relationship of the Iceni, nor how long Prasutagus had reigned. It is only an assumption that he was the king who knelt before Claudius at Camulodunum, but it is a logical one. As we have seen, it may be that Caesar's reference to the Cenimagni, the Great Iceni, may mean that there was a Ceniparvi, too, a cadet branch or sept of the tribe which could represent a more defiant splinter group. Had Prasutagus led the Iceni rebellion in 48, it is highly unlikely that he would have been allowed to continue on his throne until his death eleven or twelve years later.

The surrendering of weapons is never an easy exercise. It implies loss of face and loss of hope: soldiers reversed their swords and handed the hilts to their enemies only when defeat was certain. In Britain in a much later period, one of the astonishing military achievements of Wellington is that he never lost a gun. We are still waiting, five years on, for one bullet to be handed over by the IRA in the so-called decommissioning process. So we can conclude that 'decommissioning' in 48 would not be carried out peacefully by request. The serving soldiery of the legions, or perhaps the veterans from Camulodunum, would march into villages and hamlets, ransacking homes and hearths for swords, spears, scythes and sickles, *anything* that could be construed as a weapon. And this among the Iceni who, Tacitus reminds us, 'had entered alliance with [Rome] willingly'.

There must have been harsh words at the tribal council. Wherever Prasutagus had his court, furious tribesmen would have come to him, complaining at the insult. Boudicca would have been there and, knowing what we do of Celtic women's rights and Boudicca's personality, she too would have spoken. Perhaps Prasutagus and his queen reminded the hotheads of the risk they ran, that up to this point life alongside Rome had been tolerable. Perhaps the hotheads had voluble, persuasive chiefs of their own and, for a time at least, their words prevailed. 'The surrounding tribes', Tacitus tells us, 'followed their lead' and open revolt broke out. Who these tribes were we do not know, but logically they would have been elements of the Trinovantes to the south, where the veterans' colony at Camulodunum was already making its brutal, licentious presence felt. They may have included the Catuvellauni, deprived of both their kings – Togodumnos dead and Caratacus who-knew-where. There may have been levies from the Coritani.

This last tribe occupied the area of the east Midlands in densely forested land from the Trent to the Nene. Most of their larger settlements were built without hill forts, the capital probably at what the Romans later called Ratae Coritanorum, today's Leicester. The tribe's coins are confusing, the first inscribed silver versions appearing about forty years before Claudius arrived. They carry names or part names like AVA AST and ESVP ASV, but whether these are kings or mints and in which order they were made is unknown.

We do not understand how these groups joined with the Iceni – perhaps it was with Druidic organization – but the short-lived confederacy should have rung alarm bells in the ears of Publius Ostorius Scapula. He sent the auxiliaries from IX Hispana north to deal with it. Tacitus, as ever, is unhelpful in placing this first shock of arms between Rome and the Iceni. It was the latter's choice, he says:

. . . a site for a battle enclosed by a rough earthwork and with an entrance narrow enough to prevent the cavalry getting in. The Roman general set himself to break through these defences even though he was commanding allied troops without legionary strength.[3]

We cannot say decisively whether this was a factual statement – if so, where was IX itself? – or whether Tacitus merely wanted to play down the calibre of troops needed to put down such a footling rising. In the event, the Iceni proved a lot tougher than the Romans had bargained for. The battle may have been fought at Stonea, a fortified island in the treacherous fen country near March in today's Cambridgeshire. Here, the River Nene ran through open watercourses which may have been a local tribal centre of the western Iceni.

The general, presumably Scapula himself, drew up his infantry units and dismounted his cavalry to fight on foot, which usually rankled with cavalrymen. The Romans hit the ramparts and palisades and penned in the Iceni. Whoever their leader was, the Icenic commander was finding out the hard way that British hill forts from the days of Caesar were death traps when facing Roman attacks.

Aware that they were rebels and with their escape routes blocked, the Iceni fought with prodigious bravery. Their bodies perhaps still lie awaiting discovery in the peat of the east Bedfordshire levels.

Among the honours won that day, Marcus Ostorius Scapula, the general's son and probably a tribune in 48, was given a wreath for saving 'the life of a citizen'. A renowned swordsman and athlete, the younger Scapula would fall on his sword in 66, one of the many victims of the unstable Nero.

If Scapula senior was pleased with his success at Stonea, he had no right to be. A friendly people, the Iceni had been alienated by his high-handed actions. We do not know his brief. Claudius' almost casual injunction to Aulus Plautius to conquer 'the rest' presumably gave him the authority to take whatever action he deemed necessary. In that sense, the whole policy following Prasutagus' death in 60 is part of a *continuum* – conquest by any means. Perhaps the general believed the losses at Stonea were worth it. Historian Peter Salway credits Scapula with an unusual victory in that he had defeated a tribe without open battle on the large scale and without a full legion. Against that, he had made enemies where there were none and these enemies were now in his rear.

Content that all was well in the eastern and central areas, Scapula marched against the Deceangli in what today is north Wales. Tacitus wrongly calls these people the Decangi, and they were clearly more barbaric than any tribe the Romans had encountered so far. The hillmen had a different appearance from the Iceni, the Trinovantes or the Atrebates. They were dark, thickset and swarthy, of a height with the Romans, so that some geographers believed they originated from Spain, and had drifted north in the prehistoric migration of peoples over which much argument still turns. Their territory lay between the rivers Dee and Clwyd and the incentive for attacking them was that they had been metal miners since the Bronze Age, an underlying motive in Roman expansion. Silver, lead and copper were all mined inland of the north Welsh coast, yet no coins have been found. The Deceangli fought no pitched battles with Scapula and he, like Tacitus in his account, probably made short work of them:

> Their territory was ravaged and booty was seized far and wide. The enemy did not dare to engage in open warfare and, if they attempted to plant ambushes harassing the army on the march, each subterfuge was punished. The Romans were now not far from the coast facing Ireland . . .[4]

There are few archaeological remains to help us plot the path of Scapula's advance. He was still using auxiliaries and they must have found the mountain fortresses of Snowdonia infinitely more difficult than lowland England. If the holy island of Mona was Scapula's target, as it would be his successor Paulinus' twelve years later, he was denied it. To his north-east, the Brigantes were on the warpath.

This was the largest tribe in Britain according to Tacitus, whose father-in-law, Agricola, knew them well. They spanned the Pennines, occupying what today is both Lancashire and Yorkshire, and gave their name, via a rather circuitous route, to the concept of the brigand, a wild and ruthless outlaw.

Clearly, they had septs such as the Votadini, who lived between the rivers Tyne and Forth, and the Parisii, of the East Riding of Yorkshire. Until twenty years ago, relatively little archaeology had been carried out in Brigantine territory, but the settlements that have been excavated conform to a type first known six centuries earlier – small, circular or rectangular enclosures with a wooden stockade defence. Further north, on the bleak Northumbrian landscape, similarly shaped areas were built of stone and cut into terraced hillsides, probably as a defence against the biting winters.

These no doubt were the primitive people who grew no crops according to Caesar and, in comparison with the south the hill farms remained unprofitable until well into the twentieth century. They were herdsmen, relying for their survival on a semi-nomadic existence. The Parisii, however, were relatively recent arrivals from Gaul, as their name implies, and they brought the idea of the distinctive chariot burials mentioned elsewhere. These people were clearly not a sept in the true sense, and some experts, H.H. Scullard, for instance, maintain that the Votadini, too, were a separate tribe, along with the Novantae, Damnonii and Selgovae of lowland Scotland, the area that would one day be bisected by Hadrian's Wall. The Brigantian capital was probably at Stanwick in North Yorkshire. The site covered seventeen acres, but would be significantly expanded under the Romans. It is difficult to be certain, but perhaps already by 48/49 Stanwick and its people had embraced what Guy de la Bedoyere calls the 'Coca-Cola culture of the Roman Empire'.[5] Amphorae have been found, and fine dishes of pottery from Italy and Gaul. It is likely that the owner of this excessive display of consumerism was the Brigantian queen, Cartimandua.

As we have seen, the name Cartimandua means 'sleek pony', which reinforces our view that forenames were given among the Celts for totemic or shamanistic reasons. The queen's character is fascinating. Of the tribal leaders who opposed the Romans in the years immediately after 43, two of them are women and both of these at first were client queens of the invaders. It is possible that Cartimandua and Boudicca were related, if, as we have conjectured, the Iceni queen came from another tribe. Antonia Fraser posits the notion that they were cousins, two powerful rivals foreshadowing Elizabeth and Mary of Scots in the sixteenth century. But there is no evidence to support this, and we are sadly in the unknowable world of British tribal politics.

Had Cartimandua been among the eleven kings who submitted to Claudius, surely some ancient writer would have mentioned the fact. There is little doubt that she was won over soon after, however, so that, as with the Iceni in the previous year, the revolt of the Brigantes was not of their queen's doing. It is fascinating to speculate that Caratacus may have been behind this rising, as he may have been behind that of the Iceni and whatever resistance the Deceangli may have put up, but this credits him with a mercuriality which probably stretches the truth too far. Scapula halted his advance on the west coast of Wales, deliberating, whether to turn back to deal with the Pennine problem, but the flame of rebellion seemed to go out. Tacitus is infuriatingly vague on the mechanics of this development, writing that the Brigantes 'returned to calm once those who had resorted to arms had been killed and the others had been pardoned'. Does this mean Scapula's troops executed a few ringleaders 'to encourage the others', or did Cartimandua exercise what may have been her regal right to hang rebels? For the time being at least, the Brigantes stayed peaceful. Not so the Silures. And this time, Scapula needed a legion.

This tribe has more written about it than any other in Tacitus' *Annales* because they offered the most resistance. These were the hillmen of Gwent, adept at using their mountains and valleys to excellent effect. And their new leader was Caratacus. From the Towey to the Wye, the fighting spirit of these people would blend in the centuries ahead into the legends of Arthur. The same spirit forced Offa of Mercia to build his defensive fortifications and gave rise to the longbows which were the secret weapon of medieval English kings against the French.

We know that Caratacus was in south Wales by 49 and that he was a hero to the Silures. We do not know enough about the language of the Celts to know whether, as a Catuvellaunian a long way from home, he could make himself understood. It may be that the Druids, the spiritual and political advisers of all the Celtic tribes, acted as interpreters and go-betweens. The man had a fearsome reputation as a warrior and no doubt impressed the Silures as he was to impress the citizens of Rome itself in 51, towering over most of them as he probably did.

The only writer whose works have survived to shed light on the Celtic warlord is Tacitus, who, as always, glosses over a great deal:

> The Romans now moved against the Silures, whose natural spirit was reinforced by their faith in the prowess of Caratacus, whose many battles against the Romans – some of uncertain outcome and some clear victories – had raised him to a position of pre-eminence amongst the other British chieftains.

This is actually quite extraordinary. A writer who usually extols Roman arms and valour almost as nauseatingly as Caesar, Tacitus is forced to concede that the Catuvellaunian's battles were either victories or draws. He mentions no defeats. Scapula and the subdued tribes probably received a worse drubbing at his hands than any Roman was willing to admit.

With his forces still in north Wales and no doubt anxious to be reassured by Cartimandua that all was well with the Brigantes, the obvious route south for Scapula would have taken him through the large kingdom of the Ordovices in mid-Wales. As yet this tribe had made no move against Rome, although the presence of Caratacus in the south and the Deceangli defeat in the north ought to have told Scapula that their friendship was unlikely to last long. Not wishing to cross that particular bridge yet, he ordered a legion, which was probably XX from Glevum, to advance across the Severn and up the Wye in search of the hit-and-run enemy.

Little is known of the Ordovices. It is possible that their tribal territory extended as far north as Mona, but archaeology has yet to reveal any sizeable capital. Unlike most other areas which would be conquered by Rome in due course, no *civitas* (Romanized capital) was set up, implying perhaps that the hillmen on the Brecons and Snowdonia were too nomadic to have established any real centre. Somewhere in their territory, Caratacus rallied to him as many disaffected Britons as he could – and this fact alone raises tantalizing questions about the nature of the tribes.

All modern commentators on the period stress that we cannot condemn people like Prasutagus, Cogidubnus and Cartimandua as traitors and quislings, because there was no concept of 'Britain' for them to betray. Steeped as we are in a thousand years of nationalism, it is difficult for us to see such leaders in any other light; but we have to remember that intertribal fighting was the norm in pre-Roman Britain, and the extension of power achieved by Caratacus' father Cunobelin, whether realized by battle or politics, may still have rankled with the lesser tribes. Nor can we see things from the perspective of a Cartimandua or a Prasutagus. The history of the last five centuries has only served to underscore the insularity of the British. We have a tradition now of resisting invasions, be they French, Spanish, German or asylum seekers. The empathy we can manage only takes us so far, and most readers will sooner identify with Caratacus as a proto-Henry V or Nelson or Churchill. We do not even know *how* Caratacus rallied men who were not of the Welsh tribes to him, although we are starting to see the Druids as more influential in all this than did the scholars of previous generations.

Tacitus gives us no information about the early phases of Scapula's campaign against Caratacus. His primary concern is the events in Rome, to which Britannia was almost a footnote. Graham Webster estimates realistically that three summers of fighting preceded the Armageddon that brought Caratacus down, and it is likely that the Celtic successes in these piecemeal clashes persuaded Scapula to unleash not one, but two legions. We have seen that Tacitus' descriptions of the country, given to him by the observant and efficient Agricola, are astonishingly reliable. Even so, pinpointing the *exact* site of the battle is difficult. Caratacus, wrote the historian,

selected a site whose numerous factors – notably approaches and escape routes – helped him and impeded us. On one side there were steep hills. Whenever the gradient was gentler, stones were piled into a kind of rampart. And at his front there was a river without any crossings. The defences were strongly manned.[6]

Again, the river, with its mystical power for the Celts and its practical problem for the Romans. Again, the clever use of the land – and the footslogging legionaries would have to march uphill.

From the description it seems this was no hill fort. Caratacus had watched Roman battle tactics since the Medway seven or eight years before. He knew he could not defeat the legions in open battle; neither could he withstand a siege in a Celtic fort. No doubt his wild and less-experienced troops were anxious to do battle with the Romans once and for all, and Caratacus knew he could inflict enormous damage to halt Scapula's advance.

Malcolm Todd offers various sites for the battleground – perhaps in Montgomery (today's Powys) at the congress of three valleys; perhaps at Abertanat or Llansanffraid nearby. He was following a long list of historians and earlier antiquarians who have tried to pinpoint the place. The Tanat, however, is a small river and would have presented Scapula with few problems. Graham Webster opts for the hills above Newtown, in particular the valley around Caersws, as the most likely setting.

Scapula had with him his XIV Gemina and XX, perhaps with cohorts from II and IX as well. Together with their mixed infantry and cavalry auxiliaries, this gave him a formidable force of between 20,000 and 30,000. Webster is perhaps a little too dismissive when he writes 'Had the Britons been four or five times that number, it would not have caused Scapula any serious qualms.'[7] We cannot help wondering how heavily the ghost of Publius Quinctilius Varus lay on the shoulders of any Roman general. Scapula would have been a boy when Varus' three legions were annihilated in the Teutoburger Forest. And there was no one among the victorious Germans who could hold a candle to Caratacus.[8]

In fact we know from Tacitus that Caratacus was outnumbered at Caersws: 'His deficiency in strength was compensated by superior cunning and topographical knowledge.' As with Boudicca's oration to her army, Caratacus and the other chiefs went among their men, whipping them up to the fighting frenzy the Romans knew was awesome:

> Caratacus, as he hastened to one point and another, stressed that this was the day, this the battle, which would either win back their freedom or enslave them for ever.[9]

No doubt a man as charismatic as Caratacus would have done just that, but Tacitus' next sentence reveals his misunderstanding of earlier Romano-Celtic history:

> He invoked their ancestors, who, by routing Julius Caesar had valorously preserved their present descendants from Roman officials and taxes – and their wives and children from defilement.[10]

Caesar of course had never got further west than Middlesex, and it was stretching a point to absurdity to claim he had been routed. The tribes who had collapsed before him – the Cantiaci and Caratacus' own Catuvellauni *had* paid tribute on an annual basis. No doubt these little white lies were overlooked in the exhilaration of the moment. Tacitus says, 'These exhortations were applauded, then every man swore by his tribal oath that no enemy weapons would make them yield – and no wounds either.'[11]

Tacitus paints a picture common in Roman history – the brave stalwarts in the cohorts urging on their own commanders to battle. The point was – and Scapula knew it even if his grunting, sweating legionaries did not – that the hill ahead, even once they had crossed the river, was a formidable obstacle. Even the progress of the *testudos* would be slow. They would have to clear away the newly built ramparts and walls as they marched, all the time being hit by the spears and stones of the Ordovices.

Scapula led from the front, a risky decision, and the shields locked over his head. Tacitus admits that the Romans came off worst in the next few minutes in terms of casualties, but the constant training paid off and they prised out the loosely knit walls with their picks or javelin points and scrambled over them. By contrast:

> The British, unprotected by breastplates or helmets, were thrown into disorder. If they stood up to the auxiliaries they were cut down by the swords and javelins of the regulars [legions] and if they faced the latter they succumbed to the auxiliaries' long swords and spears.[12]

Tacitus' 'great victory' does not ring true. Caratacus knew exactly what would happen once the legions reached the crest. From the description of the countryside, it is reasonable to assume that cavalry would have been next to useless here, so the whole encounter was probably a bloody infantry melee, giving time for Caratacus to pull most of his army back to melt into the forests south of today's Welshpool to fight another day. He had inflicted serious damage on Scapula's troops, and the hollowness of the Roman victory was possibly one factor that contributed to the governor's death some months later.

We have to recognize in Caratacus a strategist of ability. Not content to hit the Romans in foraging parties as they tried to establish bases in Wales, he almost certainly had an overarching plan which involved collaboration with the Brigantes and the wilder tribes of the north. For those who lament the Roman conquest of Britain and its tendency to eclipse the Celts, such a confederation would have worked. Years later, the Romans were forced to withdraw from Scotland because of the ferocity of the Picts. With those tribes massed against them as well as the Brigantes and the Iceni, it is doubtful whether any Roman force could have stood. But, it would be many centuries before a leader could weld together a nation in that way. There are shadowy glimpses of such a figure in Arthur, and altogether more definition in Alfred; but Caratacus was not that man, if only because he put too much trust in the slippery Cartimandua.

A section of the Brigantes had already proved awkward and rebelled against their queen, and it is not inconceivable that some of these men were with Caratacus at Caersws. Whether through them or the Druids, the warlord put out diplomatic feelers to the queen, hoping perhaps to win her over with the support of her husband, Venutius. Knowingly or otherwise, Caratacus was stepping into a hornets' nest here. The relationship between the two was tempestuous and our understanding of it is not helped by the fact that we do not know the exact hierarchical structure of Brigantian politics. Was Venutius merely Cartimandua's consort or did they rule jointly? The same question has already been posed about Prasutagus and Boudicca, and we cannot know the answer. From subsequent events, we know that the royal couple, if that is what they were, detested each other, but it may have been Cartimandua's treatment of Caratacus that led, in modern terms, to the irretrievable breakdown of the marriage.

Tacitus gives two slightly different accounts of Caratacus' fall. In the *Annales*, the warlord is grabbed, chained and handed over to the Romans, who were Cartimandua's masters. In the *Historiae* (II 45) he is captured by trickery. In both cases the great white hope, the last of the Celts, was gone.

In Venutius, however, Caratacus had a worthy successor. Tacitus had written about this Brigantian in a volume that has not survived, writing in the *Annales* (XII 33) that he remained loyal to Rome while he was married to Cartimandua. He gives no accurate timescale, but, assuming that Caratacus was taken prisoner in 51, it was that year or the next that the pair divorced. Again, we have only the Roman angle on this situation and Tacitus does not elaborate. In the Roman Empire, divorce was easy and could be instigated by either party. Although there are exceptions, most of the legal framework was devised by men, especially in the case of adultery, and children always lived with their fathers. It was only in the reign of Augustus that the law was changed, forbidding execution of an adulteress by her husband or even her own family. So we have no idea of its application in Brigantian territory. Inevitably, Tacitus sees the marriage breakdown in typically Roman, sexist terms:

But [Cartimandua's] enemies, infuriated and goaded by fears of humiliating feminine rule, invaded her kingdom with a powerful force of picked warriors.[13]

This attack was in fact in response to Cartimandua's seizure of Venutius' brother and other family members, and cannot have come as a surprise. What is very telling, however, is that the Romans had to go in to bail her out: 'We had foreseen this,' says Tacitus, perhaps knowing more about Cartimandua's weakness than we do, 'and sent auxiliary battalions to support her.'

In the meantime, the world had moved on and Caratacus appeared in Rome. His reputation, Tacitus tells us, 'had spread beyond the islands and through the neighbouring provinces to Italy itself'.[14]

Claudius was happy to mount any spectacle that would add to the lustre of his name, so accordingly what amounted to a triumphal entry for the Celtic warlord into the city very much suited his plans. Only by allowing Caratacus to show his greatness could Claudius prove his own. In the north-east of Rome lay the impressive Castra Praetoria, the camp of the Praetorian Guard and its imposing parade ground. The remains of its walls today are some 50 feet high, although the higher part was added by the Emperor Maxentius in the fourth century. The modern garrison of Rome is still housed there, and the camp in Claudius' time was about two-thirds the size of a legionary fortress, perhaps housing up to 12,000 men in two-storey barracks.

The route to the parade ground and its square was lined with the Guard itself, an honour not accorded since the death of Augustus. They probably wore the armour carved on bas-reliefs from the Arch of Claudius erected in the same year (and now in the Louvre), with the ornate 'Attic' helmets, so beloved of Hollywood, and their round-cornered, rectangular shields. Dr Boris Rankov[15] doubts whether this is more than artistic convention and believes that troops taking part in celebrations like this merely wore belted tunics, the emperor wishing to play down the presence of troops in Rome. This is possible, but everyone knew the Praetorians were there, were an elite force and had killed the previous emperor and put the present one on the throne. 'Dressing down' after that seems peculiarly pointless; Tacitus says they were 'in arms'.[16]

Claudius sat on his throne, no doubt under a canopy, wearing, according to Petrus Patricius, a Greek-style chlamys.

More importantly for those who feared for Roman politics, his wife Agrippina sat near him, nodding self-importantly as the Praetorian standards were lowered in front of her.

At the end of the long column of captives and booty from Britain came Caratacus and his family. One outcome of Caersws was that the king's wife, daughter and brother had fallen into enemy hands, perhaps because of the speed with which the legions had advanced up the hill. Many of these captives, says Tacitus, 'degraded themselves by entreaties'. But there were no downcast looks or appeals from Caratacus. Instead he made a speech.

Like the oration made by Boudicca before Camulodunum and at Manduessedum, we cannot accept Tacitus' or Cassius Dio's words verbatim. Both men wrote histories for public declamation, and the making of speeches before epic events was a histrionic device Shakespeare would still be using fifteen centuries later. Caratacus spoke from the dais, almost certainly with the aid of an interpreter:

> Had my lineage and rank been accompanied by only moderate success, I should have come to this city as friend rather than prisoner, and you would not have disdained to ally yourself peacefully with one so nobly born, the ruler of so many nations. As it is, humiliation is my lot, glory yours. I had horses, warriors and gold. Are you surprised I am sorry to lose them? If you want to rule the world, does it follow that everyone else welcomes enslavement? If I had surrendered without a blow before being brought before you, neither my downfall nor your triumph would have become famous. If you execute me, they will be forgotten. Spare me and I shall be an everlasting token of your mercy.[17]

A clever speech, and from the heart. We have no idea how much, if anything, Caratacus knew about Claudius' character, but the concept of an everlasting memorial appealed to the emperor's vanity and to the historian in him. A century earlier, another Caratacus had stood before an emperor-in-waiting: the Gaul Vercingetorix before Caesar in 46 BC. The 'divine' Julius exhibited the warlord as a freak and had him ritually strangled. Perhaps, also, there was a genuine streak of compassion in Claudius which was wholly missing from the clinical conqueror of Gaul. Caratacus, by his bearing, his battles and his fine words, had indeed proved his greatness. Now Claudius would be even greater. Perhaps he heard the whispered words of the slave riding in his triumphal chariot nine years earlier: 'Remember, you are mortal. Look behind! Look behind!'

Caratacus and his family were pardoned, and, according to Tacitus, lived out their lives in Rome, the king himself probably dying of natural causes in 54. Perhaps Caratacus' most poignant summation of the Roman conquest was said to have been made when he first saw the glittering city on its seven hills: 'When you have all this, why do you envy us our poor hovels?'

Among those poor hovels, all was not well for Ostorius Scapula. While he was voted an honorary triumph in Rome and the Senate were once more wild with eulogizing Claudius' greatness, the reality of the guerrilla war was that Caratacus' legacy had begun to kick in. Perhaps the governor's command relaxed; perhaps the Ordovices and Silures, no doubt spurred on by the Druids, were determined to avenge Caratacus' capture. It may be that Claudius considered the public defeat of the British king who had harried his troops for nine years as the end of Celtic resistance in Britannia. After all, the only fighting leader whose name has come down to us was wandering, open-mouthed, amid Rome's ostentatious wealth. If Venutius was a possible successor, he was content at the moment to go to war only with the Brigantes, a military extension of what was merely a 'domestic'. All the tribes south and east of the Trent–Severn frontier were quiescent and Wales was boxed in. And as Agrippina flexed her maternal muscles to ensure the succession of her son, Nero, her husband became more isolated and withdrawn. With his hands full and ever more often looking behind him, Claudius either ignored Britain or perhaps called a halt to Roman expansion.

In the event Scapula was compelled to build as many forward positions along the Welsh marches as the warring tribes would let him. This was the kind of warfare Caratacus' levies liked best, picking off small units, especially when the Romans' prime concern was engineering works.

Most of the trouble came from the Silures in the south. Tacitus wrote:

> Battle followed battle. They were mostly guerrilla fights, in woods and bogs. Some were accidental – the results of chance encounters. Others were planned with calculated bravery. The motives were hatred or plunder. Sometimes these engagements were ordered by generals; sometimes they knew nothing of them.[18]

Hit-and-run tactics like these ground down the nerve of the overstretched Romans, and, in one particular incident noted by Tacitus, a unit, probably of XX Legion from Glevum, was hit and almost wiped out before rescue arrived from a neighbouring marching camp. As it was, the *praefectus Castrorum*, third in command of the legion, and no less than eight centurions were killed, along of course with many more legionaries. Graham Webster estimates that this probably represented a quarter of the legion. The Silures vanished into their forests and mountains as fast as they had attacked. Two whole auxiliary units, probably foraging cavalry, were wiped out hard on the heels of this débâcle, and again the long-suffering legions had to be sent in.

We can sense here the Roman commander losing his nerve. Scapula may not have been a well man by the time of Caratacus' defeat – campaigning takes it toll. And we can sense the frustration the Romans felt too. Scapula was known to have said on several occasions that the Silures must be exterminated, and Tacitus gives a parallel example of the Sugambri, a German tribe from the Rhine whom Augustus effectively destroyed in 8 BC. The Germans were all the more determined to die – and to take the maximum number of Romans with them – because they knew themselves to be marked men.

In the midst of these events, with an elusive enemy scoring victories against him and their strength growing daily, Scapula died. Tacitus gives as the cause that he was 'exhausted by his anxious responsibilities'. The Celts of course were delighted, and no doubt both sides took his death as a sign from their gods. This had been a new kind of warfare for Scapula, and perhaps for Rome itself. The Silures, perhaps because they did not share the same hierarchical structure as other tribes, operated randomly and without warning. The marching legions, the *testudo* and the harrying lines of horsemen could not operate effectively against that.

By the time the new governor arrived, a large unit under Manlius Valens had been defeated. Some authorities claim that this was a whole legion, probably II Augusta. Tacitus noted, anxious to play it down, that

> Reports were magnified, the enemy magnified them to frighten the new general; and the new general magnified them to increase his glory if he won and improve his excuse if resistance proved unbreakable.[19]

If both sides claimed the blow was a serious one, one wonders what evidence Tacitus was using to claim that the situation was exaggerated.

The new general was Aulus Didius Gallus, dispatched quickly by Claudius but arriving too late to save Valens, whose subsequent career was frozen – he died, still a legionary commander, at the astonishing age of 89! Tacitus clearly disliked this man, maintaining that Didius was 'incapacitated by age' and was 'content to act through subordinates and on the defensive'. He was probably chosen by Claudius because he had been with the emperor in Britain back in 43. He had already been suffect consul in 39 and governor of Moesia in 46 when he had invaded the Crimea, which was as far northeast as any Roman commander had marched. He had earned the *ornamenta triumphalia* and had been a proconsul in Asia before the British command came through. The rhetorician Quintillian claimed that Didius had specifically asked for the job, but details are obscure and this may merely be an assumption. Didius was a friend of Hosidius Geta, who had distinguished himself on the Medway ten years earlier, and his particular military specialism seems to have been cavalry. He had commanded such regiments of *alae* in North Africa under

Tiberius and was possibly well over sixty by now, which would explain Tacitus' comments and would make him genuinely too old for an effective field command. While Didius achieved almost nothing in Britain, it is possible that the general may have lost popularity by adopting a noxious son, Fabricius Veiento, who would be exiled by Nero in the year after Boudicca's rebellion for misuse of public office.

The situation that Didius inherited in the summer of 53 was, to say the least, shaky. He may or may not have known that a section of the Iceni still smarted over the loss of their weapons, but in the north the Brigantes were hopelessly split between the factions of Cartimandua and Venutius, the latter at that stage, known to hate Rome and all it stood for, having the best of it. Much more worryingly, the Silures, Ordovices and countless rebels who may have drifted to them were raiding deep into 'friendly' territory, attacking isolated Roman units whenever the mood took them.

Tacitus skates over Didius' governorship. At a time when it was necessary for the commander to take the situation by the scruff of its neck, he seems to have done nothing. Tacitus refers to a battle fought by a 'regular brigade' [a legion] under Cassius Nesica, but this may have been in support of Cartimandua and not against the Silures. He also says rather limply that this had a 'satisfactory ending', which is hardly the same as a decisive victory. Again, we are left facing the historian's bias head on. Were Didius' successes actually hollow or was Tacitus merely concerned to do him down?

There can be no doubt, however, that events in Rome itself called a halt to further advances in the autumn of 54 with the death, probably by poisoning, of the Emperor Claudius. His successor was his stepson, Nero, son of Agrippina and the 'entirely detestable' Gnaeus Domitius Ahenobarbus. Since his mother was the daughter of Germanicus and the niece of her now deceased husband, Claudius, Nero's credentials were fairly impeccable. Personally tutored by the brilliant philosopher-writer Seneca (restored to imperial favour by Agrippina's wheedling), he was betrothed to Claudius' daughter Octavia and officially adopted by the emperor when he was thirteen, and renamed Tiberius Claudius Drusus Germanicus Nero Caesar.

He was sixteen when Agrippina's mushrooms did their work, and three years after Caratacus appeared there the boy was proclaimed emperor by the Praetorians on the parade ground of their camp. The Prefect of the Guard was Sextus Afrianus Burrus, a soldier from southern Gaul who had obtained his post through Agrippina's machinations, and he and Seneca acted as advisers to the boy-emperor for the first five years of his reign. With hindsight, Romans like Trajan remembered those years – the *quinqueanium Neronius* – as a golden period that promised much. Nero made positive speeches, written by Seneca, to the Senate, had Claudius officially deified, supported the arts, appeared to have a progressive attitude to the death penalty and, best of all, put more faith in Burrus and Seneca than in his dangerous mother.

During the hiatus that the beginning of the new reign inevitably represented, Didius probably carried out a holding operation in Britain. Scapula's troops, harassed though they had been, had built a number of forts along the Wye Valley in an effort to check the Silures. It was probably Didius who built the 50-acre legionary depot at Burrium, today's Usk, where workshops and granaries have been excavated in the area of the modern prison. This building almost certainly superseded the base at Kingsholm near Gloucester, which would have been too far from the new frontier to be effective. In the north, Didius built a fortress for XIV Gemina at Virconium Cornoviorum (Wroxeter), five miles south of Shrewsbury. Eventually, this base would become a civilian centre, the *civitas* of the Cornovii and, at 170 acres, the fourth largest town in the country. It was probably under Didius' governorship that II Augusta set up its large base at Isca Dumnoniorum (Exeter) as the most westerly legionary base, backed by a series of smaller forts on the open bleakness of Dartmoor to the north.

Slowly, surely, the Roman grip was tightening.

What of the invisible Boudicca in these years? When Caratacus fought at Caersws we estimate she would have been twenty-four. When members of her tribe rebelled over Scapula's seizure of their weapons, she was nineteen or twenty. Working back from the outrage committed on her daughters in 60, it is likely that she gave birth to both of them during those years of Scapula's governorship. Whether she had other children is not recorded, and without a written record we know little of the mysteries surrounding pregnancy and childbirth among the Celts. There are numerous superstitions found all over Europe which *may* have their origins in Celtic religious belief. Doors in houses where births took place were left open to allow good spirits to enter. The mother in labour would have been assisted by midwives who would have untied knots in her garments to make delivery easier. Perhaps an axe, made of the magical iron, was laid blade up under the queen's bed; perhaps salt was sprinkled into her palm, or silver coins stuffed into the bedstraw. Perhaps she delivered on the bare floor so that her children would gain extra strength from the earth. Perhaps she gave birth propped on one knee by midwives – who were still known in medieval Ireland as 'knee-women'. Was the afterbirth studied to determine how many other children Boudicca would have? Was it burned to divine the same information? Or was burning the placenta considered unlucky by the Celts? The time of the girls' births would certainly have had significance for the Iceni, as for any other tribe, given the rhythm of the seasons and the importance of their great festivals. Would Druids have been in attendance, muttering magical incantations as the babies took their first breaths?

And how, if at all, would the childhoods of these little girls, whose names we do not know, have differed from that of their mother? Boudicca bursts onto the pages of history as a woman wronged, and her flame is soon extinguished. The rest of her life, along with much else in Celtic history, is silence.

6

'Tall and Terrible'

> But the Roman came with a heavy hand,
> And bridged and roaded and ruled the land.
> 'The River's Tale', Rudyard Kipling

Prasutagus the king died in 59 or 60. The vague impression we have of him, as Antonia Fraser notes, is of a man much older than his wife, perhaps a rather weak figure falling into dotage. This is possible, but apart from his name and his apparent wealth, we actually know nothing about him. We cannot see his capitulation to Claudius as an act of weakness; it might just as easily have been the pragmatism of sensible statecraft. Militarily, Rome had the edge in 43, and if Prasutagus and his family had continued in a wealthy and comfortable lifestyle for the next sixteen years, that merely proved Prasutagus' point.

We have no knowledge of how the king died or where or how his funeral was ordered. In all probability, his body was cremated, in common with as many as 90 per cent of the inhabitants of Iron Age Britain, but his grave is likely to be sumptuous and it awaits discovery somewhere in the flat fields of Norfolk.

What we do know is the arrangements that Prasutagus left in his will, which tells us a great deal about the development of Romanization in the area since the Iceni rebelled over the weapons issue in 48. The 50s was the first decade when Celts volunteered for service in the Roman army; from the Roman point of view, this may have been a necessity because of the army's relatively large size and the need for more recruits. We have no casualty figures from Tacitus from the frontier fighting against the Silures, but this must have been a consideration for any commander. Guy de la Bedoyere estimates that by the time Trajan invaded today's Romania, forty years after Boudicca's death, fourteen units (up to 10,000 men) who had been recruited in Britain were serving with the eagles. A rare named example is Lucco the Dobunnian, a soldier of Cohors I Britannica in 105. A section of the Dobunni had of course defected to Aulus Plautius in 43, but we have no way of knowing whether any of the Iceni served with the legions.

Two years before Prasutagus' death, Quintus Veranius Nepos was made governor. Presumably, Didius was pensioned off, or perhaps he died; his fate is unknown. We know from Veranius' tombstone that he died after only a year in office. Tacitus was unimpressed:

Quintus Veranius had only conducted minor raids against the Silures when death terminated his operations. His life had been famous for its austerity. But his testamentary last words were glaringly self-seeking for they grossly flattered Nero.[1]

He added that Veranius, if he had lived two years longer, would have presented the emperor with the whole province.

Various commentators have expressed doubts that Veranius was being literal here, but Tacitus seems pretty clear and Veranius did have something of a 'go-getter' reputation. He had fought in the 40s in the mountains of Cilicia, and the Greek military theorist Onasander[2] dedicated his book on generalship to him, a work which remained popular until the Renaissance.

However vainglorious Veranius' boast to Nero may have been – and this could merely have been a throwaway line to

The statue of Boudicca by J. Havard Thomas, sculpted between 1913 and 1915, shows the queen appealing to her people for vengeance against Rome. One of a series of serravesa marble statues, it was unveiled by Lloyd George in October 1916 as one of the 'heroes of Wales'! *(© Cardiff City Hall: photograph Rob Watkins)*

The bronze head of Claudius found in the River Alde in Suffolk. It was probably smashed from the Temple in Camulodunum (Colchester) during Boudicca's attack on the town. It may have been placed in the river as a votive offering.
(© The British Museum)

An artist's impression of the Temple of Claudius, the 'blatant stronghold of alien rule' as Tacitus called it. Colchester castle, today's museum, was built over the vaults below the steps. The temple was completely destroyed by Boudicca in 60 AD. *(© M.J. Trow)*

Iceni coin with horse-style design.
(© The British Museum)

Celtic horse bit and terret found at
Verulamium. An excellent example of
the skill of Celtic craftsmen and the
importance of the horse in Celtic
society. (© St Albans Museum)

One of the most beautiful relics of the Iceni is this torc (neck-band) made of gold
and found in Snettisham, Norfolk. Large numbers of these aristocratic and military
symbols have been found in the area, confirming the wealth, status and
craftsmanship of Boudicca's people. (© The British Museum)

The gravestone of Marcus Favonius Facilis, centurion of XX Legion. Erected by grateful slaves freed on his death, it was toppled by the iconoclastic Iceni during Boudicca's attack on Camulodunum.
(© Colchester Museum)

The tombstone of the cavalryman Longinus Sdapeze of the Ala I Thracia, cast aside in Boudicca's attack on Camulodunum.
(© Colchester Museum)

An Iceni hoard from March, Cambridgeshire, shows distinctive patterning on the pot and a collection of 872 silver coins. It may have been buried for safekeeping during Boudicca's rebellion. *(© The British Museum)*

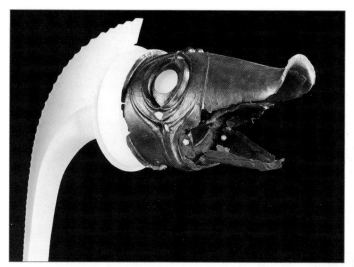

The bronze head of a carynx or Celtic war horn, found at Deskford, Scotland. This example has a wooden tongue which rattles when it vibrates and was designed to terrify the enemy by its noise. Horns of this type would have been used at Manduessedum, Boudicca's last battle.

Verlamion. A modern artist's interpretation of the Romano-Celtic centre of the Catuvellauni at the time of Boudicca's attack. All the buildings are based on archaeological evidence.

Manduessedum, the possible site of Boudicca's last battle. Aulus Plautius' legions would have formed up at the edge of the forest on the left; the Iceni would have taken ground on the Anker's flood plain to the right. *(Photograph Carol Trow)*

Skulls in the Walbrook. Were these heads found in the Walbrook stream tributary of the Thames, victims of Boudicca's attack on Londinium?
(© Courtesy of the Museum of London)

A typical round house of the type built throughout Iron Age Britain. This one, reconstructed at Butser Hill in Hampshire suirvived the storm of 1987 and would be virtually identical to Iceni houses at the time of Boudicca.
(© *Butser Ancient Farm*)

Boudicca as imagined in the Civil War period. An illustration from Thomas Heywood's *Exemplary Lives*, 1640. The torc is now a necklace and the queen looks like a courtesan of a royal court. *(© The British Library)*

Thorneycroft's Boudicca – the most famous depiction of Boudicca and her daughters was erected on the Thames Embankment in 1902. There is no historical precedent for the knives on the wheels. *(Photograph Taliesin Trow)*

impress the increasingly erratic emperor or to keep him quiet – the new governor actually achieved nothing and was replaced in 58 by Gaius Suetonius Paulinus.

Three lines after introducing him to us, Tacitus has the new man launching an attack on the Druids on Mona. But he had already been in the province for two and a half years by then and, had he been wise, would have paid a complimentary visit to all the client kings to remind them whose side they were on. Whether he went to meet Prasutagus and Boudicca is unrecorded. Tacitus tells us he was, Corbulo's rival in military science, which makes everybody compete. He was ambitious to achieve victories as glorious as the reconquest of Armenia.[3]

Gnaeus Domitius Corbulo was governor of lower Germany in 47 and had a reputation as a martinet. In the year that Paulinus landed in Britain, Corbulo took up a similar position in Cappodocia and established a client king, Tigranes, on the Armenian throne. Had Paulinus been able to augur the future, however, he might not have been so keen to compete with Corbulo. Like others who were too successful, Nero became jealous of him and ordered him to commit suicide in October 66.

The very fact that Prasutagus left a will is an indication of how far the Iceni client kingdom was already developing into a *civitas*. It was merely Nero's greed and high-handed Roman handling of the situation locally that put this development, however temporarily, on hold. Although Caesar wrote that the Druids used a written alphabet, largely Greek, to carry out business and mundane matters, and it is likely that will-making might have been a function of the priesthood, there is no hard evidence that this was so. In view of how Prasutagus bequeathed his kingdom, it is likely that the drawing up of the will was done with the connivance of Roman officials.

Until the law was changed in the empire in favour of Greek in the third century, all wills had to be drawn up in Latin. We do not know if this was the case in Prasutagus' arrangements, but it seems likely. Wills were very specific and sometimes drawn up with all the spite endemic among 'nearest and dearest' to this day. Antonius Silvanus of Ala I Thracium, who died in 142 in Alexandria, wrote:

My son, Marcus . . . shall be the sole heir of all my military and household possessions and all other persons are hereby disinherited . . . As for my slave, Cronio, after my death, if he has performed all his duties properly . . . then I desire him to be free . . . Let no malice aforethought attend this last will and testament . . .[4]

Prasutagus had no sons, and so he bequeathed half his kingdom to his two daughters, whose names we do not know, and the other half to Nero. There is no mention of Boudicca, but whether this smacks of spite, as in Shakespeare's famous 'second-best bed' left to Anne Hathaway, or whether for some reason Celtic queens could not inherit, we do not know. It seems likely that Boudicca would have been expected to act as regent until her daughters were of age, although Roman attitudes to women, as we shall see, made this problematic. In theory, the client-kingdom situation of the Iceni could have gone on into the next generation. Assuming as we do that the daughters were twelve or thirteen when their father died, they could reasonably expect to take husbands within a year or so. The Roman age of consent as laid down by Augustus was twelve, although we have no way of knowing how much, if any, Roman law was practised by the Iceni.

It was perhaps the policy of Nero by 60 to absorb a client kingdom into a province upon the death of its native ruler, as a means of natural selection. On the other hand, Iceni territory was a long way from Rome and local officials may have overstepped the mark.

The fact was that Rome's relationship with the Iceni, indeed with *any* client kingdom, was in a state of flux. Rome needed client kings as leaders of buffer states against warlike neighbours on their frontiers. We know that Romans from Caesar onward exploited the ancient hostilities between the tribes and maintained a fluctuating status quo as a result. The army in Britain, even four legions and their auxiliaries, could not hope to have held the province any other way. It would be wrong to assume, however, that Romanization meant an equal sharing of wealth, culture, civilization and comfort. Magnificent villas, Samian ware and amphorae full of wine found their way no doubt to Prasutagus and his family, and to the anonymous ruler of the Trinovantes to the south, as it already had to Claudius Tiberius Cogidubnus. In gratitude for that, the native rulers were expected to watch their frontiers, pay tributes and taxes and generally be grateful. Until *everyone* could feel indebted to Rome for its civilization, however, the situation was volatile and fraught with danger. We have already seen how the compliant Cunobelins was replaced by the rebellious Togodumnos and Caratacus.

But there were particular problems in the late 50s and these can be laid squarely at the door of avaricious Romans from Nero to Catus Decianus. The emperor was twenty-three when Prasutagus died, and he was showing signs of impatience with his wiser advisers, the philosopher Seneca and the Praetorian Burrus. He had had Claudius's natural son, Britannicus, murdered five years earlier and had turned on his own mother, Agrippina, in 59 when she opposed his divorce: she was stabbed to death. There is no need to look much further than this unstable man for the cause of a deterioration in relations between Rome and its client kingdoms. The only remarkable thing is that Prasutagus contemplated leaving anything to him!

Burrus died, possibly poisoned, in 62 and Seneca lived a miserable existence under house arrest at Nero's court before being forced into suicide over an alleged conspiracy three years later. Even before this, however, Seneca was at the centre of a cash crisis in connection with the client kingdoms. Under Claudius, large sums of money had been given to the client kings, but how much or indeed why is unclear. It may be that these were cash incentives to persuade the kings to buy their way into the Roman administration, perhaps up to senatorial level. Alternatively, they could have been to enable payment of taxes in an economy which, despite the existence of coins, probably still relied heavily on barter and land as a means of trade.

A build-up of tension in the late 50s suggests that the Romans were calling in their debts and expecting the client kings to pay up; the Iceni were in the front line. Exactly why this cash crisis should have developed is unclear – perhaps the expense of holding and policing the British frontier was larger than expected – but Paulinus seems to have added to the problem not only by his own greed, but in the appointment of a high-handed *procurator*, Catus Decianus.

The *procurator* was an agent whose specific responsibility was the collection of taxes; tax gatherers from the dawn of civilization have been justifiably reviled. The Bible brands them with thieves and prostitutes as the dregs of society. When officials visited the scattered villages of William the Conqueror's England in 1086, people thought the Day of Judgement had come. This reputation did not develop because of man's natural antipathy to 'death and taxes', but through the brutal and uncaring way that men like Decianus went about their business.

Prasutagus' will has not survived, but the style of it is typically Roman, and it was designed, no doubt, so that at least part of the Iceni lands, and Prasutagus' own family, would be protected. Decianus seems to have moved in quickly to help himself to the proceeds of the imperial section and, indeed, the rest. Under him were unknown numbers of *publicani*, men of the equestrian class who operated on behalf of the army, providing food and equipment and collecting taxes to pay for it. In the case of resistance from the natives, no doubt these men were accompanied by legionaries or auxiliaries or both, and the *caligae* of Rome were felt heavily across Norfolk.

Tacitus paints a grim picture:

> Kingdom and household alike were plundered like prizes of war, the one by Roman officers, the other by Roman slaves . . . The Icenian chiefs were deprived of their hereditary estates as if the Romans had been given the whole country. The king's own relatives were treated like slaves . . . As a beginning [Prasutagus'] widow Boudicca was flogged and their daughters raped.[5]

That this appalling incident happened is beyond dispute, and it acted as a spark to the mutinous Iceni, leading to the most serious attack on Roman power the empire had ever seen from within. Only the Batavian rebellion ten years later would equal it for fierceness, and only the Judaean revolt for heroism.[6] To understand why it happened at all we need to look beyond the uncontrolled antics of Paulinus' 'brutal and licentious soldiery' – this was brutality with a carefully measured purpose. We need to look at Roman attitudes to women.

The first clue is found in the numerous grave markers throughout the empire. In Rome itself one such marker declares, 'Here lies Amymone, wife of Marcus, most good and most beautiful, wool spinner, dutiful, modest, careful, chaste, stay-at-home.' This reads like a Nazi eulogy to wives and mothers in the 1930s and '40s. Even the awarding of mothers' crosses for producing children for the Fatherland has its echoes in the 'three children' privilege of tax exemption granted by Augustus. Also in Rome, the grave of Mus is a haunting reminder of attitudes to girls:

I lived dear to my family, I gave up my life yet a maiden.
Here I lie dead and am ashes, and these ashes are earth.
But if the earth is a goddess, I am a goddess, I am not dead.
I beg you, stranger, do not desecrate my bones.
Mus, lived thirteen years.[7]

Marcus Antonius Encolpus struck a more modern note, perhaps, in carving the grave of his wife, Cerellia Fortunata:

Do not pass by this epitaph, wayfarer,
But stop, listen and learn, then go.
There is no boat in Hades, no ferryman Charon,
No caretaker Aeacus, no Cerberus dog.
All we dead below
Have become bones and ashes, nothing more . . .

The nearest female figure to Boudicca that we have in the Roman world is the 'emancipated but respected' matron, the upper-class woman of the early empire. Her Roman contemporaries do not call Boudicca a queen, merely the widow of Prasutagus, which indicates their attitude to 'pushy females'. To them, the perfect woman was Cornelia, the daughter of the great general Scipio Africanus, who produced twelve children as the wife of Tiberius Gracchus and became an accomplished expert on Greek culture, enjoying a chaste widowhood and turning down an offer of marriage from Ptolemy Physcon, the king of Egypt. Motherhood, loyalty to her husband, beauty and intelligence were the ideals to which all upper-class Roman women adhered.

Men, however, had an altogether more cynical view. Physiologically the weaker sex, women were subject to *infirmitas* (weakness) and *levitas animi* (frivolity), and, as a result, enshrined in Roman law from the fifth century BC was the notion of the *paterfamilias* and *manus*. The former literally meant 'father of the family', the eldest male relative (not always the actual father), who literally had the power of life and death over a daughter or niece. Although this total control had lessened by the reign of Diocletian in the late third century AD, we still find it as an anchor in Shakespeare's plays 1,300 years later, and elements of it in Victoria's reign in the appalling father of the poetess Elizabeth Barrett. *Manus* (meaning literally 'hand') similarly represented the physical power of a husband over his wife, so that the move from *paterfamilias* to *manus* has the air of frying pans and fires. Roman history is awash with examples of men who cudgelled their wives to death for drunkenness or adultery. In 186 BC, when thousands were sentenced to death for taking part in Bacchic rites, the females involved were executed by their own menfolk. We have already seen that in 57 the irreligious wife of Aulus Plautius was put on trial by her husband for her alleged crimes.

Given this stranglehold of men over women in well-to-do Rome, it is not surprising that marriages were almost always arranged for political or economic reasons, and in particular the strengthening of dynasties. We have seen that similar arrangements probably existed among the Celts, too, and the marriage of Prasutagus and Boudicca can be seen in this context. Claudius betrothed his daughter to Lucius Silanius when she was one year old because the boy was Augustus' great-great-grandson. There were, however, examples of love matches in this class, and certain high-spirited girls probably bullied their fathers into agreeing to their choices. Divorce was likewise straightforward and could be instigated by either husband or wife. The quarrel between Cartimandua and Venutius of the Brigantes caused no surprise among Roman officials, only the need to send in troops to protect their interests. Children always lived with their fathers in the event of divorce. The comparative ease of divorce is at odds with the notion, implicit in the blameless life of Cornelia, that a woman remain faithful to her husband only and for ever. When Caecina Paetus was called upon by Claudius to kill himself, his wife Aria rammed a dagger into her own breast first and died with the words, 'It does not hurt, Paetus.'[8]

Direct comparison between Roman examples and Boudicca is difficult. We know from Caesar that Celtic marriages were polygamous in his day, and this had probably not changed by 60. No other wives are mentioned, but it is likely that Boudicca was only the principal consort of Prasutagus. This fact alone would have appalled the Romans, but it was Boudicca's *political* stance that outraged Paulinus' people, because there was no precedent for it in Roman society. Intelligent women were not in short supply in Rome, although clearly they were not popular with men. The satirist Decimus Julius Juvenalis (Juvenal) wrote in his treatise on the immorality of women (Satire 6)

Still more exasperating is the woman who begs, as soon as she sits down to dinner, to discourse on poets and poetry . . . Professors, critics, lawyers, auctioneers – even another woman – can't get a word in . . . Wives shouldn't try to be public speakers; they shouldn't use rhetorical devices; they shouldn't read the classics – there ought to be some things women don't understand. I myself can't understand a woman who can quote the rules of grammar and never make a mistake and cites obtuse, long-forgotten poets – as if men cared about such things. If she has to correct somebody, let her correct her girlfriends and leave her husband alone.[9]

And if intellectualism among women left a bitter taste in men's mouths, politics left a worse aftertaste. Still discussed in

Boudicca's time was the extraordinary episode in 488 BC when Gaius Marcius Coriolanus marched on Rome at the head of a huge Volscian army and was turned back by the intervention of his mother Venturia and several hundred women who would become widows otherwise. In 195 BC Roman women had staged the first known feminist demonstration, complaining about the Oppian law which limited female wealth to half an ounce of gold and prevented them from riding within a mile of Rome in carriages and from wearing purple-trimmed dresses.

In the supposedly more enlightened third century, the Emperor Elagabalus, on the prompting of his grandmother Julia, set up an all-female Senate alongside the real one. Its sole agenda, however, was etiquette – what sort of clothes should be worn on which occasion, who could be carried in a litter and of what should the litter be made, and so on. The institution was promptly shut down when Elagabalus was murdered by the Praetorians.

For most chauvinistic, sexist Romans, however, the careers of two of Claudius' wives were enough to make them for ever wary of female politicians. We have seen them at work already and, even allowing for the prejudice of male Roman historians, Messalina and Agrippina do not emerge with glowing records. The nymphomaniac Messalina, pilloried by Juvenal in Satires 6 and 10, was publicly married to consul-designate Gaius Silius while still the emperor's wife. She finally committed suicide – 'what's fine, what's Roman', to quote Shakespeare – but only with the help of a Praetorian officer and her own mother! Caligula banished his sister Agrippina for her involvement in a conspiracy against him. Marrying Claudius in 48, she persuaded him to grant her unprecedented honours, was given a seat in the Senate and was called Augusta as though she were the emperor's equal. We have already seen that celebrated captives like Caratacus were expected to bow before her. For the first five years of her son Nero's reign, in other words almost until Prasutagus' death, Agrippina was virtually as powerful as her noxious son. Tacitus put the story about, and it may have been true, that she tried to cling to power in 58 by seducing the emperor herself.

The political women we have been judging Boudicca by so far have all been Roman – the queen of the Iceni was not. Can we learn anything by comparing her with another foreign queen who loomed large in Roman history, the *fatale monstrum*, Cleopatra? The seventh Egyptian ruler of that name and the daughter of Ptolemy the Piper, Cleopatra, with her brother and co-ruler Ptolemy XIII, aided Pompey in his civil war against Caesar. After the former's rapid collapse, the queen, still only seventeen, became Caesar's mistress and was brought to live in a villa in Rome. After the dictator's assassination in 44 BC, she returned to Egypt, arranging for their son Caesarion's succession by murdering her brother. From 37 she was in a permanent relationship with Marcus Antonius, Shakespeare's Mark Antony, by whom she had three children. In the muddled aftermath of Caesar's murder, his nephew Octavian, the Emperor Augustus, pursued Antony and defeated his and Cleopatra's fleets at Actium. She committed suicide, according to legend with an asp, after Antony had fallen on his sword, on 10 August 30 BC.

Contemporary coins show that Cleopatra was not the beauty of legend, but the written record proves that she was certainly a highly enterprising and manipulative woman who used her sex to seduce powerful men and more than held her own in politics. Her choice of Antony was a mistake, politically, but he was an accomplished general, and hugely popular, and it was largely the wholesale defections of his legions that led to his defeat.

Even here, however, we have no exact parallel with Boudicca. Cleopatra was a competent ruler and Egyptians remained loyal to her, but she got close to the centre of Roman politics in a way that Boudicca never could and never intended to. Seduction was not part of her game plan, and had the Romans bothered to know her better they would probably have been impressed by her virtue. On the other hand, what would horrify them later was her ability to command troops in battle. Cleopatra was probably present at Actium (though there is no evidence for the legend of her barge hoisting sail and starting a retreat, but it is unlikely that she actually led troops in the conventional sense. Boudicca did, and she terrified them.

We do not know the exact circumstances of the beating that

Boudicca received. It is likely that this was public, wherever her capital was, intended as a deterrent and certainly a humiliation for those who would oppose Rome. Scourging – whipping with rods or thongs – was a mark of profound dishonour, normally reserved for slaves, and it was no doubt in this context that the punishment was administered, probably by Catus Decianus' thugs. There were a number of different whips in the Roman world, the *flagellum*, made of ox leather, which cut deep into the flesh; the *scutica*, made of parchment; the *ferula*, a flat leather strap. Refinements were sometimes added, such as leather thongs knotted with metal pieces, bones or lead balls, to increase the pain.

Today, we are perhaps more appalled by the rape of Boudicca's daughters than the ritual whipping of the queen herself. No doubt this was done in private, Decianus' people perhaps drawing lots for the privilege. The girls cannot have been more than fourteen and were possibly as young as eleven. It may have been Roman law that forbade sex with Boudicca herself. It was a rule of the great Augustus that sex with a widow was illegal; although it is likely that this did not apply to conquered peoples or even citizens of client kingdoms. The law on rape was even more unforgiving than it is today. Prosecutions for the crime, known as *iniuria* (wrong) and *vis* (force), could only be brought by a male relative of the rape victim, and of course the whole of the law was created by men. Under Constantine, the Codex Theodosianus differentiated between girls who were at first willing and those who were unwilling. The former were publicly burned, the latter whipped because they should have screamed for help. Against this inflexibility, Boudicca's girls stood no chance at all. According to John Matthews and Bob Stuart,[10] the daughters of disgraced consuls were habitually raped before being strangled or thrown to their deaths, and executioners deflowered virgins before they killed them in case they gave offence to the gods. Matthews and Stuart also speculate that deflowered virgins would be less attractive to would-be husbands who might be subsequent leaders of revolt, but we do not know Celtic attitudes on this. Roman men certainly preferred their wives to be virgins, but Celtic society seems altogether less rigid.

'So', wrote Tacitus, '[the Iceni] rebelled.'[11] It is now that problems arise with the timing of the revolt. Tacitus and Cassius Dio are unhelpful here, which is a pity, because our understanding of what happened, and why, depends very much on the exact sequence of events. The consensus among historians seems to be that Paulinus moved against the Druids and the discontented on Mona, and that while he was preoccupied there Boudicca and the Iceni rose behind him, creating a serious problem in what was assumed to be a safe area. Boudicca's first serious biographer, Lewis Spence, assumed that Paulinus marched against Mona in March 61, the same month in which the queen was flogged and her daughters raped. Between then and May, while various legions were marching across country into north Wales, the dismemberment of the Iceni territory continued, and at some point between May and June other tribes flocked to Boudicca's horse or boar standard. Paulinus' destruction of Mona took place in June and at the end of that month he had news of the rising. Not until early July did Boudicca attack Camulodunum.

Little of this makes sense. Certainly the time of year is in accordance with a Roman spring offensive, but virtually everything else begs all sorts of questions. Spence was following Tacitus who says that the rising took place in the consulships of Lucius Caesennius Paetus and Publius Petronius Turpilianus and that the whole campaign happened in that year. He seems to have been a year out – the rising began in 60 and was not finally put down until 61. This stretching of the time sequence opens up other possibilities as to what happened.

Mona, as the 'granary' of Caratacus' stand with the Ordovices and Silures and as a sacred place to the Druids, was a legitimate target for Paulinus. We have seen in a previous chapter how the island probably became a sanctuary for anti-Roman Celts, the focus of discontented refugees from Caratacus' campaigns and elsewhere. We have no accurate idea of the odds facing Paulinus, but his first problem was to cross the Menai Strait. Offshore islands seem to have fascinated the Romano-Celtic world. Mona was clearly special to them; Ireland was the *insula sacra*, the holy isle, and later

Christian monasteries were deliberately built on Iona and Lindisfarne as pious sanctuaries from a wicked world. Even the Isle of Wight, Roman Vectis, has legendary associations with the late imperial cult of Mithras.[12]

The strait has a strong tidal flow and swift undercurrents, and Tacitus must have ignored considerable problems encountered by Paulinus with his cursory 'Flat-bottomed boats were built to contend with shifting shallows and these took the infantry across.' Tacitus called the island *novitate aspectus*, a strange sight, and probably learned details from those who were there. Eighteen miles wide by eighteen miles long, the narrowest crossing point is the 249 feet across which Thomas Telford built his bridge in 1821. What dominates the skyline today is the virtually impregnable castle of Edward Longshanks at Beaumaris, reminding the Welsh to behave themselves, but a cluster of burial chambers, at Lligwy, Pressaddfed, Barclodiad-y-Gawres and Bodowyr, testify that Mona was an ancient hallowed place. Tacitus does not tell us precisely where the Romans landed or the exact nature of the opposition, but what he does tell us sounds unlikely. After the infantry crossed the strait in their boats, which they would have had to make or commandeer from the locals on the mainland side, the cavalry followed – 'some utilized fords, but in deeper water the men swam beside their horses'. Allowing for the possibility that Menai was not as deep or treacherous as today, all this preparation seems to have been watched by the Celts with a curious inaction. The island, Tacitus says, was 'thickly populated' and 'had also given sanctuary to many refugees', and we have seen that those men were likely to have been the hardbitten veterans of Caratacus' Silures. The time to have stopped the Romans would have been to hit them as their boats hit the shingle and before they had time to form their battle stations. Floundering in the surf, even a Roman legion could have been destroyed – Boudicca achieved this weeks later on dry land.

That Tacitus does not mention this event probably means that no such attack happened. The shrieking of the black-robed women, the curses of the Druids and the crackling of their firebrands was perhaps a cheaper alternative. If there was no attack by the Celts, the hardened Silures stood their ground, sure in the belief that their Druids' magic would work. If various classical writers were right, that the Druids foretold the future and were arbiters in peace and war, this tactic made sense. And it almost worked. Tacitus commented that:

> This weird spectacle awed the Roman soldiers into a sort of paralysis. They stood still – and presented themselves as a target. But then they urged each other (and were urged by the general) not to fear a horde of fanatical women. Onward pressed their stewards and they bore down their opponents, enveloping them in the flames of their own torches.

The Roman chronicler makes it sound easier than it must have been. In three lines, Mona fell:

> Suetonius [Paulinus] garrisoned the conquered island. The groves devoted to Mona's barbarous superstitions he demolished. For it was their religion to drench their altars in the blood of prisoners and consult their gods by means of human entrails.

There appears to have been no time for the defenders to withdraw to Holyhead mountain, whose 720 feet might have given them an advantage. Caer-y-Twr is an ancient hill fort on its ridge and might have been defensible in Paulinus' time. The destruction of Mona seems to have been swift and total; and, if so, it fell with only a little more difficulty than that with which Vespasian had taken Vectis sixteen years earlier.

The fact that Decianus decided to deal so high-handedly with the Iceni at exactly the time Paulinus was burning the sacred groves may be no more than coincidence. But can we really believe that the governor would take his key troops 300 miles away from a state about to be absorbed by force into the Roman Empire? Allowing for the fact that Paulinus had not actually issued orders for the flogging and raping of the royal women, he had the mutinous experience of 48 to go by and surely would have waited while his rear was secured.

It is possible of course that the two episodes were linked, planned with a precision that would have impressed

Caratacus. With the Druids themselves as go-betweens on the 'gold road' between Mona and Norfolk, what would have been easier than to orchestrate the whole episode to maximize Paulinus' problems? If, as we believe, Prasutagus died in 59, and if Tacitus is right that the rebellion *began* (but did not end) in 60, then we have a longer time lapse than the Tacitus/Spence version allows. It would not only give Boudicca time to get the Trinovantes and other tribes on her side, but would enable the surprise attack on Camulodunum to take place. There is no evidence of any attack until the veterans' colony there was hit, so, if Spence is right, a possible two months had gone by while the Iceni-Trinovantian army was assembling. Were the Romans at Camulodunum oblivious to this? Possibly. But Decianus' officials were busy evicting the Iceni during this period, confiscating property and collecting Claudius' and Seneca's loans. Would they not have noticed the arrival of armed troops?

The only sustainable explanation is that Boudicca was playing a waiting game. Rather than hotheadedly reacting to the outrage against her and her children, the queen and her chiefs used patience. Kept informed of Paulinus' movements, they went about their business, surrendering tribal areas to the *publicani* when they arrived, while messengers, probably Druids again, went south into Suffolk and Essex and west into Brigantian country to spread news of the outrage and enlist support.

Historians cannot be certain when, if at all, Boudicca spoke to rally her growing army. From Dio, however, we have the only physical description of the woman who so terrified Rome:

> In stature she was very tall, in appearance most terrible; in the glance of her eye most fierce, and her voice was harsh. A great mass of the tawniest hair fell to her hips. Around her neck was a large golden torc and she wore a tunic of many colours over which a thick cloak was fastened with a brooch. This was her invariable attire . . .[13]

We do not know the source of Dio's description. It rings true, and there is no reason to doubt it. Perhaps he read reports, since lost, in the Roman archive; certainly, he could not have known, unlike Tacitus, anyone who remembered the rising.

After two millennia we cannot guess at Boudicca's height. No doubt it was this fact that prompted the sculptor of the statue now in Cardiff Museum to portray Boudicca's daughters so oddly. Their breasts are well developed, but the young women do not reach much higher than their mother's waist. Archaeological evidence from Eastern Yorkshire, where the Parisii were probably clients of the Brigantes, has been gleaned from 95 female bodies. Their average height was 5 feet 2 inches as opposed to the men's average of 5 feet 7½ inches. It is possible to assume then that Boudicca was well above this, perhaps six feet.[14]

The size and ferocity of Celtic women had always terrified the Romans. Diodorus Siculus, the first century BC Greek who wrote a history of the world from the Creation to Caesar's wars in Gaul, claims that a Gallic woman was every inch her husband's equal in courage. As we have seen, Ammianus Marcellinus 300 years later gives a riveting description of a Celtic female warrior with bulging neck and grinding teeth, flailing her arms like a windmill and driving home with fists and feet like missiles from a *ballista*.

Antonia Fraser makes the valid point that mention of Boudicca's voice was probably an attempt to belittle the queen. Roman women were supposed to have soft, gentle voices, not shrieking stridency. In 1400, Leonardo Bruno wrote that

> . . . if a woman throws her arms around whilst speaking, or if she increases the volume of her speech with greater forcefulness, she will appear threateningly insane and requiring restraint. These matters belong to men, as war or battles.[15]

Bruno of course was a man, and one trained in the same Roman classical tradition that had seen Boudicca as the enemy. Cassius Dio contends that Boudicca 'directed the conduct of the entire war',[16] which puts her on a par with a warlord like Caratacus and would have been despised by

Roman men. Spelling her name Bondouika in his original Greek, Dio describes her as 'a Briton woman of the royal family and possessed of greater intelligence than often belongs to women'.[17]

The army she assembled, he says, was 120,000 strong, and if this included all the fighting men and boys of the Iceni, the Trinovantes and other disaffected tribes, this figure is not unreasonable; if accurate, it would certainly represent the largest tribal enemy the Romans had faced in Britain at any one time. Total native population figures are impossible to compute, but experts assume a broad figure of two million south of what would become Hadrian's Wall. Interestingly, Dio tells us that Boudicca delivered a speech on 'a tribunal which had been constructed of earth in the Roman fashion'. Where this was we do not know; perhaps Thetford, where we believe important ceremonies were carried out. That it was Roman is a telling comment on the degree of Celtic absorption into the ways of the empire.

We intend to quote Dio at length because it gives his version at least of Boudicca's mindset. It is *just* feasible that a garbled version of this speech came first-hand from an Iceni prisoner after Manduessedum and that a Roman official copied it down for Dio to find in the archive years later. Alternatively, it may simply be an articulate historian's assumption as to the queen's motives. Boudicca told her people:

> You have learned by actual experience how different freedom is from slavery. Hence, although some among you may previously, through ignorance of which was better, have been deceived by the alluring promises of the Romans, yet now that you have tried both, you have learned how great a mistake you have made in preferring an imported despotism to your ancestral way of life and you have come to realize how much better is poverty with no master than wealth with slavery.

How much Dio knew of the Iceni hierarchy in the assumption that Boudicca's people had no 'master' we can only guess. Boudicca's speech continues:

For what treatment is there of the most shameful or grievous sort that we have not suffered ever since those men made their appearance in Britain? Have we not been robbed entirely of most of our possessions, and those the greatest, while for those that remain we pay taxes? Besides pasturing and tilling for them all our other possessions, do we not pay a yearly tribute for our very bodies? How much better it would be to have been sold to masters once for all than, possessing empty titles of freedom, to have to ransom ourselves every year!

In theory, the client kingdoms had been paying tribute since Caesar's invasion in 54 BC and certainly since the eleven kings' capitulation at Camulodunum. The rhetorical emphasis on slavery, however, smacks more of Rome than of the Iceni. The chains found at Llyn Cerig Bach on Mona in 1943 hint at a slave culture, but they may have been simply shackles for prisoners of war:

How much better to have been slain and to have perished than to go about with a tax on our heads! Yet why do I mention death? For even dying is not free of cost with them; no, you know what fees we deposit even for our dead. Among the rest of mankind death frees even those who are in slavery to others; only in the case of the Romans do the very dead remain alive for their profit.

This is the Greek philosopher in expansive mood. It is most unlikely that the queen of a tribe in East Anglia would have this concept of 'mankind'.

Why is it that, though none of us has any money (how could we or where would we get it?) we are stripped and despoiled like a murderer's victims? And why should the Romans be expected to display moderation as time goes on when they have behaved towards us in this fashion from the very outset, when all men show consideration even for the beasts they have newly captured?

Boudicca's next point is fascinating. We would love to know what her grasp of history was when Dio makes her say

> But, to speak plain truth, it is we who have made ourselves responsible for all these evils in that we allowed them to set foot on the island in the first place instead of expelling them at once as we did their famous Julius Caesar – yes, and in that we did not deal with them while they were still far away as we dealt with Augustus and with Gaius Caligula and make even the attempt to sail hither a formidable thing.

References to Caesar, Augustus and Caligula smack of the historian of Rome. Given that, Caesar's invasion had probably passed into legend even as far north as Norfolk, though Augustus made no move against Britain and Caligula's attempt to invade when Boudicca was still a child had ended in farce.[18] The queen's speech continues:

> As a consequence, although we inhabit so large an island, or rather a continent, one might say, that is encircled by the sea, and although we possess a veritable world of our own and are so separated by the ocean from all the rest of mankind that we have been believed to dwell on a different earth and under a different sky and that some of the outside world, yes, even their wisest men, have not hitherto known for certainty by what name we are called, we have, notwithstanding all this, been despised and trampled underfoot by men who know nothing else than how to secure gain.

Once again, here is Boudicca the philosopher, with a third-century classical scholar's view of the Celts and their island. She continues:

> However, even at this late day, though we have not done so before, let us, my countrymen and friends and kinsmen – for I consider you all kinsmen, seeing that you inhabit a single island and are called by one common name – let us, I say, do our duty while we still remember what freedom is, that we may leave to our children not only its appellation

but also its reality. For if we utterly forget the happy state in which we were born and bred, what, pray, will they do, reared in bondage?

Stirring stuff. It may be Dio rather than Boudicca, and it is worthy of Henry V or Churchill. It also flies in the face of historical convention, perhaps merely because Dio is writing two centuries after Boudicca. The assumption is, borne out by the fate of Caratacus and earlier attempts at resistance, that the Celtic tribes did not band together, that their long history of internecine disputes, over territory, water sources, cattle, women, precluded it, and that the Romans were simply another tribe to take on. So, although it is bizarre for the Catuvellaunian Caratacus to be leading the Silures and the Ordovices, he seems not to have done so at the same time, implying perhaps that those tribes refused to cooperate, even against a common enemy.

If Dio is right, however, that Boudicca regarded the Trinovantes and other confederate tribes as her 'kinsmen', then this puts her on a higher plane altogether. It makes her a truly national leader a thousand years before there was actually a nation. Boudicca said via Dio:

All this I say, not with the purpose of inspiring you with a hatred of present conditions – that hatred you already have – but of commending you because you now of your own accord choose the requisite course of action, and of thanking you for so readily cooperating with me and with each other. Have no fear whatever of the Romans; for they are superior to us neither in numbers nor in bravery. And here is the proof: they have protected themselves with helmets and breastplates and greaves and yet further provided themselves with palisades and walls and trenches to make sure of suffering no harm by an incursion of their enemies. For they are influenced by their fears when they adopt this kind of fighting in preference to the plan we follow of rough and ready action.

Dio was of course writing this in hindsight. The 'rough and ready action' Boudicca had in mind was the sacking of the hated veterans' *colonia* at Camulodunum as merely a starting point. And her jibes at Roman cowardice, while hardly fair, would have struck a chord with her wild tribesmen. They were certainly as brave, if not braver, than the Romans and did indeed outnumber them. What they lacked, of course, was organization and rigid discipline, but it would take more than an outraged queen and a few weeks preparation to do anything about that.

Boudicca/Dio lays on the rhetoric with a trowel:

> Indeed, we enjoy such a surplus of bravery, that we regard our tents [sic] as safer than their walls and our shields as affording greater protection than their whole suits of mail.[19] As a consequence, we when victorious capture them and when overpowered elude them; and if we choose to retreat anywhere, we conceal ourselves in swamps and mountains so inaccessible that we can be neither discovered nor taken.

Dio is using all kinds of licence here. The guerrilla tactics he is describing fit Caratacus in the fastnesses of Wales, but Boudicca's Norfolk was singularly devoid of mountains:

> Our opponents, however, can neither pursue anybody, by reason of their heavy armour, nor yet flee; and if they ever do slip away from us, they take refuge in certain appointed spots, where they shut themselves up as in a trap.

This was, of course, the problem for the Celts in their hill forts. As we have seen, since 43 if not earlier, Roman assault forces, using siege artillery like *ballistae* had little difficulty in overcoming these strongholds. Boudicca/Dio in the meantime is in full flow:

> But these are not the only respects in which they are vastly inferior to us: there is also the fact that they cannot bear up under hunger, thirst, cold or heat, as we can. They require shade and covering, they require kneaded bread and wine and oil and if any of these things fail them, they perish; for us, on the other hand, any grass or root serves as bread, the juice of any plant as oil, any water as wine, any tree as a house.

This may well have actually been Boudicca's view of the enemy. Rome, with all its sophistication, smacks of luxury and therefore softness, but we know that in reality the Roman army was physically tough and able to conquer in every climatic condition known to man. The soldiers' rations were meagre and if they provided themselves with shade, wine and oil, it was because they came prepared for any eventuality. Boudicca adds:

> Furthermore, this region is familiar to us and is our ally, but to them it is unknown and hostile. As for rivers, we swim them naked, whereas they do not get across them easily even with boats.

Again, the rhetoric gets in the way of reality. We have noted that rivers may have been sacred to the Celts (the Roman Dio would not have been aware of that), and from Caesar's time several key battles were fought across them. If there was a problem, as at the Medway in 43, the Romans had the solution, in that case the Batavian auxiliaries whom river crossing was a speciality. Boudicca may or may not have known that by this time Paulinus' troops had successfully crossed the Menai Strait to take Mona. It was now that Boudicca the battle queen became Boudicca the high priestess.

Celtic mythology is awash with warrior queens, a reflection of the neo-egalitarian status women seemed to have enjoyed. Anu, or Dana, was the mother – goddess of the Tuatha de Danaan, associated with the hills of Kerry in Munster, Da Chich Anann, the paps of Anu. In Scottish folklore she became the hideous hag Black Annis. The fact that in one of her personifications she drove a chariot links her for ever with Boudicca. Badb the crow was an Irish battle goddess appearing to the Gaelic troops of north Britain at the Battle of Clontarf in 1014. Her alter egos were Morrigan, the death goddess, wheeling as a raven over the corpses of the slain on the battlefield, and Nemain, the dreadful, the venomous. Boudicca also has her echoes in Medb, the warrior queen of Connaught. No king could rule there unless married to her, and along with her voracious sexual appetite went a calculating political and military mind. Her armies, according to folklore, invaded Ulster and killed its greatest hero, the slingshot expert Cúchulainn, the Hound of Culann. She in turn was murdered by Forbai, son of Conchobar mac Nessa, while she bathed in a sacred pool. 'Let us, therefore,' says Dio/Boudicca, 'go against them trusting boldly to good fortune. Let us show then that they are hares and foxes trying to rule over dogs and wolves.' She released the sacred hare from the folds of her dress and the path of its run delighted her audience, who whooped and clapped at the sight of the good omen. Antonia Fraser misses the point when she writes:

> There were general shouts of delight at what was clearly a favourable omen for the uprising (as it was clearly intended to be, for one imagines that Boudicca, astute enough to install the hare, was also astute enough to ensure that it ran in the right direction).

Downgrading this important augury to a cheap and cynical trick is to misunderstand both Boudicca and her times. The queen, as well as her people, *believed* in divination; it was part of their faith. And the fact that Boudicca carried out what was clearly a ritualistic ceremony implies that she was herself a Druidess with the powers of prophecy to accomplish them.

Caesar tells us that hares were sacred creatures to the British Celts and could not be hunted. *The Druid Animal Oracle*, a compilation of Celtic animalistic beliefs, tells us that in Boudicca's day the hare was the large Arctic type. The Celtic word was *'gaer'*, and it was possible that like the horse and the boar it was a totem animal of the Iceni. It was associated with the idea of rebirth, which is precisely why it was used by the queen, as a symbol of the freedom of her people from Roman abuse. It was also linked with intuition, promise and fulfilment, all of which were in the hearts of the Iceni, poised to take on the greatest military power in the world. The animal was also associated with the corn spirit, in that that was where it was seen most frequently on summer nights when the moon was full. Perhaps at first as an attempt to kill the power of Boudicca and Boudicca's name, the Romans introduced hare-coursing to their dearly won province.

Dio Cassius tells us that Boudicca, 'raising her hand towards the heaven said "I thank you, Andraste . . . I supplicate and pray for victory."' This is undoubtedly a reference to the goddess called Andasta worshipped by the Vocontii of Gaul, and may be another variant of Anu referred to above. There is one coin of the Iceni which may depict her. Boudicca's next words, however, lose all semblance of an authentic Celtic ceremony, and Dio the scholar takes over:

For I rule no burden-bearing Egyptians as did Nitocris, nor war-trafficking Assyrians as did Semiramis (for we have by now gained this much learning from the Romans!), much less over the Romans themselves as did Messalina once and afterwards Agrippina and now Nero (who, though in name a man is in fact a woman, as is proved by his singing, lyre-playing and beautification of his person).

Boudicca's grasp of Roman history and the innermost secrets of Nero's court is astonishing, and Dio tries to pretend that she has learned all this from the Romanization of the Iceni since 43; it seems unlikely. Semiramis was the semi-legendary queen of Assyria and co-founder of Babylon in the ninth century BC. She was probably Sammu-ramat, the widow of Shamshi-adad V, who ruled as regent for three years (811–808 BC).

Boudicca goes on to extol the virtues of her own people:

Those over whom I rule are Britons, men that know not how to till the soil or ply a trade, but are thoroughly versed in the art of war and hold all things in common, even children and wives, so that the latter possess the same valour as the men.

We have seen this passage before and know that the view of Britons it expresses is wrong, but it gives Boudicca a chance to scoff at the effeminacy of the Romans:

As the queen, then, of such men and of such women, I supplicate and pray for victory, preservation of life and liberty against men insolent, insatiable, impious – if, indeed, we ought to term those people men who bathe in warm water, eat artificial dainties, drink unmixed wine, anoint themselves with myrrh, sleep on soft couches with boys as bedfellows – boys past their prime at that – and are slaves to a lyre-player and a poor one too. Wherefore may this Mistress Domitia – Nero reign no longer over me or over you men; let the girl sing and lord it over the Romans, for they surely deserve to be the slaves of such a woman after having submitted to her so long. But for us, Mistress, be you alone ever our leader.

On hearing these words the Iceni roared, the Trinovantes roared, the roar of all their thousands. And they noted which way the hare ran. It ran towards the hated Colonia Victriensis, the veterans' colony, at Camulodunum.

7

Camulodunum

> When you go by the Via Aurelia,
>   As thousands have travelled before,
> Remember the luck of the Soldier
>   Who never saw Rome any more.
> 'Rimini', from *Puck of Pook's Hill*, Rudyard Kipling

Colchester today is a town like any other, with the obligatory McDonalds, KFC and River Island. But the sprawling centre offers us glimpses of colossal Victorian civic pride, timber-framed houses that witnessed the second Civil War siege of 1648, the unique tile-built keep of Eudo de Rie's castle and, tantalizingly, glimpses of the glories of Rome.

What we cannot see so easily is Camulodunon, the Iron Age settlement that grew into a significant Roman centre. This is not just because it has been built over and has disappeared with time, but because of the destructive fate that Boudicca visited on the town in 60 AD, leaving no building unravaged and, allegedly, no citizen alive. The Roman wall to protect future generations did not yet exist. It was built later by a shaken Rome fearing a repetition of the horrors of the Boudiccan revolt. So what did Colchester mean to the people who lived there, why was it such a target and how much should we believe the appalling atrocities hinted at by Dio and graphically described by Tacitus?

We have seen that Camulodunon was a significant place before Claudius chose it as his administrative centre in the autumn of 43. It covered a relatively small area of around ten square miles. The land would have looked little different from the countryside elsewhere in East Anglia, flat pasture with areas of woodland doubtless being cut down and used for building materials by the settlement's inhab-itants. The site lay between the rivers Colne and Roman, probably navigable by flat-bottomed boat.

One of the most significant features that would have been visible on the pre-Claudian and possibly, in places, pre-Caesarean landscape would have been the complex system of dykes, which if laid end to end would extend for over twelve miles.[1] Some of these were placed in parallel to create successive lines of defence, but in other places they appear laterally. This could be to do with the natural lie of the land, either presenting defence or else landscape unsuitable for building a dyke. The majority of the dykes in this area face westwards. Does this imply a large perceived threat from that direction? And if so are the dykes the defences of the Trinovantes protecting their settlement from the relentless eastward thrust of the Catuvellauni? And can we assume that the Catuvellauni, who inhabited the site by the time of Rome, had no fear of a coastal enemy? The only dyke facing east is at Berechurch, which suggests that the dykes were not functional but represented a mark of status. Whatever the interpretation, we feel that their function was probably multiple; at the Lexden dyke, for example, there is evidence of wooden palisading, but the sheer scale of the dyke system would have been virtually impossible to man fully as a permanent defence in an area with two main centres of occupation.

The dykes were developed over a period of time, undoubtedly, but it is clear from coin finds and the chronology of intersection that the system was already in place before the Romans arrived. In the surrounding area, burials at Lexden have been dated to around 15 BC. We know that Tasciovanus stamped his coins with the mint mark CAMU in the 20s BC. All evidence points to the significant levels of development Camulodunon had reached even by this point, suggesting that it may well have been singled out before that.

Camulodunon's geography is strange enough. It stands in what is largely understood to be Trinovantian territory, and, in the tribal infighting which typified Celtic Britain, the Trinovantes had traditionally poor relations with their Catuvellaunian neighbours. We must therefore see the site as having changed hands several times, telling to whoever was the dominant tribe at the time. There may have been uneasy coalitions in place from time to time, under a popular leader who could have been from either tribe. Camulodunon may have been a trophy for the Catuvellauni, who we know were one of the newest tribes in the area. However, the dykes and the hill-fort type defence at Pitchbury, possibly used as a point of refuge, reflects a climate of violent tribal warfare. It could have been a stronghold and outpost, the border defence of either tribe. The King Addedomaros has been put into the Trinovantian camp, because his coins have been found in the Colne Valley. After him, Tasciovanus and his son Cunobelin have been associated with many of the developments at Camulodunon and Verlamion, as evinced from the spread of his coins. Cunobelin, who became chief after Dubrovellanus, was possibly neither Catuvellaunian nor Trinovantian, but as we have seen he was referred to as 'king of the Britons' by Suetonius. This is borne out by the fact that his reign seems to have been peaceful and yet his death sparked infighting which in turn led to Claudius taking advantage of the situation and launching his conquest. Whatever the tribal interpretation, whether it reflects social change, territorial shifts or simply that Camulodunon was not set in Trinovantian land and has been misinterpreted, it was clearly an important site and an attractive proposition. The word 'Camulodunon' is the nearest we can come to the Celtic variant of the name, although it is heavily Romanized, the Latin ending from 43, *dunum*, meaning 'fortified place', and Camulos, the Celtic god of war. In Roman texts, the Latin ending is obviously given, but after Claudius' triumphal entry the place was renamed Colonia Claudia.

The site of Camulodunum had two foci. These were

Sheepen and Gosbecks, both to the west of the present town centre and both of which remained significant into the Roman period. Sheepen has largely been seen as the industrial centre. It was near the river, useful for the transport of raw materials and manufactured goods, but also for smithery and other industrial processes. Excavations have revealed many metal artefacts, coins, bone, glass and broken pottery alongside manufacturers' tools such as crucibles and hearths. The richness of material shows that Sheepen was doubtless a trading site, as well as an industrial one, with shops in place before the Claudian conquest. The evidence of shackles at Sheepen indicates a slave population before the advent of Rome, made up of the prisoners of tribal warfare, a find more relevant to the Iceni than the chains from distant Mona. There are also finds of helmets, broken swords and other military equipment. These have been interpreted as scrap metal, possibly junked by the legion which left the city to campaign in the west. It is tempting to accept them as the weaponry of the poorly provisioned defenders of the city fighting desperately against swarms of Celtic warriors crying for blood under Boudicca, their slaughtered bodies stripped of equipment and ritually put in one place as thanksgiving to Andraste. The evidence does not support this, however, not least because there is virtually no evidence of large-scale killing in the city as a result of the Boudiccan revolt, a fact which Dio and Tacitus and the majority of historians since have chosen to ignore.

Sheepen also has ritual elements associated with it. There were at least four temples there into the Roman period, and it seems to have become a veritable centre for ritual activity on the post-Boudiccan site after 60. This shows the complex functionality of the site, which was also defended by the large Sheepen dyke. It also explains perhaps why the Romans built their extraordinary Temple of Claudius there; we have seen the readiness of the conquerors to adapt alien religions and appease strange gods.

Gosbecks had an altogether more rural setting before Claudius, and it was likely to have been the royal and aristocratic centre, the residence of Cunobelin, his family and retainers. We are not looking at a grand centre with statues and alabaster – that was alien and Roman – but a site with a simple palatial building of timber, thatch and wattle and daub, with some houses probably defended by a bank and ditch in the best defendable position, as attested to by the arrangement of the dykes.

There is a very rich burial on the site. Could this be the last resting place of Cunobelin? Its position would certainly support such a theory and its continuing ritual importance shows that this was a significant area to all cultures. It is again close to a river whose magic waters were, as we have seen, significant in both Celtic and Roman religion.

The written record is scant on Claudius' taking of Camulodunon. Neither is there any real evidence of additions to the site's defences in the face of Claudius and his army. There may be several reasons for this. Perhaps the defences were built in a hurry and were insubstantial, which would account for their not having survived in the archaeological record. Wood does not endure, unless it is burnt, and then if it is too extensively burnt it does not survive either, but crumbles into charcoal. Perhaps the Britons were just not expecting Camulodunon to be such a target, or that it would fall easily and be indefensible against an army equipped with siege engines and modern technology. Its status after Cunobelin's death is uncertain, a clue to divisions within the next generation. As we have seen, Cunobelin's sons Togodumnos and Caratacus set up satellite states, the former north of the Thames, the latter around Hampshire. Therefore, Camulodunum could momentarily have become less important and been seen as not worth defending – or perhaps there were not enough people to defend it. Whatever the answer, Claudius and his force of around 30,000 do not seem to have met with much resistance on their entry into the city.

A temporary legionary camp was immediately set up either at Gosbecks or Sheepen. The Romans doubtless chose an area where they could make use of the existing defences, namely the system of dykes, and indeed possibly extend them. The 'triple dyke' for example may not have been triple prior to Claudius; Professor Christopher Hawkes discovered a Roman shoe and also slot marks from the use of shovels consistent with the practices of Roman engineers.

Claudius had plans for Camulodunum. The town was built

at his direct command (although this was where he ended his active part in the conquest, returning to Rome in his long, extended triumph). This made Camulodunum the flagship of Rome in Britain, a fact which contributed heavily to its destruction by the forces of Boudicca. But this is where we should leave the name Camulodunum behind. Under Rome it was first the Colonia Claudia, then Colonia Victriensis, City of Victory, although precisely why this later name was added is debatable. We shall cling to Camulodunum since this, or something like it, was the name retained by the Trinovantes.

Before it had fully developed into a colony with a centre and administrative area, Camulodunum represented an important place militarily. The camp developed into a small fort at Gosbecks, which in turn led to the development of a huge legionary base, the scale of which had never been seen in Britain before. The earlier, smaller fort at Gosbecks was near to the central enclosure associated with Cunobelin's Camulodunon, near the site of the modern zoo. It made use of the existing defences in the shape of Heath Farm Dyke at its back. As well as serving the surrounding area and keeping an eye on the tribal movements, the function of this fort could well have been to control traffic moving through the area, especially as the legions began to push northwards into Brigantian territory and westwards to the Druids of Mona. The site seems to represent a significant thoroughfare, the suggested harbour at nearby Fingringhoe a place for supplies to be brought further inland as well as being a central position in the territory where Claudius' first incursion had occurred. The internal street system also gives more evidence as to the fort functioning at least partly as an early checkpoint.

The legionary fort was built at Sheepen. It shows a huge concentration of men and materials and a level of organization and administration probably never seen by the tribes of Britain. It must have been an imposing sight to the newly conquered people of Camulodunum and the surrounding area, especially for the young, to whom the name Caesar can have been at best an ancient legend. Caesar does not mention Colchester in his *Commentarii*. Was this because it was not significant then, an important site yet to be developed, perhaps in response to the destruction of the Catuvellaunian chief Cassivellaunus' headquarters at Wheathampstead?

The fortress covered a large area, housing around sixty barrack buildings surrounded by an impressive stone rampart which would have stood out in a world of wooden structures. Such constructions were not easy to build, but the estimated 60,000 troops at Claudius' disposal were employed in its construction and for some it may well have represented their new home. Labour from the surrounding area may also have been pressed into service; the Trinovantes were, after all, a conquered people.

The v–shaped ditches were deep and wide and presented additional obstacles to the towering stone rampart. Using evidence from the present shopping centre of the Lion Walk site, we can assume that, inside, the barrack buildings were around 70 metres in length and were detached, probably to separate officers and men, each barrack holding a century. Presumably there would have been stores, workshops and outlets for the legionaries' needs, as well as a centrally located headquarters. The annexe part of the fortress built onto the barrack area could well have housed some or all of these amenities, along with a bathhouse, an important part of Roman social ritual. It was here that the new civic centre would spring up in the wake of the Boudiccan destruction.

Camulodunum was well placed for natural resources, with woodland, stone and navigable waterways nearby, so it was unlikely that provisioning the building of the fortress and then its garrison was a particular struggle. The harbour at Fingringhoe has revealed large quantities of Roman military equipment, coinage and imported pottery. The burgeoning town was doubtless a significant centre in terms of trade and a stop-off point for merchants, whose cargoes could travel further inland by smaller boats via the Colne.

Who lived in the legionary fortress? Almost certainly XX and some auxiliary units. It was perhaps a cavalry base, too, although the lack of evidence for stables does not make this easy to prove. It seems likely that before Caratacus began to resurface in the west, the garrison was larger, or at least it was used as a launch point for legions and fresh offensives.

Other evidence is more tangible. Two gravestones, destroyed by Boudicca's forces and now on display in Colchester's museum, help us answer some questions. One commemmorates Marcus Favonius Facilis, centurion of XX. The period of service on his memorial would suggest he was a serving soldier at the time of his death, and his rank would suggest that he was not merely passing through. He stands with his vine stick and his greaves, the stone erected by his devoted freedmen. The other is a cavalryman, Longinus Sdapeze of Ala I Thracium, which bears out the presence of cavalry in the town. He could have been passing through or killed in nearby conflict, but he could also have been stationed in Claudius' colony, especially considering that the horse was significant to tribes in the area. His tombstone tells us that he was the son of Matygus, from Sardica, and that he was a *duplicarius* (second in command). He had served for fifteen years and died, probably in 49, aged forty. He is depicted mounted, riding down an enemy crouching under his horse's belly, and his face has been smashed away. For several years it was believed that this was a highly personalized memento of Boudicca's attack – the destruction of the all-important head of an enemy, already dead and immortalized in stone. In fact, the face was found in 1996 and fitted back in place, its loss merely the result of the passage of time.

Whichever units were garrisoned there, they were significantly fewer at the end of the 40s. Caratacus had risen in the west, successfully and to the detriment of Rome, bearing in mind how quiet commentators are until his defeat in 51. Ostorius Scapula, the new governor after Aulus Plautius had returned in glory to Rome, was forced to call Camulodunum's forces to aid the fighting against Caratacus. Why was this done? At least six years had been put into developing the *colonia* as a military centre, and, indeed, the very enemy the Romans were fighting had his heritage in the area; even if Caratacus never ruled there, his father certainly did. Who was to say that the Catuvellauni were not going to rise in support of their absent leader?

Tacitus seems to have been under the impression that the veterans who were left to form the colony that would be laid waste by Boudicca a decade later would be able to keep the imperial flames burning among the people of Camulodunum. This was not very likely, and certainly not the case in the long term. The town may well have been left with only auxiliary forces, and these would not have withstood a concentrated attack. The probable reason for a lack of opposition in the area in the 50s, politics aside, was that, to the north, the Iceni under Prasutagus remained quiescent, whatever the actions of the breakaway group over the disarmament issue in 47/48. The legionary fortress still stood while internal developments took place. Perhaps would-be rebels were not ready to chance their arm, especially in the presence of armed and seasoned veterans, all of whom had seen active service just a few years before. So in the short term Tacitus was right; not because of the fortitude of Rome, but because of the uncertainty of the population whose fathers had lost battles with Rome, but never a war.

Despite this, Scapula's situation must have been quite desperate that he felt it necessary to pull the troops out of Camulodunum and leave it to its own devices. It was likely that Claudius intended the site to become a provincial capital, although that privilege finally went to London, and the movement of troops was just seen as a slightly earlier progression towards creating the new capital. The developments within the town reflected Claudius' personal interest, and the coordination of resources as well as the grandiose scale of building would suggest a powerful administrative body working on behalf of the new colonists. Roman provincial law benefited the colonists greatly in terms of wealth and position.

So it was that the already redundant fort became the centre of a colony that would rapidly develop and spread into a Roman city of the highest order. The principal roads of the fort were retained, but the street plan was adapted to introduce a 'high street' as well as streets for the use of private residences. The barrack buildings were developed into houses varying in quality according to size and position on the new street plan, others being removed to make way for other use such as cultivation, perhaps an early example of allotments. Although there seems to have been much extensive reuse of the structures inside the fort, bizarrely enough, the legionary defences were filled in to make room for new buildings. This of course compromised security, as borne out by burnt houses in Balkerne Lane.

Elsewhere in the town the developments were not so cavalier. The headquarters at the centre of the fort is likely to have been the focus for the forum/basilica, the annexe became the area for amenities and also the ritual and administrative centre. The theatre would have been multifunctional. In addition to staging plays, of which the Romans were particularly fond, it could also have staged small gladiatorial contests between captives, adding to the growing hatred of Rome. Theatres were often used as meeting places for administrative decisions or discussion. Rome had until recently been a republic, and the spectacle of civic leaders arguing their case in council was a sight familiar to both Roman and Celt.

Ritual also came into play in the theatre. Next to the Temple of Claudius, which became the temple for an imperial cult, it would seem highly plausible that the theatre was a ritual site as well as host to ceremonies and performances.

There are two buildings which, as yet, have not been identified properly in the annexe; they are probably civic buildings. One may have been the bathhouse, a true indication of the Romanization and indeed development of a town. The lack of a clearly identified bath house raises questions as to whether Camulodunum was in fact complete at the time of the Boudiccan revolt. It went through several phases in terms of functionality; when it became the centre for the cult of Claudius, which appears to have been after the emperor's death in 54, the town was pushed into another stage of development, and a bathhouse had not yet been built.

The town's blatant affiliation to Rome was one of its downfalls, but it also furnishes some particularly interesting and unique evidence on the Romano-British landscape. One example is the commemorative arch of the kind found in Rome itself and also in Gaul. This makes a point about Roman supremacy. As we have seen, Claudius' victory had been a great success at home, especially after the disastrous reign of Caligula, and the arch was a celebration of this. On its apex the infamous statue of victory may have stood, thought it inexplicably fell down shortly before Boudicca attacked. The arch was a powerful symbol of Rome and appears to have stood on the main road that led to Boudicca's next targets of Londinium and Verlamium.

The most significant building, however, both in terms of the town's development and its destruction, is the one to which all other civic buildings were secondary: the Temple of Claudius. Tacitus called it the 'blatant stronghold of alien rule', and locals drafted in to make daily observances to the god-emperor were traitors to their religion as well as their people. Beneath Colchester Castle lie the temple's remains. On our visit, we sat in these vaults listening to the tour guide. The arched vault is whitewashed now and floodlit; the uneven floors carpeted to settle the sand the Romans used to create the foundations – though, even today, traces of it, brought by river from the Essex coast, still coat the stonework. The mortar, whiter and stronger than the Norman variant used a thousand years later to build Eudo's castle, still contains the traces of oyster shells that may have been a Roman engineer's lunch!

A plan of the temple can be devised because its foundations were used for subsequent building. It was an imposing creation with a large altar and would have formed a strong focal point with its white marble columns and large iron doors and Victory looking out over the town. The structure would have been particularly important as it was built specifically in veneration of Claudius. If it was in place before his death, it is unlikely that it would have had a dedication to him, as he is recorded as being quite modest about personal veneration. This was the centre of the imperial cult of Claudius, which was used as an administrative and financial tool, as well as a religious precedent. The high priest, voted in by the council of the town, was often a religious leader from the Trinovantes. He was then responsible for the cult, its rituals and offerings. This made for an effective tax-collecting tool, as the high priest went out into the surrounding area collecting for the provision of the cult. It was also one of the causes of discontent among the non-Roman population which simmered away beneath the surface years before Prasutagus died and his daughters were violated.

Taxes and labour had already been taken continuously from the people outside Camulodunum. This resentment grew as their hard-earned wealth, was spent venerating the conquerors who had taken their land and, to varying extents, their liberty. The town had its own set of rules for the surrounding area, the *lex coloniae*. These would have been primarily concerned with the upkeep and development of the town, and therefore its taxation, and do not seem to have applied to Roman citizens. The *lex colomine* also dealt with the acquisition of land. A set amount of land was apportioned to each colonist according to Roman colonial law – essentially reflecting the gratitude of the state to its former soldiers – and the size of Camulodunum would suggest the colony's territory would have been very extensive. But this does not seem to have been enough. Tacitus writes of the Trinovantes being forced off their land, as were the Iceni after the death of Prasutagus. This shows that the colonists of Camulodunum and elsewhere may not have been satisfied with their lot, and wanted more; this greed was to count against them in 60. Those who managed to keep their land did so at a high price, not least because the loans that were forced on them by Claudius, Seneca and Nero were suddenly called in, with interest. The mistreatment and financial burdens, as well as cultural suppression the masses, must have turned the countryside into a seething mass of rebellion.

This may not have been the case for everyone, however. Burial sites at Stanway clearly show Celtic ritual, though with Roman influence. They contain Roman coins, and one has writing equipment, which only came with a Roman education; others contain imported wares and even Roman military equipment. These are the graves of the aristocracy, the people who collected the taxes from those who had worked their land before the Roman occupation. They had decided to throw in their lot with Rome, to enjoy a better quality of life or out of fear of losing their status. It was not necessary at this period to be a Roman to become a Roman citizen. An auxiliary trooper could afford to provide his son with a spell as a Roman legionary, which led directly to citizenship. Patronage, clientage and contacts were the cement of Roman and Romano-British society, as they remained for centuries to come.

This could be why the site at Gosbecks was left relatively untouched, because the Romans were respectful of the aristocratic heritage of the area, and indeed, after the early fort had fallen out of use, it could well have been given over to the local hierarchy. It is equally possible that the reason Gosbecks remained relatively unsullied was that the Romans feared inciting the wrath of the Celtic gods and spirits by desecrating what seems to have been a strong ritual centre for the inhabitants, and so left it firmly alone.

But the Romans were not to escape the wrath of the Britons. The first omen came as Victory fell from her pedestal to crash in the dirt of the streets of the *colonia*, as if trying, said Tacitus, to flee the town before it was too late.

The population of Camulodunum failed to follow her example, despite knowing that the Boudiccan threat was on its way. We have no details of the timescale involved, but the raising of a huge army of the Iceni, the Trinovantes and others could not have gone unnoticed. There is no evidence for refortification of the town, and the inhabitants must have regretted building theatres and shops over the old fortress' substantial defences. It is likely that they made some provision, but it has also been suggested that support for Boudicca, which had grown strong, led to the sabotage of the town defences. A kind of fifth column seems to have been operating inside the colony, perhaps dissuading the more sensible from manning the barricades. The Romans were obviously still not afraid enough to flee. Perhaps they expected the *procurator* Catus Decianus to send more than a few hundred men to their aid. Perhaps they were supremely confident of beating what they may have assumed would be a poorly armed rabble, especially as some of the colonists, veterans of Claudius' conquest, may well have remembered the ease with which they had taken the town from the Catuvellauni. Perhaps they expected the distant Paulinus to arrive with his cavalry. What they did not perhaps realize was that the tables were now well and truly turned.

Across the countryside Boudicca's army rallied to her in numbers and strength. Dio gives us a figure of 120,000, and, even if this is an exaggeration, the actual number would have been in the tens of thousands, and no less terrifying. At their heart was the flame-haired rebel queen, following the direction of the wild hare and under the divine protection of Andraste.

The population of Camulodunum probably stood at between ten and twenty thousand, a large figure by the standards of the day, of whom untold slaves, servants and other members of the rural populace may well have been Boudiccan sympathizers. The small contingent that was sent to help the colonists would not have been sufficient to stop the rebel army. Tacitus tells us there was a small garrison and that Decianus sent, probably from Londinium, 'barely two hundred men, incompletely armed.'[2]

He conjures a brave picture of a two-day siege, where the few defenders doggedly held out, a notion graphically rehearsed today in 'The Revenge', Colchester Museum's audio-visual re-enactment of the attack. But in reality such a siege must be viewed as an impossibility. We have already established that no evidence has as yet been found of refortification of the town, which would have had to be substantial to withstand such an army. The truth is far more brief, but the end for the town no less total. Tacitus wrote:

> Delirious women chanted of destruction at hand. They cried that in the local senate-house outlandish screams had been heard; the theatre had echoed with shrieks; at the mouth of the Thames a phantom settlement had been seen in ruins. A blood-red colour in the sea, too, and shapes like human corpses left by the ebb tide . . .[3]

The attack would have started as a low hum from the north, building to a cacophony of whoops and screams, the Iceni bragging of their prowess and calling on their gods. Then in the black mass that had appeared in the distance of the forests, glints, like tiny points of light, a swirling torrent of smoke pouring from thousands of flames. The mass began to break off like soldier ants and the chariots thundered into view, suddenly all too close and all too real. Screaming into the town, hurling lit torches at the buildings, chasing petrified townsfolk, hacking about them with sword and spear. Like a sea of muscle and iron, the woad-caked tidal wave that was the rebel army poured into the city through its meagre defences and joined the charioteers in putting the town to the torch. The blaze must have been seen for miles around, the flame of victory and of freedom and the sear of hellfire.

The desperate colonists probably did try to put up some kind of resistance, but the Temple of Claudius, described as the place of a valiant last stand by the veterans and auxiliary force, was more likely to have been the last refuge for cowering old women, frightened old men, crying children and desperate mothers. It was a death trap. Pouring into the sand-filled vaults to pray, it would have been only a matter of time before their city was gone and they were reduced to slavery or worse. The temple, too solid to burn easily and with a huge iron door, may have seemed the best place to hide, but the intensifying heat asphyxiated some of the people inside, consigning them to a crematorium of their own making. It would have been only a matter of time before the roof was ripped off or the door smashed from its hinges by the rebels outside screaming their bloodlust.

When it was over, the town still ablaze, burning with an intensity which must have lasted for days, nothing was left untouched. Every house, every shop was a smouldering wreck. It is difficult to recreate the actual attack and destruction of Claudius's colony and to imagine after two millennia the feelings of the people there, but the picture above is based on strong evidence. Camulodunum was undoubtedly razed to the ground. Every house and building has evidence of being burnt and many artefacts from the period are charred: walls, whose clay shells have been baked hard by fire, have cavities in them where their wooden cores have perished; glass that has become molten with the heat; even a burnt mattress at Lion Walk. The shops of Camulodunum do not seem to have been looted very extensively, but virtually all surviving material is smashed or broken. The memorial statues, of the centurion Facilis and the cavalryman Sdapeze, were smashed and pushed to the ground. A broken javelin and shield found in an oven could indicate a Briton rendering his enemy's weapons useless. The

Boudicca

presence of charioteers screaming through the city comes to us from a single terret, but it is significant.

Other questions are less easy to answer. It must be assumed that some looting did occur. We need not accept Tacitus' obvious bias: 'The natives enjoyed plundering and thought of nothing else . . . they made for where loot was richest and protection weakest';[4] but plunder has been the god-given right of victorious armies throughout time.

The lack of evidence for hoards in the *colonia* would support this, but the fact that precious materials survive elsewhere where destruction has taken place could point to other factors. The interpretation of hoards is often as secret caches meant for times of trouble, perhaps ransom money or bribery; but, by virtue of their being hidden, it is unlikely that the rebels would have waded through every burning house and extracted all the loot from the town.

There is very little evidence of domestic occupation. The appearance of the bed or couch at Lion's Walk is exceptional, not only because of its survival, but also its uniqueness in Britain. As we have already established, fire can preserve things well. There is evidence of wheat and figs and even flax, probably for dyeing. Workshops still have moulds for making commodities. But none of these have been found in exceptionally large quantities. It has been suggested that the appearance of a bed could be indicative of the sparseness of Roman living, especially among tough ex-soldiers used to army life. But where are the lamps, the tables, the stone and clay icons of the household gods the Romans venerated in large number? Surely there would be evidence of these, even if they were smashed. Obviously, the archaeological record is always yielding new evidence, especially with the keen industry of the Colchester Archaeological Trust, but why is there is not more domestic evidence? Could its absence mean evacuation? Could the colonists, receiving so little help from Catus Decianus and none from Gaius Paulinus, have decided to leave the town, abandoning perhaps the old and infirm, those too decrepit to run? It seems likely that a contingent would have stayed, as the town was so significant, but, if the colonists had been aware of the size of the force against them, even they may not have been able to stay loyal to Rome.

This brings us to the death toll. The number we are given for the combined deaths from Camulodunum and the subsequent slaughter at Londinium and Verulamium is 70,000. We have already estimated Camulodunum, by far the largest of the three places, as having a maximum population of only around 20,000, including non-Romans. Even if everyone had stayed at Camulodunum , we would still struggle to reach the figure projected by Tacitus. Reports of those deaths, like that of Mark Twain, must be presumed to be exaggerated.

What we cannot escape is the inference that all the people in the towns were killed; both Tacitus and Dio attest to this. Where, then, are the bodies? There is evidence of only one burnt skeleton at North Hill, and evidence of individual bones, possibly indicating amputation. Doubtless there was loss of life, but not anything remotely resembling the entire population. The Celts, unlike the Romans, did not use hostages, so it has been suggested that the victims were taken to ritual sites for sacrifice. Dio writes:

> And this they did, to the accompaniment of sacrifices, feasts and wanton behaviour, not only in all their other sacred places, but particularly in the grove of Andate [sic].[5]

Again we turn to the suggested figures. It would be difficult, even if it occurred over a period of time, to dispose of several thousand bodies successfully without the fact either being mentioned somewhere in antiquity or some examples being discovered by archaeologists. And logic dictates that Boudicca did not have time. She knew the Romans would send their legions against her in revenge for the act of desecration she had committed. Even based on the assumption that, on a purely logistical basis, the sacrificial sites, 'particularly . . . the grove of Andate', could not have been far from the town, carting tens of thousands of sacrificial victims while striking out at the enemy before he can organize himself would be tricky to say the least. The victors did not take hostages but, from the evidence we have seen here and will see at Verulamium, they did have slaves and these must surely account for at least some of the captives. The attack on

Camulodunum, however violent and terrible, was symbolic. It was meant, as with the majority of Boudicca's acts of destruction, to crush Rome's influence. The Temple of Claudius was a symbol of conquest and oppression and was likely to have been a major target for Boudicca and her army. It is difficult for us to imagine its strangeness in the 50s. Today the castle museum, with its Roman tiles, its immaculate gardens and its blossoming trees, has a familiarity that a thousand years has brought. Then, the temple, with its gold and white, its imported marble and its foreign statuary, was unbearably alien to the Britons – a red rag to a bull.

Dio mentions Quintus Petilius Cerialis Caesius Rufus only in passing and in a later context. He was related by marriage to Vespasian and may have been a Sabine. He was also one of the luckiest generals in Roman history. Tacitus' account is, as usual, so brief that we are left breathless at the speed of the campaign. A realistic timeline would read something like this: assuming that Boudicca did indeed launch her campaign from Thetford, it would have taken the rampant Iceni two days to march the forty miles to Camulodunum. The success of her attack depended on surprise, so in another day, two at most, Camulodunum was a smoking ruin. Graham Webster says that Paulinus ordered the only legion close enough to put the revolt down. Again, we need to slow the pace.

In the unlikely event of a watchful Roman seeing the Iceni on the march and putting two and two together, it was a 250-mile ride to Mona. Even with fresh horses or a string of gallopers passing the news like relay batons, such word would take between three and four days to arrive. Paulinus would then have to send the same or a different messenger to reach Cerialis and IX Hispana. Much more likely is that no news was sent until Camulodunum had fallen, delaying the arrival of retribution still further. Cerialis was at Lindum, today's Lincoln, developing as it was into a *colonia* for veterans, not unlike Camulodunum. Paulinus' galloper would have had to ride due east on the 160-mile journey to Lindum and tell Cerialis of the terrible events to the south. Many commentators criticize the legate of IX for his impetuous dash south, but by this time a week had probably passed since the destruction of Camulodunum, and time was of the essence. It seems from the events that followed that Paulinus was not yet ready to march to Cerialis' aid.

The IX now faced a 110-mile march to Camulodunum, unsure, of course, where exactly the Iceni were. This would have taken infantry at least three days, but it seems from subsequent events that it was a vexillation of the legion, perhaps three cohorts and 500 cavalry. They would have marched south to Durovigutum, modern Godmanchester, and then south-east in search of the enemy.

The likelihood is that the Iceni stopped them within a day's ride of Camulodunum, using the cover of the Essex forests to mount a brilliant ambush. The exhausted Romans, impossibly outnumbered, would not have been given time to deploy into battle formations and were cut to pieces. Tacitus says that all the infantry were killed, and Cerialis himself cut his way back north with whatever cavalry survived, making either for

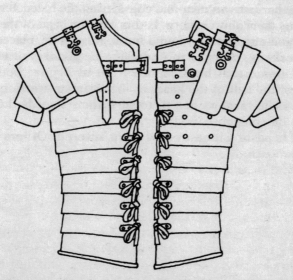

Artist's impression of a legionary's breast and back plate (*lorica segmentata*), from a reconstruction by Michael Simkins of the type found in Corbridge, Northumberland.

Lindum or the cavalry camp at Longthorpe near Peterborough. Here he hid behind his defences and no doubt believed his military career was over.

Antonia Fraser assumes that the Iceni wasted time in these weeks, sacking, destroying, getting roaring drunk; but she has fallen for Roman propaganda. If this had been the case, Cerialis would have done better and may have caught Boudicca's people napping. As it was, the rebels had clearly prefigured assistance from somewhere and planned accordingly. No doubt councils of war were held in the ashes of Camulodunum. What next? Should there be another target? And if so, where? We have no idea of how well informed Boudicca was of the state of readiness of other towns or how much she knew of Paulinus' movements. Results so far had been astonishing. Not even Caratacus had defeated a legion in the field, and the burning of Camulodunum was without precedent. Already, Rome was rocked by the events of the early summer, but the war council had not finished.

It may be that some of the Trinovantes went home, aware that the harvest was near and considering the hated Temple of Claudius their only concern. Is this why the head of the statue of the god-emperor was found in the River Alde, placed there as an offering perhaps to Andraste, the goddess of victory? Was it immersed there, ripped from its bronze body as a totem of the cult of the head, by Trinovantian warriors going home to be farmers again, to turn their swords, however briefly, into ploughshares?

The head of Claudius had been severed. Others would follow.

8

The Cities of Sacrifice

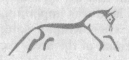

> They made a pile of their trophies
>   High as a tall man's chin,
> Head upon head distorted,
>   Set in a sightless grin.
> Anger and pain and terror
>   Stamped on the smoke-scorched skin.
>
> 'The Grave of the Hundred Dead',
> Rudyard Kipling

At the time of Boudicca's revolt, London as a city was still embryonic. Boudicca's destruction of what was there could be seen as the catalyst which ensured its development into a major centre and prime player throughout Britain's history from the second century onwards. Tacitus refers to the settlement as 'an important centre for businessmen and merchandise', but mentions precious little else except that Paulinus was forced to abandon it, which suggests it might not have been highly significant in terms of defence or indeed for any other reason.

A major problem for the archaeologist is the extensive and dense subsequent development of the city. London remains one of the largest and most powerful cities in the world and has enjoyed that status throughout almost 2,000 years of history. As a result, finding evidence of its origins is far from easy and has had to be undertaken piecemeal in an uneasy 'armed truce' with developers and construction engineers.

Londinium did not share Verlamion's and Camulodunum's illustrious heritage of royal occupation and patronage before the coming of Rome – proof of this is the fact that we do not know its Celtic name. Although Iron Age farmers did farm land along the Thames as well as the fertile land of the North Downs, the area that would develop into the city remained unoccupied. This could have been because the heavy soils were difficult to farm, and for a predominantly agricultural people the quality of land was important. Another possibility could be that only when Roman soldiers arrived in the country was the potential of the area recognized as being of strategic importance.

The Thames had obvious ritual significance for the Celts, in common with any other sizeable body of water. It may have been as much as a mile wide at high tide, with the islands of Southwark and Westminster protruding above the water. The flood plains were later developed with the likely addition of causeways and perhaps a bridge connecting Southwark to the North Bank. The river has yielded what must be regarded as ritual deposits, as well as some possible discarded or lost items. The Battersea shield, with its La Tène curls and its bronze loops, does not fall into the latter category. It is likely that the shield was deposited there as a votive offering, perhaps a memorial to a famous warrior, or perhaps by a new settler from Gaul making a supplication to ensure he would prosper in his new home. The shield reveals a high level of craftsmanship and would have belonged to a man of considerable wealth. It retains many Celtic aspects in its design but also has typically Roman elements such as the use of enamel and symmetry, which was not a feature of the Celtic style. It seems likely that this work was commissioned, possibly by a Belgic settler who would have assimilated various characteristics of Roman and Gallic style. Despite the richness of artefacts such as this one, and deposits found at places such as Wandsworth, the Thames' banks remained sparsely populated in the Iron Age. Its tributaries were occupied, and the Catuvellaunian lands spreading from Cassivellaunus' centre at Wheathampstead may well have reached as far as today's Croydon.

What we do see emerging is a recognition of Londinium as a crossroads, a remarkable frontier town almost in the tradition of the Old West, built on commerce. From the evidence of Belgic coin distribution it is possible to plot a route from Londinium to Wheathampstead, the sparse number of coins suggesting these were lost by travellers making their way along the route which would develop into Watling Street, linking the Catuvellauni settlement at Verlamion, the increasingly Romanized Cantiaci territory and possibly Camulodunum. The significance of Londinium as the crossroads of the south-east undoubtedly accounts for some of its later development.

Elsewhere, tighter and more numerous finds of coins show us where there was settlement. A strong concentration of coins is just one of several archaeological indicators that suggest large settlement areas spreading from Staines to Kew dating from around the first century BC. There are coins of Gallic/Belgic origin from what would be considered as Londinium proper, but these could well have been brought by the conquest, as local coins remained in circulation into the Roman period.

At Kew in the west and Walthamstow in the north, we have evidence of gold coinage and also, that rare archaeological commodity, 'change', tin coins. These deposits seem to represent the fullest pre-Roman monetary spectrum in the area. Walthamstow's position near a crossing point of the Lea could explain the prevalence of coinage. Perhaps a ferryman exacted a toll to cross, or there could have been a trading settlement nearby. Tasciovanus, whose son Cunobelin was responsible for colonizing most of the south-east for the Catuvellauni, had a wide spread of influence, though this seems to have extended only as far as east London.

There is evidence that Tasciovanus was in coalition with other tribes, for example, the Nervii, whose territory yields both his coins and also a specially minted coin unique to the area, presumably for the use of that tribe alone. His son seems to have gone one step further and pushed the Nervii out of their territory. So these two Catuvellaunian chiefs were obviously powerful and wanted to extend the empire of their tribe, taking in the north bank of the Thames as a matter of course.

Southwark and Westminster seem to have provided the most attractive sites for settlement due to their proximity and, presumably, their safety from the tides, but even here settlement seems to have been sparse. Southwark gives us Iron Age pottery beneath early Roman buildings, and coins associated with it giving a broad chronology of 50 years from 25 BC to AD 25.[1] The grave of a young man has been found under later Roman development,[2] and at Harper Road a woman was buried in the mid-first century AD. Her coffin contained a torc and an imported mirror, probably marking the last resting placed of one of the early post-conquest settlers. Who she was remains a mystery, but her discovery raises fascinating questions about the status of Romanized Celtic women in the years immediately before Boudicca's rising.

The lack of pre-conquest settlement evidence could well be explained by the fact that the idea of centralized sedentism still had not fully taken hold. As we have seen, Camulodunum, which grew into a very significant Roman city, was only a relatively small settlement even at the height of its Celtic life as a royal residence. It is really with the arrival of Rome that we begin to see wholesale centralization of population, industry, commerce and politics.

We have seen that the army under Plautius crossed the Thames in 43 and waited for the arrival of Claudius to march north to Camulodunum. The armys crossing place has been hypothesized by Fuentes and Higgins as somewhere between Westminster and Tilbury, but this still leaves much to speculation.

It is certain that the waiting army would have built a camp large enough to house an invasion force that was still to be supplemented by the emperor, his *comites* and his elephants, and it would not have been any smaller than the camp that was built at Camulodunum prior to the huge legionary fortress. Sadly, as at Camulodunum, no such camp has yet been discovered. However, the strategic significance of the crossing if nothing else would have been recognized by Rome, the site to be kept provisioned by some kind of settlement or fort so it would appear that here we are at the inception of Londinium as a significant place, whence its development has continued to this day.

From the Roman military perspective, Londinium was a central point for movement anywhere in the south-east; into the Catuvellauni lands in Hampshire; north to the East Anglia of the Iceni and the Trinovantes and, when it became necessary, to Lincoln; north-west to Worcester and into the West to clash with Caratacus. The huge logistical potential of the Thames could not have escaped them. From the coast, which had doubtless been carefully examined by the Classis Britannicus, the army could transport supplies far inland to a point where they could then be sent off on the major routes to provision towns and supply soldiers. It would therefore make sense to establish somewhere to control this traffic. It is difficult to determine how much planning went into establishing Londinium. It seems that Claudius had his eyes set on Camulodunum for his administrative centre in Britain, so the theories of London being established as the administrative centre of the province after the conquest may not necessarily be accurate. It probably does represent the hub of fiscal and perhaps even military organization, but the *lex colonia* of Camulodunum probably made the latter the more Romanized city. It is likely that, by 60, the *procurator* Catus Decianus was already based in Londinium.

In the absence of any immediate post-conquest settlement evidence, it has to be assured that the town grew from its road system. It is difficult to date these, as the chronology of the building of the different routes to the Thames covers a relatively short timescale. In places they could represent post-Boudiccan routes established with the rebuilding of the city after her attack, and in others it is likely that they grew with the trading town of the Claudian years.

Londinium is unlikely to have been established until the road system and a crossing of the Thames had been constructed. Evidence of such a system appears to us in the form of roads across the marshland at Southwark. These were built between 50 and 55, and it is towards the end of this

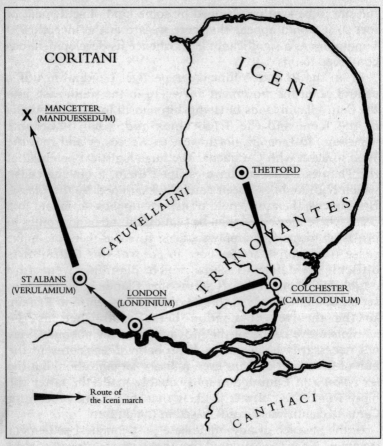

CORITANI

ICENI

X MANCETTER
(MANDUESSEDUM)

⊙ THETFORD

CATUVELLAUNI

TRINOVANTES

ST ALBANS
(VERULAMIUM) ⊙

LONDON
(LONDINIUM)

COLCHESTER
(CAMULODUNUM)

Route of
the Iceni march

CANTIACI

Boudicca's campaign, 60/61

period that the buildings probably begin to appear. This ties in with the appearance of poorly struck Claudian coins in large numbers, dating from the later years of the emperor's reign, essentially 50 to 54. Although this does not give us a definitive chronology, it does point towards expansion in trade.

Evidence to support the theory that London grew from its road system is found in the appearance of buildings along Watling Street. These were clearly planned, but do not present a purely military function, along the east–west wall. But there is also contrary evidence. There are several burials on the site which do not seem to have any formal distribution in terms of Roman practices – they occur within the site, not outside a boundary. This suggests two things: firstly, that Londinium was not typical in Roman town planning, and secondly, it had no form of defence or boundary. The second point is confused, as there is evidence of a substantial ditch at Aldgate and Fenchurch Street containing Claudian debris. Elsewhere post holes indicate a possible palisade. More telling is the evidence of burnt buildings on top of filled-in defences; again, as with Camulodunum, development over defence. The appearance of ditches and palisading could represent a fort, but inconsistencies in the material evidence, and not least the regularity of the ditch, suggest that we could be dealing with a series of small compounds, perhaps a store such as that at Richborough, a stable or even a garrison building.

The argument that Londinium is not typical is undeniable. The irregular street system jars with the notion of the town growing out of a fort, and yet there is little evidence of urban domestication. It appears that Londinium, even in our period, was emerging not as a Roman town in the truest sense, with a toga-clad officialdom, but a commercial centre run by local entrepreneurs and foreign interlopers – a cosmopolitan settlement from the first.

By 60 the centre at Cornhill, now roughly the area of Leadenhall Market, had become fully established and was beginning to spread out. It had its own water system, shown to us by an iron collar found in a pipeline under Boudiccan debris, the wooden pipe doubtless burnt away by the destructive force of the fire. Painted plaster, too, came out of the Boudiccan conflagration debris. A large building with burnt grain presents itself as a store. There is industrial debris at Fenchurch Street, from iron- and bronze-working and glass-blowing. Engraved gems and intaglios show the existence of luxury crafts, the gems doubtless coming from Europe. The production of luxury items would suggest there was a market for such goods. One burnt building has an enclosure associated with it, possibly for gardens, and it may just have been a civic building, perhaps the offices of Decianus himself. With no evidence of governmental civic buildings, however, a picture emerges of a strong mercantile population. There are richly furnished burials with ceramics, glass and other luxuries associated with them, but these could just as easily have been visiting merchants as Roman colonists. These burials appear on the perimeters of the town, which suggests that its layout became more typical, but they are associated with houses along the side of the road, which is not typical.

On the town's outskirts, there is evidence of indigenous peoples settling, the buildings contemporary in style with those of the town, but further out becoming more typically British. There is evidence of small-scale smithery here, too, with hearths, and bronze and iron debris. This suggests that the local people were taking advantage of the commercial town, and it is easy to imagine open markets on the roads to London with people selling their wares. In the rebuilding of Southwark after Boudicca, there is direct evidence for 'shopfronts' of gravel. This development would echo and re-echo down the centuries as London grew beyond its walls with ever-increasing bustle and importance.

Thus the growth of London was probably kick-started by a military presence; the plethora of 'small change' coinage and evidence of military equipment in the surrounding area supports this. It would therefore have attracted merchants and, as a good supply route, would have been useful for the army. But once it began to move elsewhere and other larger places were developed, such as the huge legionary fortress at Camulodunum, the army probably became dispersed around the country to hold the lines of an expanding frontier. By this time markets may well have already been in place, and administration would have been needed to control the flow of supplies to towns and to the army. The fact that the *procurator* Catus Decianus was almost certainly in Londinium supports this, and the fact that he was only able to send 200 badly armed troops to the aid of Camulodunum suggests that the military presence had withdrawn – either that, or Decianus feared that he would be next. He was right.

By the time Gaius Paulinus had reached Londinium, the

procurator had run to Gaul, almost certainly by ship along the Thames and across the Channel to Portus Itius. Tacitus pulls no punches in his analysis of blame: 'It was his rapacity which had driven the province to war.'[3]

The legate had marched through what Tacitus calls 'disaffected territory', although how he got there is uncertain. Mona is 250 miles from Londinium, and Graham Webster conjectures that to save time Paulinus took a galley from the Menai Strait and rowed to Deva, modern Chester, before galloping south-east with his cavalry. Behind him his tired legions slogged, licking their wounds from Mona, shaking themselves free of the memory of the Druids and their banshee women, taking the land route through the territory of the Ordovices.

Paulinus reached the ramshackle collection of huts that was Londinium before Boudicca. Again, Antonia Fraser offers debauchery and drunkenness as the reason for the Iceni's delay. It was two days' march between Camulodunum and Londinium, but there may have been arguments in the war councils as to what the next target should be, and time was needed to cope with Cerialis and IX. Graham Webster also assumes that the Iceni were out of control, bypassing strongholds, as Tacitus says, and going for the soft centres of least resistance.

When the legate arrived with his lathered, sweating cavalry, a deputation came to him begging for help; but Paulinus turned his back. 'Unmoved by lamentations and appeals,' wrote Tacitus, '[Paulinus] gave the signal for departure.' Those who could – the young, the wealthy – were allowed to follow the cavalry north in search of the legions hurrying behind. The others – the old, the very young, the women – were to be sacrificed for the sake of a province. Tacitus paints an unwittingly moving picture of these first Londoners, saying that some stayed behind because they were 'attached to the place'; it would be the same in the Blitz in 1940.

What else could Paulinus have done? He almost certainly threw out a screen of cavalry to the north, and his scouts probably reported the Iceni on their way, roaring their defiance and perhaps carrying the captured standards of the shattered Hispana and the heads of its soldiers. There was no fortress strong enough or near enough to defend, and the rough wooden warehouses along the river would burn like matchsticks under the torches of the Iceni. Cerialis and IX were beaten and had run north. Even if Paulinus had already sent word to Exeter and II Augusta under their camp prefect, it would be days before they arrived. His one hope lay in reuniting with his infantry and picking his ground and his moment to face Boudicca. And he was gone before the Iceni arrived.

We have no precise details of the attack. The Iceni, says Tacitus, 'could not wait to cut throats, hang, burn and crucify, as though avenging, in advance, any retribution that was on its way.'[4] There was no palisade to hold them, no garrison to block their way. The townspeople of Londinium were traders, metalworkers, weavers and spinners. There were no veterans here to try to organize a rudimentary defence. Tacitus tells us they were 'slaughtered by the enemy'. Dio plunges into the full horror of an early example of total war which has dogged Boudicca's reputation ever since:

> Those who were taken captive by the Britons were subjected to every known form of outrage . . . They hung up naked the noblest and most distinguished women and then cut off their breasts and sewed them to their mouths, in order to make the victims appear to be eating them; afterwards they impaled the women on sharp skewers run lengthwise through the entire body . . .[5]

The focus on women is fascinating. Does this refer to a Celtic ritual of which we know nothing? Were the female victims some sort of inverted version of Boudicca herself in that the targets seem to be high-born? Was this a punishment for Celtic women having slept voluntarily with Roman men? Or is this Dio, writing on behalf of a nation that crucified men for laughs and pitted women against lions in the arena, desperate to depict cruelty greater than that habitually inflicted by Rome?

Boudicca's forces took Londinium in what was probably less than a single day, and burned it extensively. There is significant evidence of burning along Milk Street, King Street and Oxford

Street. Boudicca, or a contingent of the Horse People, seems to have crossed the river by a bridge and burned shops in Southwark lying on the main route, heading naturally to a crossing that must already have existed. The Iceni possibly burnt and destroyed the bridge – there is no evidence for one now. But the facts are not as clear as at Camulodunum, which suggests that the destruction of Londinium was not as important, symbolically. Londinium had not taken on the overtly Roman nature of Camulodunum or indeed Verlamium. Indeed, for all Tacitus' lament for those abandoned to die by Paulinus, it is possible that on reaching Londinium Boudicca found it largely empty. It stands to reason that the merchants would have had boats, and the port may have been deserted when Boudicca arrived to put it to the torch.

The destruction of Londinium may have appealed to Boudicca as being the severance of a major commercial centre. Because we know so little of her, however, it is just as likely that she burned it because she came across it on her way to the next target of Verlamium, and we doubt she stayed to watch it burn, as the Iceni doubtless did at Camulodunum. This could explain why the evidence for burning is so sparse, because the fire was not so intense. And again, despite Dio's graphic description of wholesale slaughter, where are the bodies? If the three skulls found in the Walbrook stream are examples of the queen's handiwork – the ritual beheading of enemies – it hardly constitutes a massacre.

The single producer of Samian ware that has been identified in Londinium does not seem to reappear after Boudicca,[6] but he could just as easily have fled downriver with the merchants as gone down before an Iceni blade.

It is ironic that Boudicca's destruction of Londinium probably led to its being rebuilt with more verve. After Boudicca's attack the town appears to have remained sparsely occupied, but then it quickly developed into a prosperous and important city. The shops at Southwark were rebuilt bigger and better, and the town spread out into a more vibrant metropolis. It was already showing signs of significant progress before it was cut down in its prime by Boudicca, but it is interesting to hypothesize as to how far it would have developed. For example, Julius Classicianus has a memorial dedicated to him in London. He is known and indeed revered as being the *procurator* and primary rebuilder of London, sharing not only a definite administrative importance with the town but also a special mention in its rebuilding.

But all this lay in the future. The Iceni and their flame-haired queen were turning north-west, to Verlamium.

Verlamium, ancient St Albans, is an interesting site with varied artefacts. It is difficult to imagine the Roman city today. The excellent museum, built in Roman style at one corner of the imposing basilica erected years after Boudicca's death, stands in quiet parkland where ducks dabble in the lake and children play on swings. The modern bustle of St Albans is almost invisible from here, in the low-lying valley of the Ver, and even the roar of traffic seems curiously stilled. Home to the Catuvellauni, and a settlement with undeniable Roman influence, it is difficult to decide whether it was a key Roman centre or indeed whether its indigenous population was fully Romanized. Calling them indigenous is an anomaly, as the Catuvellauni had probably only arrived on the site around a hundred years previously, as the tribe extended its power across central Britain. The site itself had a high-status nucleus, the King Harry Lane cemetery and the famously rich Folly Lane burial showing evidence of a definite hierarchical order which may have-sharpened by strong links with Rome. It was also the site of a royal mint. The surrounding area was very rural, however, and, as Dio tells us that this was laid waste by Boudicca, it is odd that there is no evidence for destruction outside these centres.

The Catuvellauni were hostile towards those Trinovantes who marched with Boudicca, so why did they not ravage their enemies? The whole nature of Celtic tribal society was internecine. Those who see Boudicca's rising as the first struggling flame of independence and nationalism are misguided. It would be perfectly logical for the Trinovantes with Boudicca to exact appalling revenge for past slights, real or imagined. This possibility opens a veritable can of worms. We must look at the town, its history and at least partial destruction by Boudicca. But we must also examine the possible social implications and divisions that explain why Boudicca knew when to stop.

So let us begin with the conquerors, this time not from Rome. The Catuvellauni were the most heavily Belgic-influenced tribe in the area, with a hierarchy similar to that encountered by Caesar in Gaul. The Belgic peoples were associated with an undercurrent of conquest and influence both before his time and between the two invasions of Britain by Rome. Pottery from the period follows Belgic influence, and the same people have been identified as prime protagonists in the affirmation of burial rites, not just in the artefacts found in grave goods deposits but also the laying out of cremations and enclosed cemetery sites. This is important because it sheds light on the structure of tribal development. These developments, as with later Roman influence, did not preclude previous cultural undertakings, but merely set new precedents and trends. This suggests either an ability on the part of the tribal groups to adapt to external influence, a need to have a more uniform identity, or a need to develop their own culture by looking elsewhere. On the other side of the coin it could show that certain groups were easy to conquer, though willingness to capitulate does not fit overall pattern we see with the rebellions of Caratacus and Boudicca, as well as other, less well-documented disturbances. At various times the Catuvellauni, Trinovantes, Iceni, Dobunni, Brigantes, Ordovices and Silures all fought against Rome, and against each other. There is in fact little evidence that the Catuvellauni had to destroy any existing tribe to become the dominant culture, except at Letchworth. A refortified hill fort there was destroyed by fire in earlier strata. The layers contain large amounts of Belgic pottery where before there was none. This could identify the Catuvellauni as the conquering arsonists. Evidence of pitched battle rarely survives in this period (which makes Manduessedum, in the end, merely a tentative site), but it is interesting to postulate a small-scale campaign on the part of the Catuvellauni, possibly after the Roman invasion, showing a further influence, that of organized campaigning. Whether or not they had taken territory by force, the Catuvellauni had been opposed to

Caesar in modern Hertfordshire, and we see Verlamion appear as a centre after the initial conquest. This could indicate that the Catuvellauni grew, out of opposition to Rome, into a cohesive group, or that political elements led to their establishing a centre with or without Roman influence.

Verlamion was established around 20 BC by Tasciovanus, who also gives us first-hand evidence of the place being a royal mint in this period: his name was struck on coins found on the site along with crucibles and coin moulds, all on display in the local museum.

The early site was only lightly defended with small surrounding ditches, and possibly a timber palisade to the east. These light fortifications might suggest it was not a royal centre of any sort, let alone the Catuvellauni capital; however, we should not be too easily disuaded. The lack of defences could be indicative of the time. The evidence points to the overriding superiority of the tribe; in effect, there was no fear of attack, so there was no need for elaborate defence. Early cultures rarely seem to have provisioned themselves unless out of necessity, having only just emerged over the previous few hundred years from an intensely parochial and purely self-sustaining lifestyle into the trading world.

If the Catuvellauni were the undisputed dominant group in the area, Verlamion may well have been a royal site. It could equally have been a temporary palatial site for Tasciovanus while he moved around his territory, although Verlamion is really the most obvious site for a centre. The peregrinations of kings continued until the reign of Elizabeth I. Before that, rulers roved the countryside with their households and retainers, descending on castle, abbey and town. If this was true of Celtic kings, it would explain the lack of any large central capital, for example, among the Iceni.

Another possibility is that, even with meagre defence, Verlamion still presented itself as a well-protected site in terms of the surrounding area, which was very rural. As such, the appearance of palisading would make a site like Verlamion stand out. Linked with this is a well-represented idea in the archaeology of a defended site, that of status rather than protection. In effect, the defences showed that a powerful people controlled the site, and were not built to withstand large-scale attack. This is a hypothesis much suggested for the dyke built several hundred years later by King Offa of Mercia, originally supposed to keep border raiders from Wales out of his kingdom. However, gaps in its construction have led to the suggestion that this was Offa flexing his muscles rather than making an out-and-out attempt at defence. Later castles like the magnificent, moated Bodiam in Sussex *look* impressive, but they could easily be taken in the event of a real war. Essentially, any individual or tribe who could control and coordinate that amount of resource would be a force to be reckoned with, and these structures were warnings, rather than enticements, to those who had a mind to take something worth defending. This could be the case on a smaller scale with Verlamion, a big architectural fish in a small settlement pond.

The dominance of the Catuvellauni is shown not just through destruction and construction of buildings and towns. South of Verlamion, at Park Street, there was found what has been interpreted as a slave chain, similar to finds at Llyn Cerig Bach and Camulodunum. If the chain indicates regular use of slaves, then this could be a tangible reminder of the workforce employed in building defences for the town or in the manufacture of other objects. It is unlikely that this would have included high-status skilled work, as artisans were revered by the Celts. At Park Street there is evidence of skilled carpentry and metalwork, so perhaps the slaves could have been a purely agricultural workforce.

The appearance of crude burials of individuals who suffered from poor health could also indicate this slave population, along with evidence for small buildings on farmsteads too small for stores, barns or the farm centre. It is difficult to say where the slaves could have come from. They could have been the tribe in residence prior to the Catuvellaunian occupation or they could have been taken from surrounding tribal groups. They could have been criminals or political prisoners, but with no evidence of tribal interaction away from Rome and with little material evidence, this remains one of the many questions about the Celts that will probably never be answered.

The importance of the site itself can be looked at in terms of its topography, size, its development and surroundings. The River Ver, now a trickle, could well have been a significant body of water in the Late Iron Age and Roman period and, according to archaeologist Rosalind Niblett, could very possibly have been navigable by flat-bottomed boats. This would have made Verlamion an important trade centre, not an *oppida* on the scale of Camulodunum, perhaps, but a manufacturing site with raw materials such as iron coming in from the Weald and Northamptonshire. As we have seen, iron was identified by the Greek geographer Strabo as Britain's main export, and features in quality items such as the horse furniture for chariots and the brooches found at the Folly Lane burial. Equally, the centre of culture, which initially had strong Belgic and transcontinental links, could have received goods from Europe via the inland waterways, which we know to have been developing in the first half of the first century AD.

The importance of the town can also be seen in political and social terms. Tasciovanus' predecessor, Cassivellaunus, was the first Catuvellaunian leader to enter into agreement with Rome. True, he had put up important resistance to Caesar, but his negotiations, whatever precise form they took, set a precedent successive next generations of kings. As a result, Verlamion formed the civiccentre of a people who were allowed a fair amount of autonomy.

This could suggest that the town had not joined with Caratacus and that, therefore, he was acting independently of the rest of his tribe. It could also highlight the fact that the country was still very much made up of different small tribes acting independently of each other. However, it is the archaeological record which gives us an excellent indication of the real story of Verlamion's survival. There is evidence of refortification and extension of the town's defences which appears to be contemporary with the Claudian conquest. Did Caratacus' rebel army plan to halt the Roman advance into the north-west? Perhaps they were not successful enough to get to Verlamion and so did not oppose the legions when they arrived. But this did not prevent Rome from building a fort near the Ver, which adds credence to its importance as a centre of some kind by 43 or 44.

The fort was used to control supplies and troops moving to the Midlands along the River Lea which would place it probably along Watling Street at the point where it cut across the river. Initially temporary, a more permanent fort was built on quite a large scale, around 425 feet long. This was likely to have been occupied by an auxiliary cohort – military hardware of *auxilia* equipment found at the site adds weight to this idea. The appearance of a fort housing up to 500 troops would facilitate the growth of a town. However, much of the development was away from the fort. Verlamion became Verulamium, an important political centre for Rome, and self-government followed – the creation of what the Romans called a *civitas* – between 43 and 60.

Despite this new status, most settlements still existed outside the centre and remained fundamentally rural. Enclosure did increase, however, suggesting series of farmsteads and a concentration of production such as pottery and weaving. The interpretation of the fort's function is difficult. At some time before 60 it was demolished, and the material used to build other constructions. This would seem to suggest that the fort was only temporary to keep the centre in check as it had been associated, at least by affiliation, with the previous problems of Caratacus' stand. Now the political situation was stable enough to remove the fort, an action replay of the lax defences which had laid Camulodunum open to Boudicca's attack. The building that has been interpreted as having been a fort has no real proper dating evidence, although Verulamium's chronology and construction would support its being post conquest rather than post Boudicca, as Verulamium was not rebuilt for some time after the Boudiccan rebellion.

But if the centre had become politically important, why remove something that could be used for defence? It is likely that with the town now flourishing and the military population no doubt being at least partly integrated into society, the town, which had a series of internal dykes, did not need a military construction: there is no record of warfare in the area between 44 and 60.

The town's development moved on apace in the twenty years between the Claudian conquest and Boudicca's rebellion.

It is in this period that we see the importance of Verulamium in Romano-British terms, which helps us make observations for its significance as a whole. It was fast developing an organised street system, including a 'high street', with evidence of shops, including a high-status glazier's, as well as stalls that sold imported pottery. Bronze fragments found there have been from a bronze statue. Was this a Roman deity associated with Verulamium's Roman temple or a Romano-Catuvellaunian hero? It is difficult to say. It is also difficult to say if Boudicca destroyed it, as the fragments could be refuse from the statue's construction. A bronze knife from just outside Verulamium demonstrates that the Catuvellauni had a high knowledge of metalwork from the second and third centuries BC. The series of dykes has been interpreted in part as pre-Roman; for example, a ditch under the post-Boudiccan forum (*c.* 75 AD) had evidence of heavy silting, which suggests it was cut a fair time before the Claudian invasion. However, it is not clear whether these dykes were constructed contemporaneously. It seems likely, because of their scale, that they were built in phases and they could well have gone in and out of use throughout the town's history. Furthermore, their interpretation could fall in with the idea of status rather than defence as their sheer scale would suggest they were to a large extent unmanned. For example, to the north an arm runs towards the river, useful for both the pre-Claudian town and the Roman military presence there. It seems likely that these boundaries were largely in place before the arrival of Rome, but it was probably Rome, or a response to Rome, that expanded them. For example, we do not know if the substantial dykes, White and Nas, had smaller precursors. The town itself filled an area of around two hectares around the central enclosure. It lay in a valley, the plateau being dotted with lesser buildings which were probably domestic sites.

As we have seen, there is strong evidence for coin manufacture at Verulamium. In the north-east corner of the central enclosure there seems to have existed the major concentration of workshops belonging to the minters. Both Tasciovanus and Cunobelin have VIS or VERLAMIS on their coins which adds credence to the idea of the mint being in or near the town. The appearance of mould slabs, gold, silver, bronze and iron has been associated with the production of ingots and not necessarily the actual striking of coin. The name on the coins has also been interpreted as a reference to the ingot production. However, it is very tangible and it is likely that they were struck in or around here.

As with many sites of this pre-Christian period, much useful artefactual evidence comes to us from grave goods, burial sites and ritual sites; Verulamium and its surroundings are no exception.

The nature of Verulamium's ritual history and the length of use of sites suggests that its appearance must have affected the inhabitants spiritually to a large extent; this adds to its importance, essentially as a centre of religion. The landscape could well have appealed to spiritual ideas: deep woodland in the valley itself, and the banks of the Ver with its waters sparkling, almost ghostly, waiting for supplication.

At nearby Essenden an irregular ditched enclosure has yielded deliberate deposition of spears, swords, ingots, torcs and coins dating from the first century BC to the first century AD. This implies a warrior elite, perhaps connected with Caratacus, Boudicca or even the Roman soldiers who garrisoned the wooden fort on the river or its larger predecessor. The appearance of weaponry gives us an insight into the culture and history of Verulamium. Did Caratacus, fighting a rearguard action near here, make an offering to Belinos, the god of war? Did the hoard form a memorial to those lost in battle or a supplication to protect the town from Rome? Did the town's Romanized citizens make a similar offering to protect them from Boudicca?

Friars Walsh in the same area shows evidence of a triple dyke from the Late Iron Age. Strange or overly elaborate organization of an enclosure often sets it apart from others, as does artefactual evidence with it. Friars Walsh is no exception and forms a significant Romano-British cult site well after Boudicca and within the period of the new, rebuilt Verulamium. Ritual significance and the importance of spiritual culture is demonstrated best, however, in the burials found in and around the old centre.

Near the post-Boudiccan town we see the King Harry Lane

cemetery. It was excavated in the late 1960s and remains one of Europe's largest Late Iron Age cemeteries, with 455 cremations and seventeen inhumations. There is evidence of at least eight ditched burial enclosures, with others having probably been weathered away. The true extent of this burial ground could be even more substantial, but sadly modern construction precludes excavation to confirm its extent; this also makes it difficult to establish the area that it served. But there are some particularly ornate grave and pyre offerings with these burials, and the burials themselves have a strong central concentration suggesting an elite. However, unaccompanied inhumations buried in the ditches of the burial enclosures and at their entrances could be interpreted as the graves of a lower social order, possibly guards or servants of those buried opulently in the centre, servile in death as they may have been in life. Although there is no evidence from this period of deliberate killing with edged weapons, murder is not wholly impossible, as we have clear evidence in early cultures of the use of potions, for example, the Funnel Beaker culture.

Remedies and poisons alike have formed an important part of historical culture, many 'old wives' tales' being based on ancient remedy until recent times. These were used to kill as well as cure; hemlock, deadly nightshade and yew berries are all referred to as poisons in scientific works, with writers such as Shakespeare, as well as conventional historians, describinh thetimely or untimely deaths of some of history's most famous and infamous characters. As we shall see, part of the legend of Boudicca is that she poisoned herself. Why not here? The traces of most natural poisons would have vanished by now, so it would not be possible to tell. A similar possibility is ritual strangulation; if a 'victim' were willing to follow a leader into the afterlife, a strangulation would not necessarily show on a skeleton, unless the vertebrae or hyoid bone had snapped. However, most 'sacrificial' victims were normally treated with more reverence, as we have seen in the case of Lindow Man. The peripheral burials could simply be slaves, however, whose social standing precluded a properly furnished burial.

The chronology of the site was originally interpreted as running from 10 BC to AD 60, but this has since been revised to the period 25 BC to AD 43. Clearly, without archaeological access to the whole site the full extent cannot be realized, leaving full dating and social representation unprovable. It would appear, however, that there are no Boudiccan 'victims' here, which suggests we are not dealing with the wholesale slaughter described by Tacitus and Dio; after all, such a large, well-established site would undoubtedly have been a natural resting place for any victims.

St Stephen's cemetery, 500 yards east of the King Harry Lane site, shows close grouping suggestive of possible family or tribal groups, and although dating evidence puts its predominant period of use in the third century – by which time Verulamium was a fully fledged Roman town with unique theatre, an impressive basilica, forum and hypocaust system – other evidence puts initial use at soon after the Claudian invasion, and faint traces of other enclosures suggest possible earlier boundaries. Indeed, it may have been a dynastic site of the Catuvellauni. The type of person buried there appears to be neither very rich nor very poor, a middling sort who could represent the families living around Verlamion in farmsteads and individual settlements.

In social terms, burial evidence is very telling. Richly furnished burials are very often found in a central position with poorer ones occurring on perimeters, often as simple inhumations unceremoniously dumped in pits such as those outside Verulamium. The bones of these people showed signs of illnesses such as tuberculosis and osteoarthritis, diseases associated with endemic poor health. These remains have been plausibly interpreted as the bones of slaves who had no place in established burial sites within the town or outside it.

At the other end of the scale, one of the finest examples of a 'chieftain burial' comes to us from Verlamion, at Folly Lane. The so-called 'chieftain burials' were originally thought to be unique to the area around Welwyn. One such site, excavated in 1965 at Panshanger on the edge of what today is Welwyn Garden City, revealed five wine amphorae, a silver cup and thirty-six other vessels, together with glass gaming pieces which show strong Roman influence. Sites such as these show the importance of feasting and entertainment in the afterlife.

Folly Lane is a post-conquest burial that shows clear indigenous trends as well as Roman influence. The site covers two hectares and contains only a single cremated burial at its centre. The sheer size of it suggests that the site hosted a large ritual cremation. There is a rich collection of pyre goods. The sunken funerary chamber at the centre housed the cremated remains and at least thirty-two vessels, including high-status material imported from Gaul. Precious metals – 2.5 kilograms of molten silver, bronze and enamelled horse gear – also survive along with an ivory chair and a mail tunic. This last item had clearly been placed in the grave and not worn around a body. The chamber had been destroyed and filled in, the end of a reverential ritual with feasting around the body, possibly before and during the burning. Three inhumations are found at the enclosure's entrance, again showing belief in the possibility of guards in the afterlife.

This was obviously a very important individual, a prince, a king, perhaps a queen. It is not the last resting place of Boudicca, but the appearance of the mail shirt suggests an individual revered as a warrior, possibly even revered by Rome, as the site remained free from Roman destruction. A section of a lorica, a Roman breastplate, and Roman horse furniture have been found associated with the grave. The particularly tribal nature of the burial, however, suggests little Roman influence and also points to this being an individual important to the native people, as the burial seems very much in keeping with pre-Roman concepts. Could this represent the burial of Togodumnos or another rebel leader, buried with a secret identity but with all the trappings of a tribal hero, including Roman trophies he or she acquired? We know from Tacitus that Togodumnos died in or soon after the battle on the Thames in 43. As the crow flies, Verlamion is only twenty miles from the likely battlefield.

If we accept the version of commentators of the day, namely, Tacitus and Dio, we come to an event that should have caused hundreds of burials: the destruction of Verulamium. Advancing from the sack of Londinium and moving north-west, the screaming, clamouring hordes poured into the valley, the blue-painted, spike-haired Iceni destroying all in their wake. No house was left unburned, no beast left alive nor any human. Blood flowed like water, the screams of the dying and the roar of the flames fusing into some awful symphony, the blaze lighting the sky as if a beacon of death had been lit.

Dramatic? Yes. Accurate? Unlikely. This little piece of artistic licence on our part forms an implausible account of the scale of destruction at Verulamium, if the archaeology of the area teaches us anything.

The lack of a fort would seem to preclude the need for any pitched battle, although around one hundred lead slingshot of the kind used by auxiliary forces, often taken from local populations, have been found. These could be associated with the defence of Verulamium against Boudicca, but they could just as easily point to the conflict of the Claudian invasion. The lack of other weaponry suggests the site could also be a cache or training ground. Tacitus wrote:

> . . . those who stayed [in London] because they were women, or old, or attached to the place, were slaughtered by [Boudiccan forces] . . . Verulamium suffered the same fate.

Not exactly. There is evidence of possible attack burial: eight hurriedly buried individuals outside the city gates and a female burial in a ditch. This is hardly wholesale slaughter and definitely not Boudiccan. We realise that an argument for mass graves, or else the victims being burned with the town, is possible, but no mass graves have been discovered. Roman writers do not give separate figures for Verulamium, but an estimated seventy thousand reputedly died there and at Camulodunum and Londinium. Can we accept that where evidence of burning has been found we are talking about cremated thousands kept there until they turned to ash, the ashes then scattered so that no significant deposit of burnt bone could be found by archaeologists almost 2,000 years later?

It is the destruction of the town itself that helps us with some possible interpretations as to what kind of war Boudicca was waging. The shops that lined Watling Street, the producers and suppliers of high status and imported material, provide evidence of burning and destruction. Some interpreted timber buildings in the centre also carry evidence of burning, and those could possibly have been civic buildings or even temporary barracks. The bathhouse which appears under the post-Boudiccan forum, or basilica, is a clear symbol of Romanization and offers at least partial evidence of destruction.

The surrounding area, however, remains untouched – and the soft targets that were the farmsteads and settlements of Praewood, Essenden and Gorhambury would surely have offered easy pickings to the savage Iceni horde depicted by Tacitus. In fact Gorhambury appears to be a particularly high-status site, containing much imported material and the remnants of a villa of the late first century AD. However, it remains seemingly untouched, which is strange, surely, if the 'natives enjoyed plundering and nothing else'. The fact that Gorhambury has clear pre-Roman significance could answer this riddle. It has a significant enclosure and is clearly Belgic-influenced and therefore pre-Roman. Artefacts found there suggest this was a local residence of some importance before Claudius. It may well have remained so and Boudicca therefore had no wish to attack it. We would argue that Boudicca was not out for wholesale slaughter and looting, and neither were her forces. She was after all not 'fighting for [her] kingdom and wealth', but as 'an ordinary person for [her] lost freedom'. Even Tacitus admits that. Boudicca was attacking Rome and its symbols. The destruction of civic and public buildings was intended to wipe Rome from the landscape exactly as at Colonia Claudia, which had suffered a much more devastating destruction. Boudicca was not a primitive but a patriot, and had risen above tribal infighting to look at things from a higher level, to unite and be free, just as Caratacus and Togodumnos, brothers once divided, united under a shared hatred for Rome.

This theory is borne out by what happened at Verulamium after the Boudiccan revolt. It lay dormant for over a decade and then developed into a significant *civitas*, with a fort, forum and temple, the centre surrounded by villas. The reason it lay dormant for such a period could be due to Roman fear of reprisals or local rebellion again destroying what they tried to rebuild. It could be that the area lay untouched until the

Romans regained interest in it. But it is more likely, surely, that the 'dormant' period represents a period of construction and only temporary habitation; construction of a full and glorious embodiment of Rome, finally stamping on the flames of Boudicca's heritage by replacing what she had tried to destroy in glorious technicolour.

As with Londinium, the Iceni probably did not linger long at the conflagration along the Ver. They had destroyed three Roman towns and over half a legion. Surely nothing could stop them now? They marched ever north-west, to Manduessedum, the place of the chariots.

9
Mars Ultor

We know the wars prepared
On every peaceful home,
We know the hells declared
For such as serve not Rome . . .
'Ulster', Rudyard Kipling

The battle was over. We tried to picture it on the warm spring day we were there, imagining the heaps of dead on the Anker's flood plain. The bodies were thickest at the base of the hill where the shield phalanxes of XIV Gemina and XX broke through the Iceni ranks. And nearer the river, where the women and children were driven backwards and pinned against their circle of wagons, bodies were hacked by swords, skewered with javelins, arms and legs broken in the panic. Some no doubt would have been crushed under the sheer weight of numbers, their faces blue, their lips swollen, blood trickling from their noses. As we have seen, the women also fought, even the children, snatching up swords, spears, anything with which to defend themselves against the hated Romans.

We cannot accurately imagine what such a battle was like or what its aftermath must have been. Worthy attempts at re-creation, as in the opening action of the film *Gladiator*,[1] can only touch the surface. And what made Manduessedum doubly awful was the presence of so many women, so many children.

Tacitus, not uncritical of his people's empire, but a Roman first, foremost and always, writes of 'almost 80,000 Britons' dead. Paulinus' casualties reached 400 dead, more than that wounded. Many modern authorities have accepted these figures unreservedly – despite casting doubt on the numbers facing each other at the beginning of the battle – but we must remain sceptical. If we are right about the siting of the battle, and allowing for alteration in the Anker's meander over two millennia, there would not have been room for half that number of Britons on the field, still less that number of dead.

It does not detract from the enormity of Boudicca's defeat or the completeness of Paulinus' victory. 'It was a glorious victory,' Tacitus wrote, 'comparable with bygone triumphs.' And it spelt the end of the Iceni.

It was probably dusk on that long summer day before the killing stopped. Weary centurions gave orders to their auxiliaries to strip the dead, collect the weapons and burn the smashed wagons. Wounded men dragged themselves to the river, letting the cold healing water lap their cuts. But the Iceni had already gone that way and the water must have been dark with blood. As the torches were lit and the clerks wandered the field, separating the bodies of friend and foe, the only sound was the whinnying of the cavalry horses and the groans of the dying. At dawn, there would be time to take stock, count heads, answer roll-calls and decide what to do with the prisoners.

Aulus Cornelius Celsus died ten years before Manduessedum, but the eighth and final book in his *Encyclopedia* deals with the operations that the surgeons of XIV and XX carried out somewhere on the slopes near Watling Street. If these men had lived up to Celsus' ideals, they would have been:

> . . . young or at least . . . youngish. [The surgeon] should have a strong and steady hand which never shakes and he should be ready to use his left hand as well as his right. His eyesight should be sharp and clear and he should have courage. He should feel sorry enough for his patient to want

to cure him, but he should not be driven by his cries into working too fast or into cutting out less than is necessary.

Wounds were cauterized with red-hot irons as the darkness grew, searing, red-hot metal sealing the gaping gashes left by sword and spear. Lacerations were bandaged in vinegar-soaked lint to prevent gangrene. After that, it was up to the gods . . .

The Celtic warriors may have been speared or hacked to death, even after the moment of blood was over. We know from Gaius Paulinus' subsequent actions that he was a vengeful commander. He would pursue the policy of *Mars Ultor*, Mars the Avenger, for the next two years until more conciliatory hands stopped him. Tall warriors, their bodies bruised and battered, their lime-streaked hair matted with blood, their gold torcs ripped from their necks, were shackled together and forced to kneel as the legionaries swung Roman swords on their bowed heads.

Perhaps Paulinus turned his back as his troops did what they liked with the Iceni women, the wives and sisters and mothers of the men they had killed. To the victors in any war belong the spoils. The rape of two princesses had begun this war; who knows how many rapes would end it?

Exhausted, numbed by the terrible experience of the previous day, the women and children were perhaps rounded up in chains to be sold in the public auctions of the more civilized south, or in Gaul or Rome itself. These were the offspring of those who had dared to challenge Rome. They could not be allowed to grow, as their fathers had, into a sullen and rebellious people.

What of the rest? The instinct of the survivors would have been to move east, to go home. They had destroyed the hated *colonia* at Camulodunum and with it the offensive Temple of Claudius. They had burned the trading town growing up along the Thames, the likely base of the hated *procurator* Decianus, and had left a charred and blackened wasteland. They had batted aside IX Hispana and seen its commander flee the field in a clatter of horsemen and a gust of plumes. They had flattened with fire the Roman-influenced town along the Ver, the one that had dared to spring up on a sacred site of the

Catuvellauni. Now they were broken, scattered, weakened beyond hope. Andraste, to whom Boudicca had prayed, was not listening. Her place would be taken, as Romanization spread, by the panoply of Roman gods and finally by the most unlikely deity, a Christian corruption of the Hebrew god Yahweh, who had no relevance to the Iceni at all.

'Boudicca poisoned herself.'[2] With that single terse sentence Tacitus consigns the first British heroine to oblivion. Cassius Dio hints that she died from disease. Either is likely, but the weight of probability suggests the first. It is of course possible that the queen was wounded at Manduessedum or that she became ill in whatever pursuit Paulinus mounted in the days after the battle. We do not know what sort of reception the fugitive queen would have received from the Catuvellauni east of Watling Street, or how fast news of her defeat spread. Some of the isolated farmsteads may have given shelter. Others, realizing that where Celts fled, Romans would probably follow, may have barred their doors or even formed armed resistance against the fugitives.

Boudicca's options were now very limited. Her own nobility and large numbers of her people, young and old, male and female, had been destroyed. Wherever she went, Roman vengeance would follow. There were probably insufficient numbers of Iceni to make a second stand. The Catuvellauni, across whose territory her battle-scarred chariot rumbled in those August days, had probably never adopted a complete anti-Roman stance, even in the days of Caratacus, obliging the warlord to move west into Wales for military support. To the north, the Brigantes were a divided people, but their rightful queen was Cartimandua, a friend of Rome who had already handed her allies the head of Caratacus on a plate. She would, given the opportunity, do the same with Boudicca. And Boudicca must have learned by now of the destruction of the Druids on Mona and with them no doubt the flower of the Ordovices and Silures who might once have come to her aid.

She could surrender to the Romans herself. But Paulinus was in no mood to be conciliatory. The ferocity of Boudicca's attacks on Camulodunum, Londinium and Verulamium precluded the awestruck courtesy afforded to Caratacus. He had struck at Roman marching camps, and auxiliaries on the road. No one speaks of Caratacan attacks on civilians. The best that Boudicca could hope for was to be taken in chains to Rome, to be jeered and spat at by the unforgiving crowd before they killed her. Perhaps she had heard of the fate of Vercingetorix or had listened to stories of women prodded into the arena with flaming brands to face starved wild beasts. She had probably never heard of Cleopatra, who had allowed a snake to crawl over her body to avoid just such a public fate, but that did not matter. Boudicca needed no precedent. She may well have promised, as Dio insisted she did in her pre-battle speech, to die if she could not conquer.

If Boudicca were, as we believe, a priestess as well as a queen, she may have had herbal knowledge about poison and the expertise to know how to administer it. We do not know the extent of Druidic medicinal knowledge, but Iron Age Britain abounded with potentially lethal plants which could be crushed into swallowable poison. The savin of which Pliny wrote is an example; so too are hemlock, yew, bryony, buttercup and belladonna. The thorn apple and a whole host of woodland-growing fungi would have served her purpose just as well.

We are equally ignorant of the fate of Boudicca's daughters. The consensus is that she poisoned them, too, rather than let them fall again into Roman clutches. The elder girl was heiress to the kingdom of the Iceni and what that meant, in the aftermath of Manduessedum, was not to be contemplated. Other loving parents have carried out the unthinkable as the lesser of two evils, most notoriously, Joseph and Magda Goebbels in the *Führerbunker*, in Berlin in April 1945. While Magda lay upstairs, drugged and in shock, the aptly nicknamed 'poison dwarf' lovingly administered cyanide to all six of his children and stayed with them until they died. Then he burned their bodies so that their corpses could not be abused by the advancing Russians or used for the propaganda purposes at which Goebbels himself excelled. As Anthony Beevor has demonstrated admirably in his recent book on the fall of Berlin,[3] the sort of atrocities carried out by the Red Army at the end of the Second World War have been visited on the losers of wars for centuries. The Iceni would find that out.

Paulinus must have searched for Boudicca. Had he found her, he might have killed her outright. Given the Roman attitude to women, it is debatable how her appearance in Rome would have been taken. Caratacus had been a different matter; he was a formidable warrior and a man, a worthy adversary of the now divine Claudius. There was more than a hint of embarrassment that a mere woman could have inflicted so much damage on the greatest empire the world had ever known. There can be no doubt, however, that the governor wanted her head; and, failing that, her grave. The absence of Boudicca's tomb is a sore disappointment for archaeologists and, in a lesser way, almost as surprising as the missing grave of Alfred the Great.[4]

Assuming that the queen did take poison, it was probably within a week, perhaps two, of her final battle. The extraordinary female burial find at Vis proves that high-born Celtic women were honoured with the same trappings and no doubt devotion as men. But in the case of Boudicca there were two complications. The first is that the natural trend of Celtic Iron Age burials in Britain is toward cremation. So the body of Boudicca is not likely to have survived, though her ashes might perhaps have been preserved in an urn as yet undiscovered, or dug into the peat of her native fens, or scattered on the warm wind of August. The second complication is that she was a woman on the run, with the Roman equivalent of a price on her head. If Ross and Robins are right about the need for the utmost secrecy in the ritual murder of the Lindow Druid Prince, then that applies doubly to Boudicca. A large and showy funeral, with Druidic rites and much weeping, would have attracted far too much attention. There would have been vexillations and cavalry patrols all over East Anglia since the rising, which would have known, as we do not, where Boudicca's headquarters were and a careful watch would have been kept. Not for her the eternal peace of a tended grave where her ancestors slept.

The lack of a grave or any known resting place has fired ever more lurid speculation. As we have seen, even an authority like Malcolm Todd believes that Boudicca's last battle was fought somewhere just north of Verulamium, and earlier experts speculated (perhaps only because of Thorneycroft's statue on the Thames Embankment) that the battlefield was in London. Parliament Hill has been suggested, as has the area between Highgate Road and the Vale of Heath. Most unlikely of all is the area once called Battle Bridge, which was flattened to build King's Cross station on the site of a smallpox hospital in 1852. Boudicca's body is said to lie, prosaically, somewhere under platform ten!

With a little more realism, in that the following sites lie at least in Iceni territory, Soldiers' Hill near Garboldisham Heath, Norfolk, and St Andrew's church, Quidenham, in the same county, have been suggested. These villages, less than five miles apart, are equally close to a Neronian gold hoard found at Scole and the Icenian tribal centre at Thetford from where the revolt possibly began. Even so there is no tangible evidence of Boudicca at either site. She had gone and, no doubt unwillingly, left her people to their fate.

Fifteen miles south-west of the Place of the Chariots lies the village of Baginton, on the edge of Coventry. It was here in 1960 that the remains of a Roman fortification, the Lunt, were discovered, exactly 1,900 years after it was first built. Partially reconstructed by the Royal Engineers, the fort today has wooden palisades and walkways on top of its huge earth ramparts. It is likely that the original was erected in the winter of 60–61, when Paulinus' army was kept *sub pellibus*, under canvas,[5] to keep a wary eye on the natives. The Lunt's proximity to Manduessedum implies that tribes local to the area, in other words some of the Corieltavi, had joined Boudicca on her way to the battle. Given her previous success, it would be surprising if they hadn't.

Within the Lunt's perimeter are the usual signs of legionary buildings, granaries and stores, but what makes it unique is the existence of a 107-ft diameter *gyrus*, a circular paddock for training cavalrymen and remounts. It matches similar descriptions of cavalry schools by the Greek philosopher and cavalry expert Xenophon in his *Hipparchicus*, and smaller 'bulges' in the fort's earthworks may be smaller *gyri* for the same purpose. It is not too far-fetched to accept that the captured Celtic horses from Manduessedum, as well as the mounts of various Roman *alae,* were corralled here for a while soon after the battle.

The Lunt, unusual though it is, was only one of a series of forts, some new, some upgraded existing buildings, which represent the archaeological record of the aftermath of Boudicca's rising. It is likely that a second fort was built at Caesaromagus (Chelmsford) in the heart of Trinovantian territory. Another, larger and more impressive, was erected at Great Chesterford near Saffron Walden. In the south of Iceni territory, there were forts at Pakenham and Coddenham, within easy reach of each other along today's A414 (and, incidentally, very close to the posited Suffolk burial places of Boudicca quoted above). At Coddenham, the grave goods of a legionary include a mirror case relief of Nero reviewing his troops. In the heart of Iceni territory, military bases have been discovered at Worthy and Horstead, an easy day's march apart and forming a triangle with a third likely base at Caistor St Edmund, which, would become Venta Icenorum, the small, impoverished Iceni *civitas* in Agricola's time. Two of the most impressive forts were now strengthened on the Iceni's western boundary. With its incredible view for miles over the grey, gloomy fenlands, Lindum, the future Lincoln, was established as a permanent base for IX Hispana, probably in the months following Manduessedum. The original site was 43 acres, and the fort may have been built to house some of the new recruits brought over to supplement the legion's losses at Boudicca's hands. A fort that size could probably not have coped with a complete legion and its *auxilia*. At Longthorpe to the south was another vexillation fortress, where Cerialis may have ridden after his defeat. Near today's Peterborough, the base was probably already built by the year of the first Iceni revolt and, like the Lunt, may have been a cavalry base intended for quick forays into the surrounding countryside. Tile steps found here show that it was also a base of IX Legion, although exactly when is unclear.

What this fort evidence represents is a ring of the enemy fencing in the heartland of rebellion. For all that the Iceni were a people with a coastline, there is no evidence that they had a navy or any real reliance on the sea. Even so, Malcolm Todd believes that there were probably a number of forts dotted around the Norfolk coast, too. Certainly there was a base on the Wash at Branodunum, today's Brancaster, and another at Burgh Castle (Gariannonum) on the east coast. These represent the most northerly of the Litus Saxonici, the Saxon shore forts dating from the third century, but it is not impossible that these are merely the later versions of earlier fortifications.

It is clear from the written record that Gaius Paulinus was not content with a mere containment of the situation; he was out for revenge. Tacitus commented, 'Hostile or wavering tribes were ravaged with fire and sword.'[6]

Although the phrase is a stock one among classical writers, there can be no doubt that Tacitus meant it literally, and what was so damning was that wavering tribes were seen as legitimate targets. In other words, neutrality was no defence. The Britons were supposedly either for the Romans, which meant active participation against Boudicca, or they were against, in which case they had either died at Manduessedum or were hunted throughout the winter that followed.

After Boudicca, the highest-profile casualty of her rising was Poenius Postumus, camp prefect of II Augusta. The fact that the legion, based at Exeter, was commanded by him rather than a *legatus* (general) implies either that the actual commanding officer was dead or was based elsewhere, perhaps on some kind of secondment. We cannot know why Postumus failed to obey orders from Paulinus to join him at Manduessedum:

The camp prefect has many important responsibilities. He must choose a site for a camp and mark out the wall and ditch. He must organize the tents or soldiers' barracks along with their baggage. He is also responsible for seeing that medical treatment is available for sick soldiers. He must also see that the following items are always available: wagons, mules, saws, axes, spades, chisels, wood, straw, battering rams, onagers, ballistae and every type of siege machinery. As the most knowledgeable man, he is chosen for the job after many years' outstanding service. He can then teach others what he has done well himself.

This was the official description of Postumus' commissary post according to Flavius Vegetius Renatus, writing in 375 but working from centuries' worth of others' writings on the Roman army. Clearly, although we know nothing about his personality, Postumus would not have been promoted to this rank without experience and it is unlikely he would be the type to quake at rumour, however terrifying Boudicca's attack may have been. It may be that he misread the destruction of Cerialis' IX Hispana, believing a similar fate might overtake Paulinus, and decided to hold the south-west and fight there on his own terms. His realization that he had guessed wrongly led to his and his legion's shame. Postumus killed himself with his sword and II Augusta marched to join Paulinus' command, presumably under an anonymous tribune.

'The whole army', wrote Tacitus, 'was now united', although not actually in a single base. Its numbers were also swelled by reinforcements sent by a grateful Nero. Tacitus tells of 1,000 cavalry, eight auxiliary units and 2,000 regulars from the Rhine. This is either a measure of how badly damaged Paulinus' units were (especially IX) or how determined Nero was to keep order in the troublesome province. When news of Boudicca's revolt first reached Rome, the emperor seriously considered abandoning Britain. There was no talk of that now – Nero could relax.

The auxiliaries seem to have gone straight into winter quarters – although Tacitus does not tell us where – while the legions attacked wherever there were pockets of resistance or wherever they fancied a spot of pillaging. For all that the Roman army was a highly organized and disciplined force, its soldiers expected booty as a perk of the job. That they were laws unto themselves would be amply illustrated by the situation eight years later when Roscius Coelius, legate of XX Valeria Victrix, mutinied against the military inactivity of the governor Marcus Trebellius Maximus and forced him into running to Rome.

The archaeological evidence of Paulinus' terror campaign is confused because of the close proximity of dates between the Claudian conquest and the reprisals after Boudicca. Only eighteen years had passed, one legionary's serving term with the army, and archaeology can rarely be so precise. While the bodies found at Maiden Castle are presumed to belong to Vespasian's attack in 43–4, it is possible that the Durotriges refortified the site or at least made a stand there in 61. Similarly, corpses and evidence of fire at South Cadbury in Somerset may point to II Augusta wiping out resistance there. Since John Ireland, the King's Antiquary, made a romantic link with Arthur, proposing South Cadbury as the site of Camelot, there has been a sense of disappointment that nothing 'Arthurian' has been excavated. Cadbury was in fact an Iron Age fort replaced by a Romano-British temple. At its south-west gateway the bodies of thirty men, women and children were found. The existence of child bodies is important. There were none at Maiden Castle, presumably because children were sent away before the attack or because Vespasian spared them. Now even the children were legitimate targets of Rome.

With Paulinus' units in 60–61 was Titus Flavius Vespasianus, eldest son of the 'Muleteer' who would be emperor in ten years time. He was a military tribune under Paulinus and may have earned his tough reputation in the war of attrition in this period. Honest, talented and hard-working, he would later command a legion in the Jewish War and ride beside his father to a magnificent triumph in 71. Ultimately succeeding to the purple himself, his short reign was one of good government, working well with the Senate and alleviating the suffering caused by the eruption at Pompeii and an outbreak of plague in Rome the following year. He died of natural causes on 13 September 81, the 'darling of the human race'.

Nearer to the Iceni heartland, archaeological evidence tells the same depressing story. At Burgh-by-Woodbridge in Suffolk was a rectangular enclosure with ditches and ramparts dating from the century before Christ. Inner defences here were destroyed in about 60, and an artillery bolt and javelin head are signs of fighting. Similar items have been found at Thetford further north, on the ridge at Gallows Hill. Suggested by some as a possible palace of Prasutagus and Boudicca, insufficient domestic wares have been found, and, as we have seen, it was probably a religious site used for ceremonial purposes. The post holes clearly show a systematic demolition rather than wholesale burning of buildings, which would have been entirely timber-made. The shape of the holes suggests a rocking backwards and forwards of the uprights, rather as a dentist twists loose a tooth. Ditches have been backfilled, and Thetford's destruction implies the closing down of at least the visible signs of Iceni power.

Over much of Norfolk and Suffolk there are hoards of coin and precious metal which can be dated with some accuracy to Boudicca's revolt. There are few similar finds in the Trinovantian lands to the south, but we cannot accept Paul Sealey's[7] view that this implies the Trinovantes were less committed to the revolt. Coins, mostly silver denarii, have been found at Weston Longville, Scole Joist Fen, Lakenheath, Eniswell, Santon Downham, East Dereham and North Creake. They range from pre- 31 BC to examples from 61, the latest decorated with the head of Nero. The fact that none postdate 61 means that the coins were buried either as Boudicca took to the campaign trail or as Paulinus' legions hit the area looking for vengeance. We have seen that coins did not have the same significance to the Celts as they did to the Romans – perhaps to the former there was a spiritual or religious dimension – but these finds are not placed near water and have all the hallmarks of being items for later exhumation. At Field Baulk, March, Cambridgeshire, 872 silver coins have been found in a red-glazed pot with typical Iceni decoration. A similar pot at Fring in Norfolk once had a covering of flax or hemp. The fact that many of these coin hoards are a mixture of Roman and Iceni currency is a reminder that for eighteen years before the revolt, the Iceni had been a client people of the empire, and trade transactions would doubtless have gone on.

Six metalwork hoards have been found which date to the period. Four of these came from the Brecklands around Thetford, which possibly suggests that this was the epicentre for Boudicca's people. The beautiful silver wine cup, with its olive and vine leaf decoration, is a tangible reminder of transnational links. This and the other bowls from Hockwold-cum-Wilton in Norfolk were, however, deliberately battered out of shape, either in an attempt at what today we would call recycling or in contempt for the alien art of Rome. The olive and the vine, as we have seen from Dio's rendering of Boudicca's speech before Camnlodunum, were to her symbols of a vicious and decadent regime. The finds at Brandon in Suffolk were contained in an upturned cauldron, which itself had religious significance for the Celts, and one of the bowls was probably used for the making or drinking of local beer. At Saham Toney and Westhall, harness mounts, enamelled terrets and linchpins are a tangible reminder of the lore of the chariot. These were the Iceni, the Horse People, and they took their war wagons with them to the afterlife.

We cannot know who buried these hoards, exactly when or precisely why. That their owners did not come back is certain, either because they went out against Paulinus' legions or because they died of starvation. Extraordinarily, the Iceni had left their crops in the fields in the summer of 60 and no one seems to have harvested them. Practically speaking, it would have been possible to rescue some of this in the weeks that followed Manduessedum, but, conversely, harvesting could not have been done comprehensively and some areas would have been more depleted of their menfolk than others. The deaths of so many women and children, all of whom would normally have gathered the harvest, added to the problem. We have no idea of the size of the Iceni population in 60/61, but the impact of Boudicca's last battle must not have been unlike that of the plague in the 1340s. Cattle would have gone unmilked, corn ungathered, sheep wandering away from homesteads. Nowhere is this devastation more apparent than at West Stow in Suffolk. Like Butser in Hampshire, the Iron Age buildings have been lovingly reconstructed by conservationists, and breeds of pig from the period reintroduced. On the edge of the Breckland, Stow may have been at the heart of Boudiccan resistance, and, indeed until 61 it was a considerable farmstead with a number of circular buildings. There is a gap in the archaeological record of at least ten years, but no sign of destruction. Did the owners of West Stow die in their smoky huts from the famine that swept the countryside?

In Rome, the disgraced Catus Decianus was replaced as *procurator* by Gaius Julius Alpinus Classicianus. If Decianus, with his greed and high-handedness, represents all that was bad in Roman provincial administration, Classicianus was all that was best. It comes as no surprise then that Tacitus writes him off as a virtual traitor:

> Still the savage British tribesmen were disinclined for peace, especially as . . . Classicianus . . . was on bad terms with Suetonius [Paulinus] and allowed his personal animosities to damage the national interests. For he passed round advice to wait for a new governor who would be kind to those who surrendered, without an enemy's bitterness or a conqueror's arrogance. Classicianus also reported to Rome that there was no prospect of ending the war unless a successor was appointed to replace [Paulinus] whose failures he attributed to perversity – and his successes to luck.

Classicianus may have been overplaying his hand in the last remark, if indeed this was what he actually believed. The point was, however, that Paulinus had been caught napping. He had gone against Mona without securing his rear, and a little more strategic concentration from Boudicca would have destroyed his command on top of the burning of three major settlements. He knew perfectly well that he had almost lost the province, and his vengeful actions of the autumn and winter of 61 were an attempt to obliterate his mistakes and make someone else pay.

Classicianus had an altogether more sensible and conciliatory outlook. A Gaul, with an obvious understanding of oppressed peoples that Paulinus totally lacked, he realized that rebels are difficult to control and impossible to tax. His father, Julius Indus, had helped the Romans suppress the Gallic rising in 21, so there was a family history of this most difficult of jobs. The Gaul was clearly exercising his independence from Paulinus when he wrote to Nero explaining the position. Just as Claudius had sent an imperial freedman to Aulus Plautius' rebellious army to defuse a touchy situation, Nero sent his own version, Polyclitus.

Tacitus clearly did not like this man, almost certainly because of his former slave status. His escort was 'enormous' and he was 'a trial to Italy and Gaul'. He may have intimidated the army, acknowledges the writer, but the enemy found him a joke: 'The British marvelled that a general and an army who had completed such a mighty war should obey a slave.'[8]

If this was so, then the Britons had missed the point. Polyclitus, whatever his origins, carried the writ of the emperor, and any general, especially with this particular emperor, would do well to listen.

Polyclitus seems to have done a good job. He clearly agreed with Classicianus, but Paulinus was not removed immediately. The loss of some ships in a storm at sea provided Nero with the excuse he needed to replace him, and the avenger was sent back with full honours to Rome – no loss of face, everything swept under the carpet.

His replacement was Publius Petronius Turpilianus, whom Tacitus dismisses scornfully. He, 'neither provoking the enemy nor provoked, called this ignoble inactivity peace with honour'.[9] By this stage in his *Annales*, of course, Tacitus is 'psyching up' to the governorship of one of Rome's greatest generals, his father-in-law Julius Agricola, and against him lesser mortals like Turpilianus pale into insignificance. In fact it was probably the brinkmanship and steadying influence of Turpilianus and Classicianus that Britain needed in the early 60s, not an ambitious warmonger like Agricola. Both sides had been hurt. The Iceni, bloodied at Mandusesedum, their queen dead and their farms destroyed, were in desperate need to recover. Rome too had been shaken, not so visibly in men and material perhaps, but the blow had been severe, the province so nearly lost. It was a time of reconciliation and cooperation. The Iceni must never rise again, but burning and slaughter was conversely the surest way of making this happen.

Turpilianus was a relative of Aulus Plautius, the first governor. His father had governed Syria with justice and firmness. So the man's pedigree was not in doubt. And his methods proved correct. There was a much-needed hiatus while old wounds were licked and men breathed again. And the next governor, appointed in 63, was not even a military man.

Marcus Trebellius Maximus, unsurprisingly disparaged by Tacitus, was a civil servant and headcounter, having recently organized a census in Gaul. The mutiny against him by the pushy Roscius Coelius five years after his arrival is probably as much a reflection of the disintegration at the top in Rome as it is resentment at military inactivity. Tacitus says Trebellius used *'conitate quandam'*, a certain courtesy, which had never been shown to the British before, and the fact that he lasted for six years implies that he was playing his governorship right.

Boudicca's revolt, coupled with war with the Parthians and the catastrophic fire in Rome in 64, led to a debasement of Roman currency. Unfettered from the controlling influence of Seneca, Burrus and even his mother, Nero was descending into the kind of megalomanic behaviour exhibited by Caligula. While the great unwashed of Rome continued to love him because he gave them bread and circuses, an aristocratic conspiracy led by Calpurnius Piso attempted to murder him in 65. The plot failed and a rash of executions and murder followed – among the victims were Seneca, Faenius Rufus and the poet Lucan. Vespasian himself narrowly escaped death after nodding off during one of Nero's sickening lyre recitals. Wisely, he went into voluntary exile to breed mules and wait for the inevitable. That came on 9 June 68 when, declared a public enemy by the Senate, Nero killed himself at the villa of his freedman, Phaon – *'Qualis artifex pereo'*, 'what an artist dies in me', were allegedly his last words.

In Britain, there were literal as well as metaphorical fences to build. From the ashes of Camulodunum would rise the Colonia Victriensis, the colony of the victorious, although in no sense could the veterans of XX be regarded as that. Rebuilding possibly began in 64, that four-year gap itself a testimony to the totality of the town's destruction and the scale of the shock the Romans had suffered. Pottery finds around the base of the new wall show that building probably continued until about 80, and the huge defences, the oldest surviving Roman masonry wall in Britain, was striking evidence that never again could the Trinovantes attack with the impunity of 60. The wall was nearly 20 feet high in places and ran for 3,000 yards enclosing 44 hectares. The Hole-in-the-Wall pub now stands on the site of the massive Balkerne Gate built in these years. It had two large arches for horsed and wheeled traffic and two smaller ones for pedestrians.

Such a gate would be permanently manned by soldiers, tradesmen stopping here to have their goods checked and pay various tolls.

We know that, in common with many other towns, the *colonia* had its metalworkers producing jewellery, figurines and cutlery. The little carved black bear, perhaps a Celtic tribal totem, was found here, made of jet mined in Brigantian territory around Whitby. Here too was the grave of a child who was given his toys to play with in the afterlife, a group of nine grotesque little figures at a dinner, some reclining on one elbow in Roman fashion, others singing – the entertainment of the wealthy and privileged. By the early second century the town had its own sewer system and, a sure sign of peace, a theatre was built, not within the defensive walls but out in the countryside, a Romano-Gallic tradition.

Interestingly, there seems to have been no attempt to rebuild the detested Temple of Claudius. Its vault today lies beneath the giant square keep of the Norman castle, relic of another alien military power in the land of the Trinovantes. Today, fittingly, it is Colchester's museum.

London had possibly suffered as badly as Camulodunum, yet by the mid-70s, it was undergoing such a resurgence that Julius Classicianus, the *procurator*, was buried there, probably in 75. The tombstone has survived, erected by his widow Julia Pacata. Recent excavations during the building of the Jubilee Line extension have proved that the extent of the Boudiccan burning was greater than we had previously believed, but even so the site was a prime trading centre and the city would rise in time to eclipse Colchester as the nominal capital of Roman Britain. Some building began at once, as evinced by the tree-ring dating of timber from 62 and 63. Pottery continued, as if the battered survivors of her attack refused to leave but soldiered on as Londoners have always done.

It was really under Vespasian's *imperium* that the city was properly rebuilt. This was Agricola's governorship, when conquest was resumed and there could be no doubt that the Romans were here to stay. About ten years after Boudicca's attack, a wooden amphitheatre for gladiatorial displays was built on the site of the present Guildhall. The commercial focus of the town was the forum at the Cornhill nearby, the name itself proving the trading continuity of the centuries. There was a basilica by the turn of the century and perhaps the governor's residence lies under Cannon Street station. South of the river on land reclaimed from the marshes, a large stone building was probably the mansio, the residence of the province's administrators. The quay itself was quickly reopened, the huge oak timbers that formed berths for the merchant ships preserved to this day by the chemicals in the river water. This ran over 600 yards along the revetted foreshore on either side of the bridge, backed by a series of warehouses for the storage of grain, wine and all the other goods of the empire.

By 125, a grid-shaped city had emerged, with an amphitheatre beyond the Walbrook and at least two bathhouses, one at Upper Thames Street, the other along Cheapside. London was already going west, not yet defended by a wall, but by a fort built immediately after Boudicca's revolt to protect the town from the north, the way she had come.

Verulamium had to wait longer for its rebuilding. Arguably less Roman and less commercial than either Camulodunum or Londonium, activity in the valley of the Ver was limited until about 75 and implies a handful of squatters living there, no more. Along King Harry Lane, buildings were reappearing perhaps ten years after Boudicca's destruction, rubble from the fire being incorporated into the new work. A large ditch of some 48 hectares defended the town, along with the accompanying rampart, but there is no sign of a fort. In time Verulamium would rise to become Roman Britain's third largest city, with an impressive amphitheatre, bathhouse and a thriving commercial and manufacturing centre. Despite the fact that the theatre was out of use by the late fourth century and was in fact the town's rubbish dump, new building was still going on long after the legions left. A fascinating and tangible reminder that this was a Celtic holy place before the Romans came is in the striking second-century mosaic of the horned god Cernunnos, now on display in the museum and wrongly captioned as Neptune.

Whereas these Roman centres were being rebuilt as soon as peace and money allowed, there is archaeological evidence that the Iceni territory itself was deliberately turned into a relative wasteland. Paul Sealey conjectures that it may have taken centuries for the local population to reach levels likely elsewhere. Wherever Boudicca's tribal capital was, it was levelled or ignored and a new *civitas* developed near Norwich at Caistor St Edmund. This was Venta Icenorum, at a mere 45 acres deliberately and pitifully small. This was in no sense a royal residence, for the Iceni lands were no longer a client kingdom but merely a part of the empire. If Prasutagus and Boudicca had any family able to claim royal descent, they were not granted it. The Iceni were a beaten people and they were not to be accorded the usual status of town dwellers. The common grid of streets is visible in aerial photographs, but there is a sense that this place was almost a ghetto where some Iceni were perhaps forced to live and where they could also be watched. It may even be the silent testimony of the hostility of its founding that Venta Icenorum was not built upon by later generations, as though the memory of it was too grim. Athelstan minted coins in 1096 at Norwich, three miles away on the Wensum, and the Norman castle and twelfth-century cathedral followed. A mere' dent in the corner of a Norfolk field may be the site of Venta Icenorum's amphitheatre, grudgingly built at a much later date than its founding. Only the town's walls are visible above ground. Guy de la Bedoyere conjectures that the siting of the place – it is not on a recognised trade route – contributed to its failure to grow. This ignores the later commercial success of Norwich, however, as a medieval centre of the highly lucrative wool trade and at the heart of the best farming land in the country.

The archaeological record only tells us part of the story. At the heart of Roman attitudes, whether of revenge or pacification, was always the city of Rome itself, dwarfing anything Trebellius Maximus or Agricola built in Britain:

In the principate and censorship of Vespasian and Titus, in the 826th year after the city's foundation [73] the walls of Rome, embracing the seven hills, measured 13.2 miles in circumference. The city itself is divided into 14 districts and has 265 inter-sections with guardian lanes.[10]

Pliny's *Natural History*[11] paints an impressive picture:

> Agrippa in his aedileship[12] created 700 cisterns, 500 fountains and 130 reservoirs . . . Upon these structures he erected 300 statues of bronze or marble and 400 marble columns.

'Such', said the geographer Strabo, 'is Rome.'

There is a sense with the Iceni that Rome has to hold back in order to make their system work. But that holding back was merely a delaying tactic, and Tacitus had no need to be scornful of it or dismayed. The Horse People, with their boar standards, their magical hares and their warrior elite in torcs and chariots, represented a world that was past. The Romans, modern, aggressive, ever busy, wanted to move on.

Ironically, it was the Roman Tacitus who summed up the situation best, in describing the eternal discussion between the conqueror and the conquered. One of the most fearsome enemies faced by his father-in-law Agricola in his war in Caledonia (Scotland) in 83–4 was Calgacus. As Cassius Dio wrote Boudicca's speech for her, as it were, so Tacitus writes Calgacus':

> Plunderers of the world, now that there are no more lands for [the Romans] all-devastating hands, they search even into the sea. If the enemy is rich, they are rapacious; if poor, they lust for dominion. Not East, not West has sated them; alone of all mankind they covet riches and poverty with equal passion. They rob, butcher, plunder and call it empire and where they make a desolation, they call it 'peace'.[13]

Seneca, like so many others a victim of Nero's dictatorship, might have given Calgacus comfort when he wrote in his *Moral Epistles*:

> The entire human race, both present and future, is condemned to death. All the cities that have ever held dominion or have been the splendid jewels of empires belonging to others – some day men will ask where they were.[14]

10

'The Roar of our Thousands'

Till I make plain the meaning
Of all my thousand years –
Till I fill their hearts with knowledge,
While I fill their eyes with tears.
'The Recall', Rudyard Kipling

That most historically attuned poet, Rudyard Kipling, wrote of a prefect of the Weald called Julius Fabricius in his poem 'The Land':

Then Julius Fabricius died, as even prefects do,
And after certain centuries, imperial Rome died too.

Rome, perhaps, but not her culture. Throughout Europe, Roman law was practised for centuries in law courts from the Seine to the Dneiper; it formed the basis of constitutions written and unwritten down to the present day. The principal chamber of American political life is still called the Senate – a form of democracy the Romans would not have understood. Roads built by the legions have been widened, macadamized and painted to cope with modern traffic, but they are Roman at their core. Languages, our own, French, Spanish and

Italian, owe their origins to the Latin tongue – even modern Romanian has an affinity with the Roman language because of Trajan's conquest of what was then Dacia in 101–5. Rome's Empire might have abandoned its elaborate pantheon of gods for the all-powerful Christian God, and it might have split to form a breakaway rival in exotic Byzantium to the East; it might even have been sacked half a dozen times by nomadic 'barbarians' from the north; but the essence of what it stood for lived on.

For some time, we hear nothing of Boudicca. The Iceni must have mourned her, remembering the flame she lit for years. But how long does memory last? Many of those who knew her were killed at Manduessedum, or died soon after of famine or disease. Survivors of Camulodunum, Londinium and Verulamium no doubt spat at the mention of her name for the rest of their lives. To the next generation, she was a memory, a monster perhaps to terrify whimpering children or a goddess who could be translated into Badb or Morrigan, Nemain or Macha, the crow goddesses of the Celtic battlefield. By the time the legions left Britain early in the fifth century it is likely that her name had been forgotten.

The next mention of her, though not by name, comes from the quill of the monk Gildas, one of the country's first historians. Born in the 490s, Gildas is a rough contemporary of the shadowy Arthur, and his *De Excidio et Conquestu Britanniae* (The Ruin of Britain) is the only surviving history of the Celts from the Roman invasion to his own day. Written in Latin between 516 and 547, the history is laced with all the prejudices of a man born not only into the Roman tradition which saw women as inferior but into the Christian tradition which saw them as the source of all evil. He was also sickeningly moralistic: 'Britain has kings, but they are tyrants . . . Britain has priests, but they are fools.' He pointed the finger at five such Romano-British rulers faced with the increasing danger of Saxon invasions. Cuneglasus, from what had been the Ordovices territory, he refers to as an adulterer and violent maniac. Vorteporix of Dyfed to the north raped his own daughter. Aurelius Caninus from the old Dubonni lands killed his father and was a notorious fornicator. Constantine from the far west beyond Exeter slaughtered priests, and Maelgwyn of Gwynedd (the Silures' old haunt) butchered members of his family to seize power. Against such figures, Boudicca gets off relatively lightly. Gildas calls her:

. . . that deceitful lioness, who put to death the rulers [which Claudius] had left in Britain, to unfold more fully and completely the enterprise of the Romans.[1]

It is a testimony to how effective was Roman propaganda that Gildas sees the Britons (after all, his own people) as 'crafty foxes' who 'offered their necks to the sword and stretched out their hands, like women, to be bound'. It was a hopelessly distorted image that would survive for centuries.

The next references to Boudicca are vaguer still. There are no names and virtually no facts in the work of either Bede or Nennius. Bede was a monk from Durham who was ordained at the monastery at Jarrow in 703. A devoted priest and prolific writer, he was highly knowledgeable on a huge range of topics, speaking fluent Greek, Latin and Hebrew and writing articulately on the Old and New Testaments, grammar, physical science, medicine and astronomy. Such a breadth earned him the title 'Venerable' and he was canonized in 1899. His most famous work, completed in 731, was *Historia Ecclesiastica Gentis Anglorum* (Ecclesiastical History of the English People), but like all early historians, without access to original texts and devoid of any archaeological awareness, on Boudicca and the Iceni he in fact wrote fiction. Equally unreliable was Nennius, author of *Historia Britonum* in the 760s, tracing the history of Britain from mythical origins. Claiming that his sources were drawn 'from the annals of the Romans, the writings of the Holy Fathers, the annals of the Irish and the Saxons and our own traditions', Nennius' importance today lies in his amassing Arthurian folklore; Boudicca's revolt is merely mentioned in passing without any relevant detail.

By the twelfth century, the name of Boudicca seems to have been forgotten altogether, although we should not perhaps read much into the fact that Geoffrey of Monmouth does not mention her in his *Historia Regum Britanniae*. As obsessed as

Nennius with the legend of Arthur (a war leader who in practical terms achieved less than either Caratacus or Boudicca), the book is spurious hokum based on chronicles that Geoffrey alone claimed to have seen, and traces Britain's beginnings to the legendary fall of Troy.

It was the High Renaissance that rediscovered Boudicca, because it rediscovered the 'glory that was Greece and the grandeur that was Rome'.[2] Essentially a backward-looking movement of enormous complexity, the rebirth of culture it engendered actually propelled philosophy, art and especially science forward. The exploration of the physical world from the 1490s led to the discovery of the Americas and its indigenous peoples, and undertaking which led to attitudes astonishingly similar to the civilized Roman view of the 'barbaric' Celts.

Renaissance historians were the first to bring Boudicca back into the historical light, albeit at first in the scholar's language of Latin and with a great deal of confusion. The humanist Polydore Vergil de Castillo, born in Urbino about 1470, came to England in 1501 as deputy collector of Peter's Pence, one of the many taxes due to Rome. In a sense, therefore, he was the spiritual successor of Catus Decianus, whose ruthless tax collection had embittered the Iceni. Vergil stayed, however, becoming a prebendary of St Paul's and a naturalized citizen by 1513. His *Historiae Anglicae Libri XXVI* was printed in Basel in 1534 and later additions continued until the year of his death (1555). Although he was using Tacitus and Dio as his source material, Vergil unaccountably uses their different spellings of her name – in Latin and Greek – to create two different people, Voadicca from Tacitus and Bonduca from Dio. The mistake was slavishly copied for several generations.

Vergil's contemporary, Hector Boece, born in Dundee about 1465, became a friend of Erasmus, chancellor of the newly founded university in his home town and a canon of Dundee cathedral. His *History of Scotland*, written in Latin in 1527, muddied the Boudicca waters still further. Perhaps confusing the queen with Cartimandua and the Iceni with the Brigantes, Boece has 'Voada' married to Arvirsagus, the queen battered with 'insufferable stakes' and her daughters raped. Because

Boece sets the whole business near the Scots border, she begs for help from her brother Corbrede, king of the Scots. His remonstrance to Rome is dismissed as being merely from a 'barbarian people'.

In the next generation, Ralph Holinshed perpetuated the Vergil/Boece myths. Originally from Cheshire, in the heart of what had once been Brigantes territory, the future chronicler went to London and worked in Reginald Wolfe's printing office. His monumental *Chronicles of England, Scotland and Ireland* appeared in two volumes in 1577, and, although he had assistance from William Harrison, Richard Stonyhurst and John Hooker, he seems to have written most of the 'English' sections himself. Holinshed had clearly read the collected works of John Leland, royal antiquary to Henry VIII, who had amassed 'a whole world of things very memorable' on early British history. Holinshed's events more correctly take place further south than those of Boece and, without reference to either Tacitus or Dio, he invents a whole biography for Boudicca's daughters. She is still called Voada and the same name, confusingly, is given to her elder daughter, who marries a Roman of noble birth, Marius, 'who had deflowered her before her time'.[3] According to Holinshed, it was the younger daughter, Voadicca, who was the feisty one, fighting Romans on the Isle of Man and in Ireland before being killed by them. It may be that the confusion here is once again with Cartimandua, whose ongoing feud with her ex-husband, Venutius, erupted into further violence in 69.

The Elizabethan obsession with Eliza, their queen, had obvious echoes down the centuries and for the first time Boudicca was hijacked by a later society for its own purposes. Tacitus' *Annales* and *Agricola* appeared in English for the first time in 1591, translated by Sir Henry Savile, an eminent scholar who was Latin secretary and Greek tutor to Elizabeth and one of the translators of the King James Bible of 1611. Tacitus' original moral was retained and seen as being even more pertinent in the 1590s than it was in his day:

If thou dislike their wars, be thankful for thine own peace; if thou dost abhor their tyrannies, love and reverence thine own wise, just and excellent Prince [Elizabeth]. If thou doest detest their Anarchy, acknowledge our own happy government and thank God for her, under whom England enjoys as many benefits as ever Reign did suffer miseries under the greatest Tyrant.[4]

This rosy picture of England was actually far from true, but, when Savile wrote, Elizabeth was the heroine of the Armada, only ten years earlier prancing on her white horse at Tilbury to impress her troops, wearing a breastplate and promising them victory. It could have been Boudicca on her chariot at Manduessedum (even down to the red hair), except that by the time Elizabeth made her Tilbury appearance she already knew the Armada had been destroyed.

It was in this decade that John White had accompanied Walter Ralegh on his voyages to Virginia, and his beautiful drawings of the Algonquin natives he found there kick-started an Elizabethan love affair with primitivism that never quite went away. Samuel Daniel in 1612 made the comparison between the natives of Virginia and the Celts, was drawing not only on the artwork of White, but also that of the Dutch artist Lucas de Heere, producing in 1575, *'les premiers Anglois comme ils alloyment en guerre du temps du Julius César'*.[5] Stuart Piggott pronounces these drawings to be of 'very woe-begone naked savages', but in fact de Heere's representation of the woad-painted warriors, with their oval shields, spears and heavy moustaches is extraordinarily close to Roman descriptions of them – only the genitals have been 'glossed over' for the sake of modesty. John Aubrey continued the Celtic/Native American analogy into the next generation when he wrote:

They [the Celts] knew the use of iron. They were two or three degrees, I suppose, less savage than the Americans.[6]

The analogy was far more accurate than either Daniel or Aubrey knew. Neither the Celts nor the native Americans were savages except in the prejudice and preconceptions of the Romans and the British who wrote about them. Both peoples wore warpaint in battle, with a similar ritualistic purpose, and both, at least at times, fought naked. In terms of the Celtic obsession with the head, the native American penchant for taking scalps is another similarity.

It was perhaps inevitable that a character at once so exciting and yet so vague as Boudicca should be hijacked too by poets and playwrights. Edmund Spenser refers to her as 'stout Bonducca', a reference to her courage rather than her build, and, interestingly, heightens her as a doomed figure by alleging treachery among her followers:

> By reason that her Captaines on her side
> Corrupted by Paulinus, from her swerv'd.[7]

Her end is suitably romantic:

> And yet, though overcome in hapless fight
> She triumphed on death, in enemies despite.

Spenser and Ben Jonson in the next generation were the first to be upbeat about Boudicca and indeed the Celts in general. Others, like John Aubrey, without the wisdom of archaeological discoveries and inclined to swallow Roman propaganda wholesale, were depressing. He wrote:

> Let us imagine what kind of a countrie this was in the time of the ancient Britons . . . a shady, dismal wood: and the only inhabitants almost as savage as the beasts whose skins were their only raiment.[8]

Aubrey's generation assumed that the Druids built Stonehenge, and the wild mixing of millennia continued into the Age of Reason. In 1714 the skeleton of an elephant was found, complete with flint-headed spear, near Battle Bridge in London. The assumption was made that this was the site of Boudicca's last battle against the Romans, in which Claudian elephants were believed to have been used.

The historian William Camden ploughed a lonely furrow in his *Britannia*, a ground-breaking topographical survey published in 1586 in Latin and which was translated into

English in 1610. Camden was Clarenceux, king of arms and second master of Westminster School, and his sources included Tacitus, Dio and Gildas. Boudicca and the Iceni for the first time appear exactly where we know they were – Norfolk. He does confuse the veterans' colony at Camulodunum for Maldon in Essex, but he is at least in Trinovantes territory.

It says much for how history treats its subjects that Boudicca's star shone only as long as Elizabeth's. No sooner had she been rediscovered by scholars of the Renaissance, than Jacobean male chauvinism attempted to bury her again. By 1603, when James VI of Scotland became James I of England, the mood of the country was such that people were tired of the tetchy, melancholy old woman that Elizabeth had become. 'Women's worth', wrote Anne Bradstreet, the extraordinary Puritan who became, unknowingly,[9] America's first poetess, 'disappeared with our queen.' This was not strictly a first-hand observation – Mrs Bradstreet was born nine years after the death of Elizabeth. And Boudicca was left to the bitter misogyny of the Puritans Fletcher and Milton.

John Fletcher was the third son of the dean of Peterborough, born in Rye, Sussex, in 1579. Along with the more famous Christopher Marlowe, he was a graduate of Corpus Christi College, Cambridge and he died of the plague in 1625. Coming as he did from a literary family and known to have collaborated on various plays with Philip Massinger and William Rowley, it is difficult to disentangle Fletcher's work from theirs. But while his most famous collaborator, William Shakespeare, went on to write *Cymbeline* in 1608, based *very* vaguely on Cunobelin, Fletcher produced *Bonduca* six years later. The fact that the play's central character is not the queen of the Iceni at all, but Caratach (Caratacus), tells us much about Fletcher's view of womanhood. She rides a 'cart', not a chariot, is boastful, and her own stupidity leads to her defeat. 'A woman beat 'em . . .', Bonduca shouts, 'a weak woman, a woman beat these Romans!'

Consciously or otherwise, Fletcher is parodying Elizabeth, who famously had 'the body of a weak and feeble woman', and whose sea dogs and weather had destroyed the invasion plans of the Rome of her day, Spain. Bonduca's words subconsciously pick up the boastfulness of the Celts, to whom tall stories around the winter fires were lifeblood. He also hits upon what stung the Romans most – three towns and half a legion destroyed by a *woman* was something they found utterly intolerable. Caratach's reproach, however, is pure Jacobean: 'So it seems. A man would shame to talk so.' The real Caratacus, on the contrary, would have trumpeted his victories louder than anyone else.

Caratach is unbelievably ambivalent in the treatment of the Romans who violate Bonduca's daughters, here referred to as Caratach's nieces:

Caratach: A woman's wisdom in our triumphs? Out, out, ye sluts, ye follies, from our swords filch our revenges basely?*

Daughter 2: By—— Uncle, we'll have vengeance for our rapes.

Caratach: By—— ye should have kept your legs closed then.

The role of women in many Jacobean tragedies (played by boys, of course, which would have lessened their femininity anyway) is often that of the guilty party. Cleopatra's weak romanticism and selfishness sways the great Antony from his Roman duty, and Lady Macbeth, driven by vaulting ambition, persuades her husband to commit murder. So in *Bonduca* the queen herself brings about her own defeat though the flaws in her character and – the cry of chauvinist manhood for centuries – her daughters were somehow 'asking for' their rapes.

John Milton has come down to us pre-eminently as the author of the epic religious poetry in *Paradise Lost* and the lyric poetry of *Lycidas*, *L'Allegro* and *Il Penseroso*, but in his own day he was even better known as a radical pamphleteer, and a belligerent one at that. Born at Cheapside, London, not much more than a slingshot from the Roman town that

---

* He is furious because the daughters are torturing the rapists and he wants these men released.

Boudicca had burned, he returned to England from Italy at the outbreak of the Civil War and became the chief apologist for the Puritanical regime that followed it, defending with such virulence the men who judicially killed Charles I that he feared for his own head at the Restoration eleven years later.

His second series of blistering pamphlets was written in 1643 and entitled *The Doctrine and Discipline of Divorce*, which stemmed from the fact that his seventeen-year-old first wife, Mary Powell, had left him because her father was a Royalist. This is no doubt the origin of Milton's misogyny (although it did not prevent him from getting Mary back or marrying twice more in later life). In his *History of Britain* (1670), the apologist dismissed Cartimandua's actions of the Brigantes as 'the rebellion of an adulteress against her husband', and praised the people who sided with Venutius because they had done something positive about 'the uncomeliness of their subjection to the Monarchy of a Woman'. In Milton's day and in Milton's mind, 'good queen Bess' was a memory; Charles I's queen Henrietta Maria was a foreign idolator. The actual power in the land was Oliver Cromwell and, unsurprisingly, *Mrs* Cromwell barely gets a mention in the biographies.

Confronted with the story of Boudicca's beating and her daughters' rapes, Milton comments:

> . . . worthier silence, retirement and a Veil, than for a woman to repeat as done to her own person or to hear repeated before an host of men. . . . A woman was their commander-in-chief. For Boadicea [sic] and her daughters ride about in a chariot, telling the tall champions, as a great encouragement, that with the Britons it was usual for women to be their leaders.

Milton was usually in awe of classical writers, but he reverses this in the case of Tacitus and Dio:

> This they do out of a vanity, hoping to embellish and set out their history with a strangeness of our manners, not caring in the meanwhile to brand us with the rankest note of barbarism, as if in Britain women were men, and men women.[10]

Inevitably, to Milton, Boudicca will lose at Manduessedum:

> Hitherto what we have heard of Cassibelan [Cassivelaunus], Togodumnos, Venutius and Caractacus [sic] hath been full of magnanimity, soberness and martial skill: but the truth is, that in this battle, and the whole business, the Britons never more plainly manifested themselves to be right barbarians; no rule, no foresight, no forecast, experience or estimation, either of themselves or of their enemies; such confusion, such impotence, as seemed likest not to a war, but to the wild hurry of a distracted woman, with as mad a crew at her heels.[11]

This characterization of Boudicca as a madwoman and the Iceni as a rabble is no doubt one that Paulinus would have applauded. The Roman propagandists were admirably abetted by their counterparts sixteen centuries later.

We have placed Milton's Boudicca in this fictional category because the poet so badly misread the woman and her times. In the less rabid era of the Restoration, she is restored to something approximating a heroine. The diarist John Evelyn listed thirteen women in *Numismata* (1697) who are examples of the 'learned, virtuous and fair sex', and the first, chronologically, is Boudicca. In the same year, Charles Hopkins wrote another play about her, with leading actress Mrs Barry in the title role. Two years earlier, Fletcher's play was resurrected (and hugely adapted) at the Theatre Royal, this time with music by Henry Purcell, organist of Westminster Abbey and the Chapel Royal. It was probably his last major work for the stage before his untimely death at the age of thirty-six, and one of the songs, 'Britons, Strike Home!', became what 'Rule Britannia' was to be a century later. In this reworking, Boudicca's vainglorious rantings have been toned down, and, in a theatrical age famous for its comedies and 'froth', her daughters are weak and willowy rather than vengeful harpies.

It was in the seventeenth century that antiquarianism came into its own. The men of this generation picked up any trifle – historical, archaeological, legendary – and wrote it all down as fact. In some ways their work is infuriating because of their lack of scholarship and care; in others it is vital because it contains much that might otherwise have been lost for ever. Edward Bolton wrote in 1624, 'That STONAGE is a work of the BRITANNS, the rudeness it selfe persuades', and believed Stonehenge to be Boudicca's grave. Thirty years later the country's best-known architect, Inigo Jones, wrote a rebuttal, printed posthumously:

A mighty Prince may be buried with great Solemnity, Yet no material Monument be dedicated to his memory.

Chronologically between the two, the prolific playwright and actor Thomas Heywood wrote *Exemplary Lives* in 1640 and was happy to accept Bolton's grave idea at Stonehenge, referring to Boudicca as a 'mother and nurse of magnanimity', which is as far a cry from Milton's attitude as is yet to appear in print. More interesting is the illustration accompanying the work, which shows the queen in contemporary court dress, including plumes and sash. The come hither look on her face and the nakedness of her right breast give her more the air of a courtesan than a nurse and mother!

Nine years later the radical Leveller John Lilburne was languishing in jail having taken the 'Great Rebellion' to extremes that were not to Oliver Cromwell's taste. The petition produced by Leveller women for his release made use of Boudicca as an example of weak women who had saved the British from defeat by the Danes. The historical inaccuracy is less important than the fact that the queen had once again been hijacked for a cause, to the extent that Antonia Fraser[12] makes a distinction between Boudicca, the queen of the Iceni, and Boadicea, the legendary figure of heroism which later generations have made her. In the 1950s, Sir Mortimer Wheeler, doyen of the first television archaeologists, went further by saying he preferred the 'Boadicea' spelling, because he could never bring himself to dine with anyone called 'Boudicca'!

A much more matronly Boudicca appeared as the 'Thrice Happy Princess' in Aylett Sammes' *Britannia Antiqua Illustrata* in 1676. The engraving was by William Fairthorne and again showed a woman of Fairthorne's time, the only nod in the direction of Dio being Boudicca's long hair and spear:

To War, this Queen doth with her Daughters move,
She for her Wisdom followed, they for love . . .
But they, being ravisht, made her understand
'Tis harder beauty to secure than land.
Yet her example teaching them to dye,
Virtue, the room of Honour did supply.

It was Sammes who produced the wicker-men illustration of the Druids, happily accepting the work of Classical writers like Poseidoneus, anxious to believe in any amount of barbarity among men 'at the edge of the world'. Even so, Boudicca herself is never established as a heroine.

Poetry of the Restoration period continued the theme, even if it continued to muddy the historical waters. In 1669 Edward Howard wrote 'An Heroick Poem' with Bonduca cast as a gentle maiden. Ignoring Dio's comment on Boudicca's harsh voice, Howard's Bonduca is 'too soft to accent the rough laws of War'; in fact, war terrifies her. Her hair is 'softer than gossamer'. She is wooed by Albinius, Arthur's son, and Vortiger, a Briton chieftain, who clash in the lists to fight for her hand. Both men are killed and Bonduca dies of a broken heart before being resurrected by Merlin.

William Stukeley in the next generation did more than anyone to bring a certain 'Celtomania' into intellectual circles. His *Itinerarium Curiosum* (Journey of Curiosities) appeared in 1724 and focused on pre-Roman society. Born at Holbeach in Iceni territory in 1687 and, like Fletcher before him, a graduate of Corpus Christi College, he spent twenty years of his life carrying out fieldwork at Stonehenge and Avebury. Obsessed with the Druids, he and his circle formed The Society of Roman Knights in 1722, in which Lord Winchester was Cingetorix, Roger Gale was Venutius, Maurice Johnson was Prasutagus and John Clark was Agricola. In keeping with Celtic tradition (but not that of Stukeley's time, as it was not until the twentieth century that the Society of Antiquaries admitted women), Stukeley's wife Frances was Cartimandua and Frances Thynne, Countess of Hertford, was Boadicea, the spelling finally agreed among scholars by this time.

In 1753 Glover wrote a new play called *Boadicea*. Happily

throwing in as many Celtic names as he could, a leading protagonist is Dumnorix who was to be played by the greatest actor of his day, David Garrick. Glover's original reading with the cast was so dull and badly done that Garrick at first refused to have anything to do with it. Persistence prevailed and the play opened at Drury Lane on Saturday 1 December. Horace Walpole was in the audience and wrote to his friend George Montagu days later:

> . . . but, happily, you hear no more of her [Boudicca] after the end of the Third Act, 'til in the last scene somebody brings a card with her compliments and she is sorry she can't wait upon you, but she is dead.[13]

Even with Garrick on stage, the play closed after nine nights!

The next outing for the 'resurrected' queen appeared in 1780 when William Cowper co-opted her as a warrior heroine to stand against the American revolutionaries in his epic poem 'Boadicea'. By that year, the war against the insurgent colonists was going badly. Faced with indifferent generals and opposition in the form of France, Spain and Holland, the British knew they had underestimated George Washington's continental army. Surrender at Yorktown was only a year away. It was standing history on its head to use the analogy of Boudicca as the struggling underdog against the powerful Romans when the reality in Cowper's day was the reverse. Ignoring later American propaganda on the skill of their minutemen and the rightness of their cause, the might of the British Empire *should* have acheived an easy victory had the whole fiasco been better handled. Casting the Americans as the Romans was idiotic, but it did provide the verse later carved in stone on the Thames Embankment.

Early in the nineteenth century, Boudicca appeared as the heroine of an opera by Vincenzo Pucitta. It was not a success. The critic Augusta wrote in March 1813: 'the whole of this drama is without plot, incident or interest'. The costumes were 'absurd' and the diva playing the queen, Catalini, was past her best.[14]

Not to be outdone, the poet laureate Alfred Tennyson went

into print in 1860 with a 'fiercely brilliant poem' the metre of which was based on that of the Roman poet Catullus. His friend Benjamin Jowett visited him at his home at Farringford on the Isle of Wight in January 1861:

> I paid my annual visit to Tennyson last week. Shall I tell you about him? This year he had written nothing but a short piece called *Boadicea*, in a very wild, peculiar metre, with long lines and innumerable short syllables. It is very fine but too strange to be popular.[15]

Tennyson himself concurred. In a letter to the Duke of Argyll he wrote, '*Boadicea* – No, I cannot publish her yet – perhaps never, for who can read her except myself?'[16]

In the previous decade the sculptor Thomas Thorneycroft had begun work on the most famous depiction of the queen of the Iceni that survives to this day. Thorneycroft and his wife, both sculptors, were favourites of Albert and Victoria, the Prince Consort in particular was a keen patron of the arts and he lent the sculptor horses from his own stables to work with. Accordingly, the group which eventually found its way to the Thames Embankment shows two spirited chargers of 15–16 hands rather than the hardy little ponies that would really have hurtled over the bloody field at Manduessedum. There are no reins and the rearing animals are harnessed to a chariot that is considerably heavier and more lumbering than anything the Iceni knew. To be fair to Thorneycroft, chariot burials had not been found in Britain, nor accurate archaeological reconstructions attempted in the mid-nineteenth century. Most infamous of all, the solid wheels have murderous knives jutting from their hubs and seem to be pure artistic licence on Thorneycroft's part, an episode which has itself passed into folklore. There is no contemporary evidence for them. The queen herself, raising hands and spear aloft, appears in a diaphanous robe that may have upset the rather prudish Albert,[17] and caused Lord Edward Gleichan to write in 1928, 'One really must admire her sangfroid.'[18] Her daughters, crouching on the platform beside her, are naked from the waist up. About the only historically accurate part of the group is the heavy Celtic cloak over Boudicca's shoulders and a reasonable attempt at a Celtic spear.

Albert wanted this statue placed at the entrance to Hyde Park where the Crystal Palace had stood a few years earlier, but his own early death in 1861 put paid to that and his own memorial was erected on the ground opposite the Albert Hall. The group was still unfinished ten years later when *The Times* wrote a favourable review of it, but it was a further twelve years before Thorneycroft began work again and by 1885, the year of his death, there was the need to find considerable cash to cast the whole in bronze. London County Council wanted to put it on a tumulus, believed to be Boudicca's burial place, on Parliament Hill Fields. The Society of Antiquarians quite rightly scotched this idea as nonsense and, although a staggering £4,300 had been raised by public subscription for casting and pedestal, for several years Boudicca remained unhoused. Finally, the odd choice was made of the Embankment near Scotland Yard and the Houses of Parliament, on the northern end of Westminster Bridge. Here it was erected in 1902 with Cowper's lines carved onto its base:

> Regions Caesar never knew
> Thy Posterity shall sway.

The sculpture was highly relevant. In 1902 the British Empire was at its height, not only the largest of its day, but of any day. All the Caesars from Julius onward would have been green with envy, and although it may be straining a point to claim that the British Empire of the early twentieth century was an undiluted descendant of the territories of Boudicca, the notion had a romantic appeal which suited the times.

By the turn of the century, Boudicca was being appropriated again, on the one hand by artists, folklorists and performers of the enormously popular pageant tradition, and on the other, more dangerously perhaps, by militant feminists out for the vote. On yet a third front, Boudicca was used as a Britannia lookalike, a warrior woman with shield and spear, which itself was a curious throwback to the Celtic warrior goddesses of Irish mythology. At the height of the Boer War, in

1900, Marie Trevelyan went into print with *Britain's Greatness Foretold: The Story of Boadicea, the British Warrior-Queen*. Gone was the Jacobean misogyny, the Enlightenment's obsession with polite society and calling cards. Boudicca was a heroine against the Romans as Victoria (and both names of course mean 'Victory') was a heroine against the Boers. Again, as with Cowper, such analogies could not withstand scrutiny. Trevelyan's Boadicea is as wide of the mark as Thorneycroft's. Her rallying cry is 'For Britain, Boadicea and Freedom', the first concept at least based on the nationalism and empire of later centuries. Freedom is a rather more realistic motive for Boudicca's behaviour, but it is a very overworked word, as popular today with film makers (as in Mel Gibson's *Braveheart*) as it was for the anti-Boer imperialists.

With the Boers defeated, Victoria in her heaven and the world, at least temporarily, at peace, 1909 was a great year for pageants. In June the posters and souvenir programmes for the annual event at Colchester showed a helmeted Boudicca driving a three-horsed chariot. That same year *The Pageant of Great Women*, held in November, was not merely a chance to dress up, but was in the suffragette cause. A year after Thorneycroft's statue was erected, with her back to the town she once destroyed and facing a parliament she would not have understood, women pursuing equality with men formed the Women's Social and Political Union. Some men espoused their cause; others, like Winston Churchill and David Lloyd George, opposed them. Still others fought running battles in the streets and collected 'scalps' by tearing out their long hair and pinning it to their lapels as trophies, proving how much the Edwardians and the Celts were brothers under the skin. *The Pageant* was an elaborately staged production, written by Cicely Hamilton and directed by Edith Craig (daughter of the actress Ellen Terry). While suffragette hunger strikers being force-fed in prisons because the unacceptable face of Asquith's England, a tall actress portrayed Boudicca alongside other female warriors like Joan of Arc, the Rani of Jhansi (who had fought the British during the Indian Mutiny of 1857) and the fourteenth-century Scotswoman, Agnes Dunbar. Fifty-two actresses took part and the only male actor played Prejudice.

When the show toured the provinces, the roles of all but the three spoken parts were played by local women of the suffragist societies. No one objected to playing Boudicca, and 'St Joan' was hugely popular. In one town, however, no one wanted to play Catherine the Great of Russia: 'whatever may have been her merits as a ruler, [she] was renowned for the scandals of her private life.'[19] Since the woman reputedly slept her way through half her own army, their reluctance is perhaps understandable! When Boudicca was on stage, however, the dialogue thundered: 'Look on her who stood . . . and spat defiance at the hosts of Rome!'[20]

Three years before this, a large suffragette rally had assembled at Boudicca's statue, and on the cover of the banquet menu that night the warrior queen was shown holding a banner with the legend 'Votes for Women'. And 1906 saw the publication of Charles Doughty's *The Dawn in Britain*, one of the first times that Boudicca's name was spelt correctly. The epic poem was actually written between 1866 and 1875 and would be reissued in 1943 to bolster the morale of women in the People's War. Doughty was in no doubt that Boudicca and her daughters were consumed on a funeral pyre, cheating Paulinus' attempts to possess them even in death.

By the early years of the twentieth century, not only the name but the history was more or less accurate. Even children's histories, like that of Charles Dickens as early as 1868, were faithful to the rudiments of Tacitus and Dio, albeit inevitably glossing over the details of the daughters' rapes. Archaeology was shedding light on her people and her times, although arguably it was not until the 1960s that a truly scientific approach was adopted. Excavations before that date were sometimes sloppily done and wrong inferences drawn. Even now, however, with all the science at our disposal, we cannot find a verifiable capital for Boudicca, nor a site for her last battle, nor a grave.

And she was still, throughout the twentieth century, all things to all men. In May 1895, at a meeting of the Women of the Primrose League (the Conservative organization devoted to the memory of Disraeli) Mrs Lucas Shadwell made a speech that began:

> Dames of the Primrose League, women of England, look
> back to the time when Boadicea, the British Warrior Queen,
> sought vengeance of her country's Gods for the insults and
> injuries of the Roman Conquerors.[21]

In the First World War, a stretch of the Western Front was
known to the British as 'Boadicea Redoubt', and in both world
wars the navy used a destroyer called *Boadicea*. A much less
warlike statue than Thorneycroft's was unveiled in Cardiff in
October 1916 as one of eleven distinguished figures from
Welsh history, taking 'Welsh' in its broadest Celtic, sense
presumably, and ignoring the East Anglian associations of the
queen. In that same year, the first prototype of the tank was
undergoing trials, an ironclad version of Boudicca's war
chariot, appropriately enough at the first tank-training ground
at Thetford, an important centre for the Iceni. In the 1930s
Shell Oil used Boudicca as a symbol – mechanical horses
thundering forward, pulling a shell-adorned chariot; sixty
years later the Japanese raided Celtic history to advertise their
Mitsubishi Colt – 'It's what Boadicea would have driven.'

In the post Second World War world, the warrior queen was
hijacked yet again. The arrival of Margaret Thatcher at
Number Ten, entering the history books as Britain's first
female prime minister, inevitably led to comparisons. After the
Falklands War in 1982, Griffin in the *Daily Mail* portrayed a
smiling Maggie with a metal brassiere and curved sword
driving two spirited horses forward, and five years later, Gale
of the *Daily Telegraph* showed a curiously Romanized 'Iron
Lady' in toga and laurel wreath dragging behind her chariot in
chains leading members of the opposition.

In the same decade Judy Grahn, a feminist poet, came to
the conclusion that the queen of the Iceni was a lesbian. She
wrote that:

> Boudicca, was a barbarian [sic] and a Celt and her pudenda
> would have been active, unashamed and radiating with female
> power all her life . . . Considering Celtic custom it would have
> been unnatural of Queen Boudicca *not* to be a lesbian. She
> was, after all, a queen and a military leader of her people.

Allowing for the fact that, apart from heterosexual polygamy, Celtic customs are a closed book, it is difficult to know what customs give Grahn her grounds. Further, she attempts to tie the slang term 'bulldyke' (for aggressive lesbian) with Boudicca ('*Bo*' meaning 'cow' in Gaelic). According to Brigid McConville and John Shearlow in *The Slanguage of Sex*, the actual origin of the word is American and intended as a term of abuse with appropriate accompanying jokes. Lesbians have turned the term to their own advantage, wearing it as a badge of pride.

Thug, murderess, boaster, barbarian, harpy – Boudicca has been all these things to different generations. Queen, wife, mother, general, goddess, freedom fighter – she is all these things too. How, after 2,000 years, can we hope to give her her rightful place in history? In the list-obsessed twenty-first century, in which members of a sadly uneducated public are asked to vote on the '100 best' or '100 worst', television's Channel 4 broadcast the *Hundred Worst Britons* on 10 May 2003. The *Daily Mail* invited celebrities to select their own individuals and Conservative MP Ann Widdecombe wrote:

> It was difficult to choose between Cromwell and Queen Boudicca, as they were both so brutal and ghastly. She was hypocritical about the appalling treatment of her own people in the name of 'liberty'. I don't really dislike her for standing up to the Romans, but she slaughtered her own while being hailed as a great fighter. If you begin to argue that her strength and achievement make her a great leader and cancel out the bad things she did, you are on dangerous ground – you could argue the same for Hitler![22]

This assessment, no doubt hurried and rather tongue-in-cheek, highlights our problem. Ms Widdecombe clouds the issue by inviting comparison with Hitler and is guilty of applying the examples of the twentieth century and supposing a historical norm for behaviour. When we visited Colchester's excellent museum on the site of Claudius' hated temple, two little boys accompanied us on the tour of the vaults. Afterwards, in looking at a diorama of the town's destruction, they had no problem in identifying with the 'goodies', the

Romans cowering in the temple precincts, and felt alienated by the 'baddies', the appalling barbarians of the Iceni sweeping from the north. Absolutes like these are perfectly natural in little boys, but not in mature politicians. We shall be sending a copy of this book to Ms Widdecombe with our compliments in the hope that she will reconsider.

But why should she? First, we have to discount the notion that Boudicca was a nationalist in the modern sense of the word. She was the military and spiritual leader of her people, the Iceni, and in no sense did she preside over the destruction of 'her people', as Ms Widdecombe says. The quisling Trinovantes of Camulodunum, the Romanized merchants of Londinium and the client Catuvellauni of Verulamium were the enemy in every sense. They always had been in the internecine tribal disputes of Iron Age Britain and to see it any differently is to misunderstand the temper of the times. Second, we have done our best, in terms of archaeological evidence, or rather lack of it, to dispel the myth of Boudicca's slaughters. We have found no mass graves, we have found no sign of mass burnings of people. The notion of the 70,000 dead comes to us from two historians, Tacitus and Dio, neither of whom were eyewitnesses and both of whom were the woman's enemies. It is rather like reading a biography of Winston Churchill written by Josef Goebbels – and long before the Nazis, the Romans were past masters at propaganda. Third, we have Dio's vivid description of torture and mutilation in the towns Boudicca destroyed, which ranks her with monsters of history like Vlad Dracula, Ivan the Terrible and Genghis Khan. Again, we have *one* account, that of the Roman 'historian' Dio, writing three centuries after the event, and we have no idea of his source of information.

We have no doubt that Boudicca was a queen 'more sinned against than sinning'. She was the wife of a client king content to live peacefully with Rome. Selfish, greedy and corrupt officials took her kingdom and, when she complained, they thrashed her and raped her teenage daughters. Who, in the event, 'cast the first stone'? History is largely a male preserve. It has essentially been carved by men and written by men. When a *woman* has made the headlines, the tendency is inevitably to corrupt the truth, play her down, play up the atrocities.

Such a one is Boudicca of the red hair, queen of the Horse People. And one day we will find her grave and that of her girls. And one day, all hurt gone, all tears wiped away, they can sleep peacefully in it.

Notes

Chapter One

1. Tacitus, *Historia* I i. in Church and Brodribb (trans.), *Complete Works* (University of Columbia, 1942).
2. Michael Grant, *The Ancient Historians* (London, Duckworth, 1995), p. 344.
3. All quotations from Cassius Dio are from Epitome of Book LXII, trans. Scott-kinert, (Penguin, 1987).
4. Tacitus, *Annales*, XIV 3, trans. Michael Grant (Penguin, 1975).
5. Flavius Vegetius Renatus wrote his *Epitome Institutionum Rei Militaris c.* 375. Based on the work of a number of earlier writers, including Caesar, it was still being read as a military handbook as late as the fifteenth century.
6. Quoted in Hughes and Forrest, *The Romans Discover Britain*, (Cambridge University Press, Cambridge, 1981) p. 35.
7. For instance, Ala I Thracium was the first regiment of Thracian cavalry from modern Bulgaria.
8. Flavius Josephus was the son of a rabbi and a member of the Pharisee party in Jerusalem. Involved in the Jewish revolt of 66, he was defeated by Vespasian and 'defected' to honourable service in the Roman army. His *History of the Jewish War*, written in Hebrew and Greek, provides a fascinating glimpse of Judea at the time of Christ.
9. Job 39: 19–25.
10. Publius Virgilius Maro (70–19 BC) was the foremost poet of Rome, even in his own lifetime. His *Georgics* dealt with the

Notes

pastoral world of agriculture but his reputation stands on the epic *Aeneid* chronicling the fall of Troy and the subsequent mythical founding of Rome by the Trojan hero Aeneas.

11. Tacitus, *Annales* XIV, 34.
12. Polybius (*c*. 205–123 BC) was a Greek held as a political hostage in Rome where he became utterly absorbed by the City, writing a monumental history of Rome and accompanying Scipio on his campaigns in Africa.
13. Quoted in Stephen Allen, *Celtic Warrior* (Osprey, Oxford, 2001), p. 12.
14. Strabo, Geographica 4, 178–9, trans. H.L. Jones (Loeb Classical Library II, 1923).
15. Poseidonius was a stoic philosopher who died *c*. 51 BC. An athlete and extensive traveller, he settled in Rome in 86 BC and became a friend of Cicero and other scholars of the day. He wrote on a whole range of subjects from geometry to history.
16. Quoted in Allen, *Celtic Warrior*, pp. 16–17.
17. Diodorus Siculus was born in Sicily and travelled widely, collecting material over thirty years for his *History of the World*. Of the forty volumes only the first five have survived intact.
18. Quoted in Allen, *Celtic Warrior*, p. 20.
19. Ibid., p. 22.
20. Julius Caesar, *De Bello Gallico*, trans. S.A. Handford (Penguin Classic, 1951).
21. Ibid.
22. International Rugby, with its wedge formations, rucks and mauls, is merely a slightly less bloody version of a Romano–Celtic battle!
23. Quoted in Allen, *Celtic Warrior*, p. 28.
24. Titus Livius (59 BC–17 AD) was born in Padua and, despite his association with the court of Augustus, was foremost a republican. Probably the best historian that Rome produced, his 142-volume history of Rome, although incomplete, is a fascinating survey of power, corruption and nobility.
25. Quoted in Allen, *Celtic Warrior*, pp. 28–9.
26. Ammianus Marcellinus, born *c*. 330 in Antioch, served as an officer and travelled widely before settling down in 378 to write a continuation of Tacitus' *Histories*. He is the last great historian the empire produced.
27. Quoted in Peter Berresford Ellis, *Celtic Women* (Constable, London 1995) p. 82.
28. Tacitus, *Annales* XIV.

29. Quoted in Allen, *Celtic Warrior*, p. 30.
30. Ibid., p. 32.
31. Ibid., p. 45.

Chapter Two

1. Julius Caesar, *De Bello Gallico* V 12, trans. Hansford.
2. Ibid.
3. This was a Greek invention used extensively by the Romans. It was based on water dripping from one container into another at a constant rate, so providing a method of calculating time. The variant used in Caesar's day was probably the three-tank system of Ctesibius.
4. Caesar, *De Bellico Gallico* V 13.
5. Strabo, *Geographia*.
6. Ibid.
7. Horace, *Odes*.
8. Dio IX 19–22.
9. Tacitus, *Annales*, 1, 58.
10. The mutiny in Pannonia has, reading Tacitus' account, a modern 'trade union' ring to it: 'Next, in a confusion of voices they complained of the fees for exemption from duties, the smallness of the pay, the strenuousness of the work, mentioning specifically the rampart, trenches, the gathering of fodder, timber and firewood and the other duties which were imposed by necessity or devised to prevent idleness in camp.' *Annales* 1 xvii, xxxi, xxxv.
11. Dio.
12. Camulos was the totemic god of the Remi, a tribe from northern Gaul who may have settled in the Trinovantan area between the Roman invasions. Latinizing the Celtic gods as we know the Romans did, he was associated by them with Mars, the god of war. In another tradition, the fortress of Camulos became Arthur's legendary Camelot.
13. The Virgins were a privileged female elite, drawn from the best families, whose duties centred on the preservation of a sacred flame kept burning in honour of Vesta, goddess of the hearth.
14. The classic example in history must be that of Napoleon defeating the armies of Spain and Portugal in 1807 to return home ignoring the arrival of the British under Arthur Wellesley.
15. *Oppida* in Latin refers to large fortified strongholds, not towns in the modern sense of the word.

16. Suetonius, *Lives of the Caesars*, *Vespasian* 4.
17. Vidkun Quisling (1887–1945) was the puppet prime minister of Norway under Nazi occupation in the Second World War.
18. Eutropius was secretary to Constantine and wrote a *Brief History of Rome* which may have been intended for use in schools.
19. Quoted in Peddie, *Conquest: The Roman Invasion of Britain* (Sutton, Stroud, 1998), p. 148.
20. Tacitus, *Annales* XIII, 30.
21. Annales XIII, 30.

Chapter Three

1. Tacitus, *Annales* XIV, 30.
2. Tarquinius was the seventh and last king of Rome, thrown out by a popular revolt in the sixth century BC.
3. John R. Clarke and Harry N. Abrams, *Roman Sex: 100 BC–AD 250* (2003) argues that Roman women were fairly liberated in this period, but strictly within the social hierarchy.
4. G. Rattray Taylor, *Sex in History* (Thames & Hudson, London 1968), p. 85.
5. The open season on this complicated subject has led theorist Keith Laidler in *The Head of God* (London, Weidenfold & Nicolson, 1998) to conjecture that the pre-Celts were the fleeing followers of the monotheistic pharaoh Akhenaton. The evidence for this seems virtually non-existent.
6. Quoted in John Davies, *The Celts* (Cassell & Co., London, 2000) p. 43.
7. This group, from the Seine, gave their name centuries later to the French capital. In Yorkshire, they are famous for their chariot burials.
8. Scollar 1968, quoted in Davies and Williamson, The Land of the Iceni (East Anglia, 1991).
9. Gregory and Gurney 1986, ibid.
10. Brown 1986, ibid.
11. Martin 1988, ibid.
12. *The Song of Taliesin*.
13. Quoted in Ellis, *Celtic Women*, p. 78.
14. Ibid.

Chapter Four

1. Tacitus, *Annales* XIV, pp. 327–8.
2. Caesar, Book VI, 16.5.
3. Ibid.
4. Guy de la Bedoyere, *Gods With Thunderbolts* (Tempus, Stroud, 2002) p. 16.
5. In 1966–7 Ian Brady and Myra Hindley used the moor as the burial place for child victims. Two of them have still not been found.
6. Or is it a grave pit? Archaeologists are divided over the Gundestrup design. A number of these vertical pits, containing animal and human bones as well as votive offerings have been found throughout Britain and Europe. They seem to be more deliberate than mere rubbish deposits, despite Guy de la Bedoyere's salutary warning that 'rubbish pits came before anything else in human settlement except eating and sex'. Quoted in Bedoyere, *Gods and Thunderbolts*, p. 41.
7. Anne Ross, *The Life and Death of a Druid Prince*, (Guild, London, 1989) p. 125.
8. Chrystostom, trans. T.D. Kendrick 1927, *Orations* XLIX.
9. Marcellinus, trans. T.D. Kendrick 1927, *Wales* XV, 9, 4–8.
10. Trans. T.D. Kendrick 1927, *Vitae,* Introduction 1.5.
11. *De Situ Orbis* III, 2, 18, 19 Pomponius Mela, T.D. Kendrick 1927.
12. Strabo, *Geographica*, trans. W. Dinan, IV, 4, 197–8.
13. Siculus, *Historia* V, 28, 31 trans. T.D. Kendrick 1927.
14. The mistletoe (*viscum album*) is an evergreen semi-parasitic member of the Loranthaceae family. Its usual host trees are black poplar, apple and Scots Pine. Its aphrodisiac and fertility associations clearly survive in Christmas kissing. William Coles wrote in *Adam in Eden* in 1657: 'Most powerful of all against evil is the rare oak-mistletoe, which should be gathered at New Moon without the use of iron and never allowed to touch the ground . . . Some women have worn mistletoe about their necks or arms, thinking it will help them to conceive.' Quoted in Charles Knightly, *The Perpetual Almanack of Folklore* (Thames & Hudson, London, 1987) for the day of 14 December.
15. Selago seems to have been selaquinella, a moss-like evergreen flowerless plant. Its properties were clearly similar to mistletoe.
16. References to cannibalism in the Iron Age are rare. At the time of writing a *Time Team* programme for the BBC screened in

February 2003 found what appears to be archaeological evidence for it in a possible Iron Age sacrifice site in Gloucestershire.

17. Julius Caesar, *De Bello Gallico*, trans. S.A. Handford.
18. An extraordinary story involving Dr Anne Ross is recounted in the Introduction to *Folklore, Mythys and Legends of Britain* to which she contributed in 1973. Two years earlier she had been asked to examine two carved stone heads from Hadrian's Wall. Both she and her daughter were terrorized by a huge dark shape, half-man, half-animal that hovered in their house and leapt over banisters, landing on soft, padded feet. For a hard-headed scholar like Dr Ross to have had an experience like this is perhaps a tantalizing glimpse of the power of the cult of the severed head and of the old gods.

Chapter Five

1. Tacitus, *Annales*, XII, 31.
2. Ibid.
3. Tacitus, *Annales*, xiv, 30.
4. Ibid.
5. Guy de la Bedoyere, *Eagles over Britannia* (Sutton, Stroud, 2001), p. 39.
6. Tacitus, *Annales, XII, 33*
7. Webster, *Rome Against Caratacus*, p. 30.
8. The German chief Arminius who had destroyed Varus' legions was an impressive soldier, but his personality inspired enemies among his own people who eventually killed him in 21.
9. Tacitus, *Annales*, XII, 33.
10. Ibid.
11. Ibid.
12. Ibid.
13. Tacitus, *Annales*, XII, 37.
14. Ibid.
15. Boris Rankov, *Guardians of the Roman Empire* (Osprey, Oxford, 1994), p. 20.
16. Tacitus, *Annales*, XII, 33.
17. Ibid.
18. Tacitus, *Annales*, XII, 37.
19. Ibid.

Chapter Six

1. Tacitus, *Annales*, XIV, 26.
2. Onasander's work was among the first to discuss the importance of psychology and a leader's character in waging war.
3. Tacitus, *Annales*, XIV, 26.
4. *Études de Papyrologie* VI (1940), quoted in *Roman Civilisation Source Book 2*, ed. Lewis and Reinhold, p.279.
5. Tacitus, *Annales*, XIV, 30.
6. The revolt in Judea that began six years after Boudicca's and lasted for years, was caused by similar economic and maladministrative issues to those which incited the Iceni to rebel. Plagued by internal squabblings, the Jewish revolt was put down ruthlessly by Vespasian and his son Titus, but not before the 960 Zealots defending the hilltop fortress of Masada had committed suicide rather than surrender to Rome.
7. *Corpus Inscriptionum Lutharium*, Berlin 1862, vol. 6, no. 35 887, quoted in *Roman Civilisation Source Book 2*, ed. Lewis and Reinhold.
8. Pliny, quoted in *Roman Civilisation Source Book 2*, ed. Lewis and Reinhold, p. 381.
9. Juvenal, 6 434–56 trans. Killian, Lynch, Rowland and Sims.
10. John Matthews and Bob Stuart, *Celtic Battle Heroes* (Firebird, Poole, 1988).
11. Tacitus, *Annales* XIV, 30.
12. The complex and mysterious cult of the Persian god Mithras was a late imperial development, centring on an all-male military elite, running Water, worship of the sun and the sacrifice of bulls.
13. Dio, Book LXII.
14. An interesting comparison can be made with the five female victims of 'Jack the Ripper' in Whitechapel in 1888, the tallest of whom, probably because of her height, was known as 'Long Liz', at only five feet seven.
15. Quoted in Antonia Fraser, *Boadicea's Chariot* (Weidenfeld & Nicolson, London 1988), p. 60.
16. Dio, *Roman History*, Epitome, Book LXII.
17. Ibid.
18. Like Aulus Plautius' troops in 43, it is likely that Caligula's refused to sail across the haunted Channel. He ordered them to collect sea shells from the beach as spoils of war instead.
19. It is rather ironic that Dio has Boudicca talking of Roman suits of mail when it was probably the Celts who invented it.

Notes

Chapter Seven

1. Philip Crummy, *City of Victory* (Colchester Archaeological Tust, 2001).
2. Tacitus, *Annales*, XIV, 30.
3. Ibid.
4. Ibid.
5. Cassius Dio, *Epitome* Book LXII.

Chapter Eight

1. Beard and Cohen 1988, quoted in Peter Salway, *Roman Britain* (Clarendon Press, Oxford, 1982).
2. Goodburn 1978, quoted in John Morris, Londinium (Weidenfeld & Nicolson, 1982).
3. Tacitus, *Annales*, XIV, 30.
4. Ibid.
5. Dio, *Epitome* Book LXII. The act of impalement, associated with Vlad Dracula, the fifteenth-century Wallachian warlord, is actually notoriously difficult. There is no record of it as a Celtic means of execution or torture and it was Romans who used crucifixion. In the absence of other evidence, we doubt whether this is much more than fiction.
6. Perring, quoted in Morris, *Londinium*.

Chapter Nine

1. *Gladiator* starring Russell Crowe, Dreamworks Films, 2000, dir. Ridley Scott.
2. Tacitus, *Annales*, XIV 34.
3. Anthony Beevor, *The Fall of Berlin* (Viking, New York, 2002).
4. Alfred the Great, the Saxon king who halted the Danish invasion from his heartlands in Wessex is supposedly buried in Winchester, but no trace of his grave has been found.
5. *Sub pellibus* literally means 'under skins': Roman tents were made from cow hide.
6. Tacitus, *Annales*, XIV, 34.
7. Paul R. Sealey, *The Boudiccan Revolt Against Rome* (Shire Books, Bucks, 1997).
8. Tacitus, *Annales*, XIV, 39.
9. Ibid.

10. Pliny Natural History iii, v. 66–7.
11. Ibid.
12. Aedileship: the magistracy responsible for water supply, public baths and games.
13. Tacitus, *Life of Agricola*, xxix–xxx.
14. Seneca, *Moral Epistles*, lxxi.

Chapter Ten

1. Gildas, quoted in Fraser, *Boadicea's Chariot*, p. 153.
2. From Edgar Allen Poe, 'To Helen'.
3. Holinshed, quoted in Fraser, *Boadicea's Chariot*, p. 217.
4. Savile. Quoted in Fraser, *Boadicea's Chariot*.
5. Quoted in Stuart Piggott, *The Druids* (Thames & Hudson, London, 1975), p. 129.
6. John Aubrey, 1649, quoted in Piggott, *The Druids*, p .130.
7. Spenser, *The Faerie Queen*.
8. Quoted in Piggott, *The Druids*, p. 130.
9. Unknowingly, because the Bradstreets had emigrated to America before her work was published by a cousin.
10. Milton X, 68, quoted in *Yet Once More: Verbal and Psychological Patterns in Milton*, Edward S. Le Comte (Liberal Arts Press, New York, 1953) p. 68.
11. Ibid., 68–9
12. Fraser, *Boadicea's Chariot*.
13. Letter to G. Montagu 6 December, 1753.
14. Quoted in Theodore Fenner, *Opera in London 1785–1830* (S. Illinois University Press, 1994).
15. Abbott and Campbell (eds.), *Letters of Benjamin Jowett*, quoted in Cecil Y. Lang and Edgar F. Shannon Jr. (eds) in *Letters of Alfred Lord Tennyson*, vol. 2 (Clarendon Press, Oxford, 1981).
16. A. Tennyson, Cecil Y. Lang and Edgar F. Shannon (eds.) *Letters of Alfred, Lord Tennyson*, (Claredon Press, Oxford, 1981).
17. Contrary to our misuse of the word 'Victorian' to mean strait-laced, it was Albert who was easily shocked by nudity, not Victoria herself.
18. Quoted in Fraser, *Boadicea's Chariot*, p. 299.
19. Ibid., p. 301.
20. Ibid., p. 300.
21. *Morning Post*, 18 May 1895.
22. *Daily Mail*, Saturday 10 May 2003.

Bibliography

Allen, Stephen. *Celtic Warrior*, Osprey, Oxford, 2001.
Françoise Audouz and Olivier Buchsenschtz. *Towns, Villages and Countryside of Celtic Europe*, Batsford, London, 1991.
Bloom, Clive. *Violent London*, Sidgwick & Jackson, London, 2003.
Braningan, Keith. *The Roman Chilterns*, Spur Books, Bucks .
Brereton, J.M. *The Horse in War*, David & Charles, Newton Abbott, 1976.
Brown, Alan. *Inside the Wicker Man*, Macmillan, London, 2000.
Carman, John & Harding, Anthony (ed.), *Ancient Warfare*, Sutton, Stroud, 1999.
Clarke, John R. and Harry N. Abrams. *Roman Sex: 100 BC to AD 250*.
Clayton, Peter. *A Companion to Roman Britain*, Phaedon Press, Oxford, 1980.
Cotterell, Arthur. *Encyclopaedia of Mythology*, Lorenz Books, London, 1996.
Crummy, Philip. *City of Victory*, CAT, Colchester, 2001.
——, (ed). *The Colchester Archaeologist, 14, 15 & 16*.
Cunliffe, Barry, *Iron Age Communities in Britain*, London, BCA, 1975.
——. *Rome and her Empire*, BCA, London, 1994.
Timothy Darville, Paul Stamper, Jane Timby, *England, an Archaeological Guide*, Oxford University Press, Oxford, 2002.
Davies, John. *The Celts*, Cassell & Co., London, 2000.
Davies, John and Williamson, Tom (eds). *The Land of the Iceni*, University of East Anglia, 1991.
De la Bedoyere, Guy. *Eagles Over Britannia*, Sutton, Stroud, 2001.
——. *Gods with Thunderbolts*, Tempus, Stroud, 2002.
——. *Roman Towns in Britain*, Batsford, London, 1992.

Dilke, O.A.W. *The Ancient Romans*, David & Charles, Newton Abbott, 1975.

Dio, Cassius trans. Scott-Kilvert. *The Roman History*, Penguin, London, 1987.

Dunnett, Rosalind. *The Trinovantes*, Duckworth, London, 1975.

Ellis, Peter Berresford. *Celtic Women*, Constable, London, 1995.

Fraser, Antonia. *Boadicea's Chariot*, Weidenfeld & Nicolson, London, 1988.

Gilliver, Kate. *Caesar's Gallic Wars*, Osprey, Oxford, 2002.

Goldsworthy, Adrian. *Roman Warfare*, Cassell, London, 2002.

Grant, Michael. *The Ancient Historians*, Duckworth, London, 1995.

Green, Miranda J. *The World of the Druids*, Thames & Hudson, London, 1997.

Hazel, John. *Who's Who in the Roman World*, Routledge, London, 2001.

——, *Historical Map of Roman Britain*, OS.

Hughes, Mike and Forrest, Martin. *The Romans Discover Britain*, Cambridge University Press, Cambridge, 1981.

Hutchinson Dictionary of Ancient and Medieval Warfare, Helicon Publishing, Oxford, 1998.

Jones, Jack and Johanna. *The Isle of Wight*, Dovecot Press, Wimborne, 1987.

Jones, Moragh. *Power of Raven, Wisdom of Serpent*, Floris Books, Edinburgh, 95.

Keightly, Charles. *The Perpetual Almanac of Folklore*, Thames & Hudson, London 1987.

Larousse Encyclopaedia of Mythology, Hamlyn, London, 1960.

Lewis, Naphtali & Reinhold, Meyer (eds), *Roman Civilization Source Book 2,*
The Empire, Cambridge University Press, 1966.

Mac Cana, Proinsias. *Celtic Mythology*, Chancellor Press, London, 1996.

Matthews, John. *The Druid Source Book*, Blandford, London, 1997.

—— and Stewart, Bob, *Celtic Battle Heroes*, Firebird Books, Poole, 1988.

Morris, John. *Londinium*, London, Weidenfeld & Nicolson, 1982.

Niblett, Rosalind. *Verulamium, Roman City of St Albans*, Tempus, Stroud, 2001.

Peddie, John. *Conquest; the Roman Invasion of Britain*, Sutton, Stroud, 1998.

Pentacle, Samhain, Winter 2002/3.

Perring, Dominic. *Roman London*, Seaby, London, 1991.

Bibliography

Peterson, Daniel. *The Roman Legions*, Crowood Press, Marlborough, 1992.

Pickering, David. *Cassells Dictionary of Superstitions*, London, 1995.

Piggott, Stuart. *Ancient Britons and the Antiquarian Imagination*, Thames & Hudson, London, 1989.

——. *The Druids*, Thames and Hudson, London, 1975.

Pomeroy, Sarah B. *Goddesses, Whores, Wives and Slaves*, Pimlico, London, 1975.

Rankov, Dr Boris. *Guardians of the Roman Empire*, Osprey, Oxford, 1994.

Richardson, John. *Roman Provincial Administration*, Macmillan, London, 1976.

Ross, Anne. *Pagan Celtic Britain*, Constable, London, 1992.

—— and Robins, Don. *The Life and Death of a Druid Prince*, Guild, London, 1989.

Salway, Peter. *Roman Britain*, Clarendon Press, Oxford, 1982.

Scott, George. *A History of Torture*, Senate Press, London, 1995.

Scullard, H.H. *Roman Britain*, Thames & Hudson, London, 1979.

Sealey, Paul R. *The Boudiccan Revolt Against Rome*, Shire, Bucks, 1997.

Sharp, Mick. *Holy Places of Celtic Britain*, Blandford, London, 1997.

Simkins, Michael. *The Roman Army from Caesar to Trajan*, Osprey, Oxford, 1984.

Tacitus, trans. Grant. *Annals of Imperial Rome*, Penguin, London, 1975.

Tacitus , trans. Church and Brodribb. *Complete Works*, University of Columbia, 1942.

Taylor, G. Rattray. *Sex in History*, London, Thames & Hudson, 1968.

The Times History of War, London, Harper Collins, 2000.

The Times London History Atlas, London, BCA, 1991.

Wacher, John. *Towns of Roman Britain*, London, BCA, 1976.

Webster, Graham. *Boudicca: the British Revolt against Rome*, London, Routledge, 1999.

——. *The Roman Invasion of Britain*, London, Routledge, 1993.

——. *Rome Against Caratacus* Batsford, London, 1981.

Werner, Paul. *Life in Rome in Ancient Times*, Geneva, Minerva, 1978.

What Life Was Like When Rome Ruled the World, Time Life.

Wilcox, Peter. *Rome's Enemies: Gallic and British Celts*, London, Osprey, 1985.

Williams, Derek. *Romans and Barbarians*, London, Constable, 1999.

Wilson, Roger. *Roman Remains in Britain*, London, Constable, 1974.

Windrow, Martin & Hook, Richard. *The Foot Soldier*, Oxford, Oxford University Press, 1982.

Index

Index